WILLt ... e

Matthew Ames

Prior to becoming a quadruple amputee, Matthew Ames was an executive in the energy and resources sector, an industry in which he worked for almost 20 years as an environmental engineer and safety professional. He shares his story in the hope that it inspires positive attitudes towards adversity and disability. He is actively engaged in all aspects of family life with four children. Matthew and his wife, Diane, are determined to grow old together.

Diane Ames

Diane Ames is a civil engineer with more than 10 years' experience in the property sector. She worked in her father's engineering business before running her own consulting firm. After the birth of her third child, she left paid employment and is currently a stay-at-home mother. She is also the full-time carer of her husband, Matthew.

Kate Ames

Kate Ames has worked in magazine editorial, and as a journalist and editor. She is a senior lecturer in Professional Communication at Central Queensland University, and has been a Public Affairs Officer in the Australian Defence Force (Army Reserve) since 2001. As a magazine feature writer and photographer, her work is published regularly. This is her first book. She lives outside Brisbane with her husband and two children.

WILL to LIVE

MATTHEW and DIANE AMES
with Kate Ames

MICHAEL JOSEPH
an imprint of
PENGUIN BOOKS

MICHAEL JOSEPH

Published by the Penguin Group
Penguin Group (Australia)
707 Collins Street, Melbourne, Victoria 3008, Australia
(a division of Penguin Australia Pty Ltd)
Penguin Group (USA) Inc.
375 Hudson Street, New York, New York 10014, USA
Penguin Group (Canada)
90 Eglinton Avenue East, Suite 700, Toronto, Canada ON M4P 2Y3
(a division of Penguin Canada Books Inc.)
Penguin Books Ltd
80 Strand, London WC2R 0RL England
Penguin Ireland
25 St Stephen's Green, Dublin 2, Ireland
(a division of Penguin Books Ltd)
Penguin Books India Pvt Ltd
11 Community Centre, Panchsheel Park, New Delhi 110 017, India
Penguin Group (NZ)
67 Apollo Drive, Rosedale, Auckland 0632, New Zealand
(a division of Penguin New Zealand Pty Ltd)
Penguin Books (South Africa) (Pty) Ltd
Rosebank Office Park, Block D, 181 Jan Smuts Avenue, Parktown North, Johannesburg 2196, South
Africa
Penguin (Beijing) Ltd
7F, Tower B, Jiaming Center, 27 East Third Ring Road North, Chaoyang District, Beijing 100020, China

Penguin Books Ltd, Registered Offices: 80 Strand, London WC2R 0RL, England

First published by Penguin Group (Australia), 2014

10 9 8 7 6 5 4 3 2 1

Text copyright © Matthew Ames, Diane Ames, Kate Ames, 2014
Cover photography copyright © Paul Harris, 2014
All other photographs are property of the Ames family unless otherwise stated

The moral right of the author has been asserted

Cover design by Alex Ross © Penguin Group (Australia)
Cover photography by Paul Harris, Seesaw Photography
Typeset in 11/17 pt Sabon by Post Pre-Press Group, Brisbane, Queensland
Printed and bound in Australia by Griffin Press, an accredited ISO AS/NZS 14001 Environmental
Management Systems printer.

National Library of Australia
Cataloguing-in-Publication data:

>   Ames, Matthew, author.
>   Will to live: an inspiring story of courage, resilience
>   and love / Matthew Ames, Diane Ames, Kate Ames.
>   ISBN: 9780143799658 (paperback)
>   1. Ames, Matthew. 2. Amputees – Biography.
>   3. Courage – Anecdotes. 4. Love – Anecdotes.
>   5. Families – Anecdotes.
>
>   Other Authors/Contributors:
>   Ames, Diane / Kate Ames, authors.
>
>   362.43092

penguin.com.au

To Luke, Ben, Will and Emily.
Thank you for the light you bring into our lives.
We hope that this answers some of your questions about what
happened, and provides you with inspiration to make the best of
what life brings, no matter how hard it may seem at the time.

CONTENTS

Life is too short to be anything but happy.
Falling down is a part of life, getting back up is living.

– JOSÉ N. HARRIS

MY WISH

My 10-year-old son, Luke, was helping me pack our suitcase. The following morning we would be ending our short trip to Melbourne and returning home to Brisbane. My husband, Matthew, Luke's father, was around the corner in a rehabilitation hospital, and in our hotel room, the night was quiet.

My other three children, Ben (9), Will (7), and Emily (3), were asleep after a busy day. It was just the two of us – Luke and me.

We were closing up the suitcase when Luke asked me about wishes. It was a question that, as they often do with young children, seemed to come out of nowhere.

He had obviously been thinking about things.

'You know, Mum, if you could have one wish in the whole world, what would it be?'

I didn't have to think for very long.

'Oh, sweetheart. My one wish would be that your daddy had never become sick.'

Luke was quiet for a short time. He looked at me directly.

'That's my wish too, Mummy.'

I felt heartbroken for both of us at that moment.

That wish won't ever change. I had it when our world was turned upside down two years ago, and I have it now. What happened to Matthew has changed our lives forever.

But I do believe how we look at things is a choice.

We chose life for Matthew.

The rest of it is up to us.

PART ONE

DIANE

CHAPTER I

LIFE
INTERRUPTED

Shortly before lunchtime on Saturday 16 June 2012, I signed a Consent for Procedure form authorising the removal of three of my husband Matthew's limbs.

It was the second such form I had signed in 24 hours.

At 11 p.m. the previous night, I had agreed to an operation to remove Matthew's left arm. Doctors told me the arm had become necrotic and had died – the term they used was 'not viable' – and now, half a day later, the rest of his limbs were suffering the same fate.

This particular form made the specific risks of the operation on Matthew very clear. The words 'Death – intraoperative, or post-operative' were handwritten halfway down the page. I had been counselled about what they meant earlier that morning.

I didn't hesitate. My hands were numb, and my fingers trembled slightly as I placed my signature at the bottom of the form.

In signing, I was acknowledging that I was aware of and accepted the fact that Matthew Ames, my husband of 17 years and absolute love of my life, the father of our four children, and someone who hadn't yet reached his fortieth birthday, was very likely to die today.

I handed the folder on which the form was clipped back to Dr Brett Collins, one of the orthopaedic surgeons who would be involved in the operation.

As I walked back to the family members who had gathered with me, I wondered how we had come to this.

*

Just a fortnight earlier, Matthew and I were living a busy, happy life in Brisbane. Matthew had been promoted to the executive team at Origin Energy a few years earlier and was enjoying his role as a health, safety and environment professional. I was busy being a full-time mother, having put my career as a civil engineer on hold while we waited for our youngest child, Emily, to start school.

Everything in our life was great. We had finished building our dream house from the bones of an old Queenslander, which had taken us over 10 years. For the first time in our marriage, we weren't working on any particular project except an upcoming family trip to Disneyland that Matthew and I had been planning for a few years. It was timed to coincide with my fortieth birthday, and our good friends Gayle and David Schabe and their two daughters would be travelling with us.

So there was a lot to look forward to and life was very full.

Our journey to the point where I shakily signed the consent form for the removal of Matthew's remaining limbs started on Monday 4 June, when Matthew went to a doctor. He was normally very healthy but over the weekend had begun to feel really unwell with flu-like symptoms and a very sore throat. He was due to go away for a few days with work, to Roma, in western Queensland, where he was involved with a gas project. Roma is quite isolated, so Matthew sought medical advice that morning to make sure he was okay to travel to the project site. He got the clearance to fly and, as he would only be away for a couple of days, he decided to go later that day.

Matthew travelled most weeks, as his headquarters was in Sydney, so the routine of him leaving and coming home was familiar to the family. The upside to him leaving was that he would come home, and his homecomings were a celebration. The kids would run to the door as soon as they heard the taxi pull up at the front of the house. Matthew would come through the front door where they would all be waiting, and they would cover him with kisses and hugs. He would bring them lollies, and they would be allowed to stay up just that little bit later – the house would be full of love and laughter. I loved those moments.

When he returned from Roma on Wednesday 6 June, though, I noticed that he looked tired and run-down, although he still put 100 per cent into his coming-home moment. I'm pleased he did, now. It's a memory I'll always have of our former life.

Matthew went to bed early that night, and over the next couple of days he continued to go to work. On Friday, however, he told me he didn't think he would last the day. He did, but upon coming home, he went to bed. It was very unusual for him, and because he was worried that what he had might be contagious, he moved into our eldest son Luke's room, which is at the furthest end of our house, while Luke moved in to sleep with Will.

The next morning, Saturday 9 June, we were due to meet up with Gayle and David Schabe after Will's soccer, to do more planning for our trip to Disneyland in the September school holidays. The children had already picked out the rides they wanted to go on, and were very excited. Now we just needed to finalise some logistical details, such as how we as a family with four children would manage.

Matthew, however, said he felt too unwell to meet, so we postponed our get-together and he stayed in bed. This was really unusual – Matthew was rarely sick. He didn't smoke, and was only a social drinker. He was fit – when he was working in Brisbane, he would normally cycle from our home in Camp Hill to the Origin offices in Milton, a ride of around 10 kilometres.

Matthew was not improving but instead getting worse. He was tired and nauseous, with some vomiting and diarrhoea. He had a headache and his joints were aching. He had a fluctuating high fever and I was concerned about his hydration.

Sunday 10 June was our seventeenth wedding anniversary. Matthew had planned that we would have dinner at the Stamford Plaza Hotel in Edward Street in Brisbane's city centre. With four young children, we didn't get the opportunity to go out a lot, and he had put some effort into organising a lovely night. Matthew's mum and dad, Christine and Roy, lived close by in Morningside, and the kids were going for a sleepover, as the following day was a public holiday.

As Sunday afternoon went on, however, Matthew's condition deteriorated. Even though we were both looking forward to our night out, I felt really concerned and did something that I had never done before. I rang 13 Health and after describing Matthew's condition received advice that he needed to go to hospital. The nurse questioned both of us about whether he had a rash and we told her that we weren't aware of any. We decided that we'd drop the children at Roy and Christine's house and go to the Mater Hospital emergency department. While Matthew was changing, he noticed a small red rash on his left wrist.

It was six-thirty in the evening. Once at the hospital, we didn't have to wait long to see a doctor, who told us much the same as the doctor a week previously – that Matthew had a case of the flu, and that Panadol and bed rest were what he needed.

I wasn't convinced, but we went home and Matthew went back to bed, where he stayed for two days. On Tuesday night, he was still very unwell and complaining of pain. The rash on his arm had spread and was the size of a full handprint. I again called 13 Health and they advised me to call a doctor to the house, or go to the nearest emergency department. We called a doctor to the house, and were told the same story – that he had the flu.

Matthew and I chose the after-hours doctor because the children were asleep. Now when I look back, I think, *If only we had gone back to the hospital on Tuesday.* But we didn't, and we accepted what we had been told, again. We now know that hours would have made a difference.

The following day, Wednesday 13 June, Matthew was even worse, so I took him again to a local GP.

This time, the doctor agreed to do a blood test to see if anything else might be responsible for the symptoms, but again, sent us home. By this stage, Matthew was finding it really painful to walk. He was aching all over, complaining that his joints were getting difficult to move. The rash had increased in size and was also really painful.

The second State of Origin for 2012 was being played that evening. Normally, we would be getting excited about the game, and setting ourselves up for a night in front of the television with our boys, barracking for Queensland. We were all at home, but Matthew was in a great amount of pain, and just after dinnertime, I called his parents to ask their advice about painkillers. I wanted to know if there was anything stronger than Panadeine Forte because Matthew's pain was increasing. Christine was concerned and suggested I take Matthew to hospital again, saying she and Roy would come over to look after the children. They arrived at our door around 15 minutes later.

Matthew's face and the skin on his chest and arms were red in colour. He looked hot, and the rash near his wrist had spread up his left arm. He was uncomfortable, and he knew that something was very wrong. He didn't argue about going to hospital, so we got him ready to go.

This would be our second, and final, attempt at a hospital visit. Matthew needed help to get to the car. He could still walk but had to be supported. Roy came with us while Christine stayed behind to look after the children.

It was the last time Matthew saw our house for almost two months.

*

Between the fourth and thirteenth of June 2012, I made two calls to 13 Health, on both occasions being advised to seek further treatment immediately, and Matthew saw four doctors. All the doctors dismissed his symptoms as being the flu: one on Monday 4 June before the trip to Roma; one on Sunday 10 June at hospital emergency; one after-hours on Tuesday 12 June; and one earlier on the day of Matthew's final admission to hospital, Wednesday 13 June. I have sometimes since wondered whether things would be different if I had a different personality – more forceful, perhaps. If I had been more insistent that the doctors made absolutely sure that other possibilities were ruled out before simply diagnosing Matthew with the flu. They said his symptoms were viral, but how could they be so sure? We both trusted their advice at the time.

So while I knew Matthew was really ill, and I was concerned, I don't think either of us recognised the full seriousness of the situation even at this point – after all, everyone had kept telling us that Matthew just needed to take pain relief and go to bed.

By the time we arrived at the hospital and got Matthew out of the car, he was unable to walk at all. During the short drive, his condition had deteriorated, and when we arrived at the Mater, it was extremely busy. We drove into the emergency area, and Roy went to get a wheelchair. We helped Matthew into it and went directly to the triage nurse to tell her who we were and why we were there. We wheeled Matthew into the waiting area, but were only there for a short time before we went through some sliding doors and saw a second nurse for an initial consultation. Roy remained in the waiting room.

Matthew put his arm out to show the nurse his rash. It was a large purple bruise-like area on the inside of his left arm. Red marks had spread up his arm, covering his entire inner forearm from his wrist to his elbow. Showing the nurse this is the last thing Matthew can remember; he says it's a clear cut-off point from which he has no further recollection until he woke up. From my perspective, how-ever, he was still completely coherent. He was alert but in pain, and he was able to talk about how he was feeling and explain his symptoms.

A nurse wheeled Matthew to a cubicle, and I followed. The bed was close to the nurse's station. Matthew wasn't moaning or complaining. He was just very calm and quiet, as he usually is, but I could tell he was in a lot of pain.

The rash didn't appear to be of major concern. No one looked at it and said, 'Oh my God, that means you have septic shock.' We had what appeared to be a junior doctor assigned to us. With the nurses, she took all the readings, and they were obviously letting her do a thorough analysis so she could figure out what the problem was.

She had problems getting Matthew's blood pressure. A nurse came over to have a look, and informed the young doctor that the reading was wrong – in doing so, the nurse seemed to assume the doctor must have done the measurement incorrectly. I remember thinking, *My goodness, there's a pecking order!* The nurse then did the blood pressure, but she couldn't get a reading either. She sug-gested there was a problem with the equipment and went to retrieve another machine.

While waiting, Matthew received his first shot of morphine, but this didn't provide any relief, and he received two more doses.

Matthew was lucid but still in pain. He was so patient with everyone – but he always is.

The medical staff continued to have trouble measuring Matthew's blood pressure. They were hitting his feet to see if he had any sensation in them, which he did. They were doing a whole series of tests that, to me, didn't seem to be going anywhere. Time seemed to stand still, for both of us.

I was sitting beside Matthew's bed so, between medical examinations, we were able to talk about our plans for the weekend and our role as volunteers at the upcoming school fete.

As time progressed, Matthew became concerned because Roy was missing the State of Origin game.

'Look, I think I might be here for a while,' Matthew told me. 'Can you please take Dad home, so he's not sitting in the waiting room, and then come back?'

It made sense, so I dropped Roy at our house, and got back to the hospital within around half an hour. When I returned, Matthew's cubicle was still busy.

By now, Matthew was being attended by a more senior doctor – I think the head of emergency. The doctor still couldn't get a blood pressure reading. He decided to use an ultrasound device to determine blood flow to try and detect the blood pressure in Matthew's right arm, which didn't have the rash on it. This worked. Matthew's blood pressure was critically low.

Even though he had had three shots of morphine, Matthew was still thinking clearly. He asked me to call his assistant to explain that he wouldn't be in over the next couple of days. Despite being so unwell, he had only taken two days off work at this stage.

'Can you please ring and let Sandra know I'll be in on Monday?'

He was always so full of optimism but I had a sense that it wasn't going to be over so quickly.

*

From the cubicle near the nurse's station, Matthew was taken into a much larger room at the end of the emergency unit. I followed him and the doctors through a set of swinging doors. The room was like an operating theatre – very sterile, spacious, and light – and Matthew was placed in the centre. I sat on a chair, opposite the doorway, trying to keep out of the way. Matthew was still alert, but was soon sedated so they could put a central line into his neck. Apparently this was to allow intravenous access into a large vein to administer medication.

The people around Matthew were moving quickly, and the junior doctor we had originally met a few hours earlier came over to ask if I was okay or if I needed anything.

'All the suits are coming in,' she said at one point, referring to the increasing number of people in suits coming and going at Matthew's bedside.

I was watching it all, feeling concerned. My stomach was churning. I knew something was wrong, but I still didn't have any idea that Matthew was dying. No one to this point had really explained to me what was happening, and I sensed that was probably because they didn't know themselves.

Finally, two doctors came over to me – I think they were the senior registrar and the head of intensive care for that evening. They explained to me that Matthew was going to intensive care. They advised me to call his family. I asked them to clarify how unwell he was.

'He is very ill,' was the response.

That wasn't enough for me.

'I'm an engineer. What does that equate to in figures?' I asked.

One of the doctors told me that Matthew's chance of survival was 50/50.

I thought only of the 50 per cent chance of survival. It didn't occur to me to think of the alternative, so I didn't immediately feel a sense of panic.

'Does that mean I call Matthew's family now or leave it until morning?'

'That's up to you.'

They were professional but quite clinical. They made it clear that things were bad, but even then, I still didn't get a sense that they were catastrophic.

I was desperate to talk to Matthew, but he was sedated. A short time later, just after midnight, Matthew was taken to intensive care. We definitely weren't going home that night.

I didn't realise at the time that I wouldn't have a chance to speak with him for another three weeks.

*

I didn't get to travel upstairs with Matthew because I had been talking to the doctors when they took him to ICU. So I didn't know exactly where I then had to go to find him.

The Mater Adult Hospital ICU is on Level 7. I caught the lift and walked down the hall to the doors of the unit. An intercom is situated on the left-hand wall, directly opposite a waiting room with a small kitchenette. I pressed the buzzer, and after what seemed like forever, someone answered and asked me what I wanted.

'I am Matthew Ames' wife. He's just come to ICU.'

They let me in. I met with the medical team and spent a lot of time talking about what could possibly have caused Matthew to be so ill. I couldn't think of anything specific. I went outside for a while to sit in the patient waiting area to think. I then remembered something.

The nurse on duty was called Dave. He was the father of twin babies. I knew this because we had just been talking about his children moments earlier.

I pressed on the buzzer, and they let me in. Matthew's bed was the first cubicle in ICU.

'Dave, I remembered something.' Perhaps I was clutching at straws, but I went on. 'Matthew had a vasectomy a few months ago. Could that have caused this?'

'I don't know, but thanks, Diane, that's good to know.'

I wondered why it was good to know, so I asked Dave directly.

'Because I was thinking about having a vasectomy, but now I won't.' He laughed.

It was a little bit of humour that was important, and I laughed too. I was so embarrassed to have brought it up!

Dave was very good at calming me that night. I wasn't feeling irrational, but by this stage I was really churning on the inside. I was sitting there, thinking, *I've got to call the relatives. Do I do that now or do I wait until morning?* I needed some guidance. Dave seemed to notice my angst.

'Look, Diane. I have been doing this for over twenty years. We've seen a lot worse than this. He'll be okay.'

I needed to hear these words. They gave me a huge sense of comfort and calmed me down, if only for a little while.

*

It became very busy around Matthew's bed again, so I was eventually directed back to the patient waiting area outside. This time, I left the light off, and found a dark corner of the room. I sat on the floor and leaned against the cool wall.

Oh no. What do I do?

Eventually, I rang my friend Gwen Lea. I knew she would have finished her shift in admissions at the Wesley Hospital at 11 p.m. It didn't occur to me that Christine and Roy, who were looking after the children, would have still been awake. I was also unsure about whether I should tell the family. I needed some advice.

Thankfully, Gwen answered the phone. I explained what was happening and she told me to call Christine and Roy, and offered to go over to my house and look after the children while they came in to the hospital. It was nice to have some direction.

I called home. Christine answered. It sounded like she hadn't been to sleep.

'Christine, it's Diane. Matthew is not well.'

I told her what was happening. She and Roy came straight in to the hospital, and I then sent Matthew's sisters, Rachel and Kate, text messages. I also sent texts to my sister, Jenny, and brother, Peter. Rachel came straight in to the hospital but Kate was living in Rockhampton on a property that had limited mobile coverage. She remained unaware that Matthew was ill until the following morning.

When Rachel arrived, we buzzed to go in. It was quite intimidating in that hall outside ICU. It was the still of night – the area was dark, with limited lighting. After a short wait, the head of intensive care, Dr Shane Townsend, came out to tell us that Matthew was doing as well as could be expected, and that it was best if we did not go in to see him at that moment.

'You should wait until the morning, and come back then.'

That was great news to me.

Fantastic. He is going to be OK, because if they thought he wasn't, they would be letting us in.

CHAPTER 2

MARKING TIME

I have always been optimistic. Matthew says I'm the happiest person he knows. I'm very good at showing that side of myself to everyone around me, but when I'm on my own or just with Matthew, I let my guard down. He has always been good for me in that respect – he puts a rational bent on things, and helps me get things into perspective if ever I become anxious or unhappy.

Our relationship has been that way from the beginning. We met on our first day as engineering students at the University of Queensland in February 1990, having just finished high school in Brisbane – I had attended All Hallows', an all-girls Catholic school in the inner city, and Matthew was a 'Churchie' boy, coming from a large all-boys Anglican school based in Coorparoo. We were friends for a while before Matthew finally asked me out at the start of our second semester of study. For our first date we went to the Engineering Ball, and within two weeks of actually dating, we knew we would marry.

We were both 17 and both still at home. Our families were very loving, but very different. I lived with my parents Mary and Bill Leighton, and siblings Jenny and Peter. We had always lived in Brisbane, and most of my life had been spent in our house at Chermside West in the northern suburbs of Brisbane. I had a huge extended family – grandparents, aunts and uncles, and many cousins with whom I was very close, and most were living locally.

Matthew lived with his parents, Roy and Christine, and older sisters, Kate and Rachel. They had moved a lot and had settled in Hawthorne, in Brisbane's inner east, where they lived in a Queenslander that Matthew had helped Roy renovate extensively. In contrast to mine, Matthew's extended family was very small. He had no cousins, one aunt (Ruth) who lived in New Zealand, two grandparents in Sydney, and a grandmother, Ninna, who lived with the family when I first met them. It was a household of very strong women – Ninna, Christine, Rachel and Kate. I had heard stories of how dynamic and fiery they were from Matthew. In my family, women were very strong, but fiery probably wouldn't be a word I or anyone else would use to describe us, so I was a little scared when the time came to meet them.

I had nothing to worry about. They made me feel very welcome, and I have always had a wonderful relationship with them and Roy. I was very thankful for that closeness as the family gathered around in ICU. It helped sustain me over the next few days.

*

On Thursday morning at around 2 a.m., I left Matthew in the care of the doctors at ICU and returned home to relieve Gwen. She was sitting on a couch in our lounge room under a doona with her pillow. She hadn't slept, but hadn't expected me to come home that evening so had come prepared to stay the night.

Gwen is one of three close friends I've made through being a parent at the school. We met when our eldest boys were in prep, and her three children are of similar ages to our boys. She is the most generous friend, and always the first to say, 'What can I do to help?' She, Nicole Webb, Lisa Moroney and I form a close-knit group. The four of us are like sisters and we see one another most days.

That night, when I came home from hospital, I curled up on the couch with Gwen. It was cold, quiet and dark, and she had left just one light on, over the couch. We sat toe to toe under the doona. I didn't cry, but it was so good to have her there. And she said what she always does when one of us is in trouble.

'Diane, I am not going anywhere. We'll be here for you forever.'

Gwen had a life of her own – three children, a husband and a busy job – and here she was dropping everything for me at that moment. I was so grateful.

She left just before 3 a.m., a couple of hours before her husband Anthony would have headed off to work. Like me, she would have been lucky to get any sleep before the children rose.

After seeing Gwen off, I turned on the computer to send emails to the boys' teachers. I sent each teacher the same email with the teacher's and child's names changed.

From: *Diane and Matthew Ames*
Sent: *14 June 2012 2:50*
To: *Jennifer Little*
Subject: *Keeping you up to date*

Hi Jenny,
Matthew has been admitted to hospital tonight and is in ICU. He is expected to be in ICU for the next three or four days.
Matthew and I left the boys with their grandparents (Na and Papa) when we went to the hospital. They were all having a great time.

They expect Matthew to be here in the morning so if
Will is not his usual self, you will know why.
Thanks.

Once I had sent those, I had a shower and fell into bed. I didn't sleep easily, as my mind was racing. My chief thought was, *How did it get to this point?* I must have eventually dropped off to sleep, but it seemed like only a moment had passed when Emily woke me early the next morning.

I made sure we stuck to our normal routine so the children wouldn't be too worried. Life in the mornings was chaotic. Luke was in Grade 3, Ben in Grade 2 and Will in Grade 1, while Emily was just two, having had her birthday in March. Will still needed help getting dressed and to tie his shoelaces, and Emily was completely dependent on me. Usually I prepare school lunches and get organised the night before, but on this morning, I was madly rushing around getting things ready for the day.

I told the kids their father was going to stay at the hospital because his arm was really sore, but that he was in great hands. Because Matthew travelled a lot, the morning routine without him wasn't that unusual so the kids didn't seem too worried.

Normally I drop the boys off at the 'drop and go' section of the school and keep going. On this morning, though, I dropped the boys off, drove 100 metres, and parked in the parking zone near Gwen's car. I parked there because I knew I needed to talk to Gwen and Nicole, and I went into the school to look for them. I had Emily with me, and it only took me a few minutes to find them inside the school gates.

Gwen had filled Nicole in about what had happened to Matthew. They seemed surprised that I was at the school, and they could tell I was in a bit of a daze.

They offered to meet with the school principal on my behalf, which I thought would be a great help. They would inform the school that Matthew was still very unwell and if things deteriorated, one of them would come and get the children.

Knowing that Gwen and Nicole had things at the school under control, I walked back to the car with Emily. After I had strapped Emily in, I climbed into the back seat of the car to sit with her, which is where Gwen and Nicole tell me they found me a short time later. I can't to this day remember what I was doing and why I was still sitting in the back seat.

I wonder now whether I subconsciously parked where I did that morning because I knew Gwen and Nicole would find me. Obviously I needed them to.

'Di? What are you doing here?' Nicole asked.

Nicole and Gwen have very different styles. Gwen's a bit soft like me, and Nicole's quite to the point – she says exactly what's on her mind. They make a great team and I could see they were so concerned for me.

'I'm waiting for visiting hours to start at the hospital,' I replied.

They looked at one another and back at me.

'Di, you don't have visiting hours when your husband is so unwell,' Gwen said. Since Gwen worked at a hospital, she was worth trusting on this.

'You just go when you want – all day long if you want. Just go now,' Nicole insisted.

I have never been the type of person who breaks the rules. I remember in the early days of dating Matthew that I was really excited to jump the fence when our group wasn't allowed entry into The Ship Inn at South Bank because some of us were underage. It seemed like such a huge thing to do. I normally always do the right thing. So I felt a bit unsure, but they were insistent.

'Diane Ames,' Nicole said. 'You need to drive over there right now. Matthew needs you.'

I started the car and left. As I was driving, I received a call from one of the orthopaedic doctors to let me know Matthew was going in for surgery. They were going to clean out the infection under the rash on his left arm, and this would take a few hours. I knew I had a bit of time to get organised.

I returned home. Ben and Luke had tennis lessons and Will had a birthday party that afternoon, so I collected the presents and the tennis racquets, and drove them to Nicole's house.

Nicole was again surprised to see me – 'What are you doing here? You're supposed to be at the hospital,' she said as she greeted me at her front door. I explained that Matthew was in surgery for the next few hours and I was getting prepared for the afternoon. I handed her the presents and the racquets, and asked her to organise the boys in case I didn't make it back from the hospital. I had arranged for Will to be picked up for the party, and I wanted there to be no change to the plans if that was possible.

Nicole offered to take Emily for me, but I thought she was going to be looked after by Christine for the day, so I told Nicole that I was headed to Matthew's parents' house.

Nicole told me later that she rang Gwen after I left, and said, 'Gwen, in about twenty minutes to half an hour you are going to get a call from Di, who will shortly realise that Christine, who would normally take Emily today, is at the hospital. You'll need to be ready to look after her if you can.'

And that's exactly what happened. Gwen was prepared, and happy to take my little girl, who in turn was happy to go to Gwen. It was great to have people planning and acting for me, as I really wasn't thinking too straight. It meant I could focus on the day ahead and I arrived at the hospital feeling a bit more settled.

When I got to the waiting room, I found Roy, Christine and Rachel already there. Roy had contacted Kate, and she and her husband, Jason, were travelling with their children, Maeve and Joshua, by road from Rockhampton to Brisbane. They expected to arrive later that evening.

It was a nervous time for everyone. Matthew returned from theatre just after lunchtime, and we had the opportunity to meet with the surgeons. They told me Matthew had suffered toxic shock, and explained that they were taking cultures to find out the cause of the illness because at that stage they could only find evidence of a streptococcal infection. We found out later that this in fact was the cause – that the toxic shock was a result of *Streptococcus pyogenes* (known generally as Strep A).

It's a common bug, but if it gets into the bloodstream, as it had in Matthew's case, it can be fatal. Matthew's fitness, the doctors told me, might have been the reason he was able to battle on for so long until the disease finally got on top of him. It had, it seemed, started with a sore throat before the bacteria invaded his bloodstream. The infection is generally referred to as invasive group A streptococcus, whereby bacteria enters areas of the body where they would not normally be found.

Matthew had been conscious that morning, although he says now he can't recall this. The doctors told me Matthew had signed the consent form to have his left forearm 'debrided', or operated on to clean the area of infection. They said they had left the wound open so they could flush it again if need be, and that they had been able to save his tendons but his two smallest fingers would have reduced function. This was good news to me, and I was hopeful despite the fact that Matthew was now on life support.

His entire body was a flushed red colour, and his hands and feet were turning purple. Black streaks were appearing across his forehead, and his mouth area was mottled and swollen. The tips of his ears were going black, and other areas of his body such as his genitals were starting to be affected by the infection and subsequent withdrawal of blood. His kidneys had failed, and the doctors explained that his entire system was shutting down. I remember looking at his face, thinking, *Please. I love that face. I don't care what happens – I just want that face.* I had always thought, and still do now, that Matthew was the most handsome person I had ever met. I could stare at his face forever.

It was difficult to access his body when I visited him because he was covered in lines and tubes. I could only really kiss his head. I went in on numerous occasions during the day, but I was conscious that I needed to pick up the boys from school. Anytime I could be in the room with Matthew, I would be, but there was so much they had to do to him medically that I constantly had to leave and wait in the patient waiting area with Roy, Christine and Rachel until we were buzzed back in. Each time we visited, we would talk to Matthew about continuing to fight hard.

We were taking turns to go in because the visits were draining, but it was our way of making sure that one of us was always with him throughout the day. We had our own ways of coping while we were in the waiting room. Christine and I would cry because it was so hard to see Matthew like this, and we didn't need to worry about being strong for the kids. Roy was being positive. 'Don't worry, it's all going to be okay,' he would say, before asking, 'Does anybody want any coffee?' He was the provider, and was always looking after us. Rachel needed to keep up with her work so was on the computer between visits. It was good being together.

I was glad I had made arrangements with Nicole so the boys would maintain their routine that afternoon. I was reluctant to let them see Matthew as he was – he didn't look like the father they knew, and he was progressively getting worse. I knew routine was important. My parents had died in quick succession when the children were younger, and keeping to a normal routine had helped them and me get through that period.

After leaving the hospital, I picked up Luke and Ben from their tennis lesson and then picked up Will from the birthday party he had attended, as well as a little friend of Will's, another Ben. I walked Ben into his house where his parents were waiting for him. They were concerned, and asked me how Matthew was.

I was conscious the boys were in the car and couldn't hear me, and I felt that I could talk to Ben's parents, but I didn't want to go into too much detail. I explained that Matthew was in intensive care, but said, 'He's fine – it will all be good.'

I knew from the look on their faces that they didn't necessarily believe me. *I wonder if they think I'm delusional?* I was getting a little used to that reaction – I think people confused my being positive with being a bit naïve. I left quickly and returned home.

The only sense the boys had that something was wrong was when both Gwen and Gayle (Gayle Schabe, with whom we were supposed to be going to Disneyland later in the year) visited the house that evening to offer dinner. The last time someone had brought us dinner was when Emily was born, a couple of years earlier, and here we had two lots of dinner on offer. The boys thought it was exciting, but they also had an idea that something wasn't quite right. It was unusual to have others at dinner during the week, even when their father was away travelling.

Later that night, they asked to have a sleepover in Matthew's and my room and I agreed. It would be nice to have them with me, and our boys often did their important talking from their pillows. They might have been quiet all day, but it was at that point before sleep that they would ask questions or reveal their worries – and if they were together, the other two boys could hear the answer to the question being asked. We have a rule in our house: there is no such thing as a silly question.

There were no questions that night, and the boys crashed quickly, as they usually did. I was exhausted, but I still couldn't sleep. It was quite late, and once I knew the children were sound asleep, I got up, cleaned the kitchen and got ready for the next day. It felt to me like things were about to unravel. In my mind, if at least some part of the house was in order, I would feel better – at that point whether the kitchen was clean or not seemed to be the only thing in my life that I could control.

Other than immediate members of our family, I had only told a handful of people the details of what had happened to Matthew. I really didn't know what to say. It felt like I was treading water – just waiting to see what was going to happen next. Matthew's sister Rachel stepped in to help at that early stage – she updated family members and a slightly wider circle of close friends, which left me free to concentrate on Matthew and the kids.

On Friday morning, I arranged to meet with Gwen and Nicole at Gwen's house after school drop-off. I told the girls that doctors had told me Matthew might not survive, and that I wasn't going to give up hope.

'Diane, you don't have to give up on him,' Nicole told me. They were great words from a great friend. From that day, I never did.

I asked Gwen and Nicole to make some calls on my behalf. The children still didn't know what was happening and I was worried about the story getting out of control, and the possibility that it might be mentioned on Facebook. Gwen and Nicole wanted me to tell the children the details, but I didn't know how to do that and to be honest, I was hoping that everything was going to be fine. They also suggested that they meet with the school counsellor to get some advice, so we rang and I told her that I wanted my friends to meet her on my behalf.

We agreed that Emily could stay with Gwen and Nicole, who would work together to see that she was looked after over the next few days. It was, however, Nicole's husband, David, to whom Emily was handed first. David, who works from home on Fridays, was recruited to look after their son Xavier and Emily. Another friend,

Mandi Gosling, was also coming over to help.

As we were about to leave, Emily decided to fill her nappy. I wanted to change her before I left, but Nicole took Emily from me and handed her to David, who was looking a bit shocked at how quickly everything was moving. Nicole said we didn't have time, and she turned to Mandi who was standing beside David and Emily.

'Mandi, he might need some help with that.'

We laughed – David was more than capable, but it was an unexpected and rapid return to nappy changing for him.

I was comfortable with the arrangement. Emily loved playing with Xavier, whom she knew well from play dates in the park across the road where we gathered after school every Friday afternoon. She seemed unfazed and waved goodbye as I left for the hospital, and Nicole and Gwen headed for the school.

When I arrived at ICU, Senior Intensivist Dr Amod Karnik met with me. He told me that Matthew's condition had deteriorated further and medical staff were amazed he had survived the night. I, in turn, was surprised that they thought he was really going to die – it still wasn't something I thought would happen.

From that point, it became really clear to me that I needed to be with Matthew over the next few days – I couldn't be torn between him and the children, and I needed to stay at the hospital. I believed that my being there would be of help to Matthew, so I was happy to let the children be cared for by others over the weekend.

Meanwhile, the school counsellor was advising Nicole and Gwen that it was best to tell the kids the truth – I didn't have to give them too much detail, but enough that they wouldn't be envisaging something that wasn't actually happening or that things were more extreme than they actually were. The counsellor told Nicole and Gwen the children wouldn't cope with lying and that I needed to be honest. Our plan was that Gwen would help me talk to the boys that afternoon, after school, before I took them up to the hospital.

The day passed and Matthew deteriorated further. I asked Roy if he would come with me to help when I told the children – the boys absolutely love their 'Papa', and I thought it would be comforting for them if he was there. We met Gwen at Nicole's house, where close friends from the school community had gathered for the day, awaiting news of Matthew. Gwen told Roy and me what the counsellor had said. Gwen's like me – she had taken notes, and I in turn was taking notes from her. So when the time came to collect the kids from school, we were on the verge of running late, and there was a sudden mass exodus from Nicole's house. David Webb was again handed some of the younger children as we dashed off to the school grounds.

I dropped Roy at the school gate and he went to get the boys while I found a car park. As I walked into the schoolyard a few minutes later to meet Roy and the boys, I could see that Luke was upset. I thought he was crying because of Matthew, and that upset me. I was thinking, *Oh no. Somebody else has already told Luke how dire things are. I've left it too late.*

Roy must have seen the look on my face because as they got closer, he called out to me.

'It's okay, Diane, we need to have a pizza party.'

I was confused. *What?*

Roy explained that Luke was upset because his class hadn't won a competition for the right to hold a pizza party associated with the upcoming school fete. Luke is fiercely competitive, so this was a big disappointment for him.

Oh. Wow. Okay. I felt a huge sense of relief.

We made a commitment to have our own pizza party in the park the following week, and everyone agreed, so the mood was light. As soon as we got home to our house, I sat the boys down with some afternoon tea. Gwen and Roy sat with us at the dining room table, but they let me take the lead in explaining to the boys what was happening with their father.

I started with, 'Daddy is really sick.'

I explained that we were going to see Matthew at the hospital. I took on board Gwen's advice from the school counsellor. I kept it brief, and answered any questions the children had as honestly as I could. Surprisingly, they had next to no questions. They accepted what I told them, and at the time didn't need me to say too much more.

I didn't go into too much detail because I knew the ICU social worker, Christie Barrett, was ready to meet us at the hospital. Christie had been amazing over the previous few days, liaising between the family, doctors and hospital administration when we had any questions that no one was immediately available to answer. She talked with us a few times a day, and was a great support to all of us. Christie was going to help the kids and me when we went to see Matthew. It would be the first time the boys had seen their father since his admission to hospital two nights earlier.

My explanation at home didn't take very long. Roy was trying to lighten the mood and was being a bit silly, telling funny stories about what he did when he was younger and making all the boys laugh. The boys would listen to me for a few minutes, and then turn to Roy.

'Okay, Mum,' Will would say. 'Hey, Papa, can you tell us another story?'

I was so thankful Roy and Gwen were there. I think the boys knew things were serious, but they were coping really well and were happy, and the news about their father didn't seem to have a huge impact at that point. I was surprised I didn't cry. I'm normally a huge weeper, but for some reason, I seemed to be able to keep it together. I had the most intense desire to protect these little people for whom I was responsible, and to do that, I needed to show them that I was being strong.

Emily, who had been at the park with Nicole and Lisa and some other school friends, was going to stay with Gwen for the evening. Gwen left to pick her up and Roy and I took the boys to the hospital to meet with Christie, who was waiting in the patient waiting area with Christine, Kate and Rachel.

Christie was so well prepared – she had pencils and paper, and a diary that the children could use to record their thoughts. We explained what Matthew was going to look like, and that he had a sore arm. We visited Matthew, and the boys seemed to be accepting of what they saw, if a little confused. They asked lots of questions about the machines, and we tried to answer as honestly as we could. We did not, though, tell the boys that the doctors thought Matthew might die.

We told them he was very sick, and that he was fighting very hard against the illness. It was the truth and at that stage, I thought it was all they needed to know.

The day was not yet over. Luke had rugby training, and all the boys were going to stay with Matthew's sister Rachel and her husband, Aaron, for the weekend. Matthew's other sister, Kate, and her husband, Jason, had arrived from Rockhampton and their children would join the party. Jason and Aaron were running what they called 'daddy day care' – with my three boys, there were seven cousins in total aged between two and eight. The plan was for pizza, soft drink and Scooby Doo movies. My kids were excited.

I had taken Luke to rugby, leaving him in the care of Gwen's husband, Anthony, and was on my way to drop Ben and Will with Aaron and Jason when the phone in the car rang. It was Rachel. She asked me how far away from the hospital I was, and I told her that the kids were in the car so she knew I couldn't really talk. She said I needed to come back to the hospital straight away.

I didn't know at the time that doctors had told Rachel, Kate and Christine that Matthew was going to die that night, but I knew from the tone of her voice that things were bad.

It was the first and only time that I thought perhaps Matthew had lost his battle.

I tried to be positive despite my fears, and Aaron told me later that he and Jason had no idea anything was wrong when I dropped the boys off. I gave them big hugs, told them that Daddy was fighting hard, and that I would see them tomorrow.

When I got back into the car and started driving to the hospital, I was pleading mentally – not with God, but with my parents, who in my mind were in heaven.

Please, Mum. Dad. Don't let him in. Please. His time is not up yet. If he comes, send him back. We need him to be here, with us.

I then started saying it out loud, over and over again, to myself in the car. It gave me comfort to think I could do something by praying to my parents, because I knew that really I couldn't do anything.

When I arrived back at the Mater, I was thinking of what I was going to say to him if I was too late. I was begging that he hadn't already gone but I feared the worst.

As I walked through the entrance, I ran into Kate who was returning from the chapel, which was surprising – it's not a place you would normally find her. She told me that there were conflicting ideas about what was happening to Matthew, and I was taken aback. She must have seen my confusion because she instantly stopped talking. She seemed to know that I thought he had already died.

'Oh no, no, no, Diane.' She hugged me. 'He hasn't died. He's still with us.'

We hugged and cried together for a while, and then I pulled back. I had such a huge sense of relief.

He's not dead. Great. This is different to what I was expecting.

'Right then,' I said, wiping the tears away. 'That's a different speech I'll need to give him. I had one prepared, but it's not the one I need.'

I started walking, with Kate beside me.

'I'll have to get up there and tell him to keep fighting.'

We headed to ICU, where I visited Matthew and told him, again, that we needed him to stay with us.

He was listening, I know, but I could see that he might be losing the battle.

CHAPTER 3

THE DECISION

To appreciate when life is easy, you first have to know how hard it can be, and climbing a mountain was my measuring stick.

I had travelled a lot with my family while growing up. The year I was to marry Matthew, my parents decided we would have our last family holiday together and took Jenny, Peter and me on a trip to Egypt and Israel. I was 22.

Peter and Dimity Dornon were on the same tour. Peter is a well-known sports physiotherapist, sculptor and author, and Dimity is the founder of the renowned Hear and Say Centre. They are an amazing, inspiring couple, and they shared a dinner table with us one evening.

I have always been interested in other people's life stories, and I asked Peter how he managed to achieve so much in his life. Aside from mentioning that he didn't watch television, Peter told me he had completed the Kokoda Track.

'Once you've conquered Kokoda, everything else in life seems easy,' he said.

This struck a chord and I thought that one day I would try to walk the Kokoda Track. It seemed like the greatest challenge I could attempt. Prior to meeting Matthew, I had never camped, and holidays were spent in hotels. Life with Matthew changed all that, however. We had become great lovers of the outdoors and adventure travel in our first years together.

Matthew says he got his love of the outdoors from Boy Scouts when he was young, but it seems to be in his family. He introduced me to camping when we were students, and we were regular adventure seekers before the children came along. Each year, we would tackle something more challenging. Our first trip together had been to Eastern Europe over winter a few weeks after graduating university. We had also walked the Milford Track in New Zealand, and climbed Machu Picchu in Peru.

I decided that Kilimanjaro would be my Kokoda. I liked the idea of doing something so difficult, and doing it early in our life together. I figured that if we did this, the rest of our life would be easy.

The opportunity came in 2001 when Matthew and I travelled to Africa. We were independent travellers, and Matthew had planned our itinerary down to the last minute.

The trip was to include a trek to the summit of Mt Kilimanjaro, known as Uhuru Peak, at 5895 metres above sea level. We had chosen to climb Kilimanjaro via the Machame route because it was more scenic and passed through a number of distinctively different habitats. The trek would take six days and be more challenging than other routes. That was fine with us as we had trained hard and were the fittest we had been in our lives.

The night before we set out, we sorted through all our gear and prepared for the trek. We then went to dinner and when we returned to our room, found that we had been robbed. The thieves took our cash and travellers cheques but had left our cameras and trekking gear. The positive was that they hadn't taken anything that would stop us completing the trek.

The next morning we reported the theft to the Arusha police before we started the trek. By the time we left the police station, I was not in a good mood and it took most of the first day of the walk before I snapped out of it. Matthew gave me some space during this time and seeing as our group consisted of Matthew and me, our guide, our cook and porters to carry our food and tents, the start of the trek was quite quiet.

The trek begins at Machame Gate at the low elevation of 1640 metres above sea level. It takes six hours to climb from the hot and humid base of Kilimanjaro through lush rainforest to Machame Camp at 2850 metres. Over the next three to four days, we walked for up to nine hours each day, leaving the rainforest behind and heading through different habitats – moorland, semi-desert and alpine – as we climbed to 4550 metres for the eve of our summit climb. When we arrived at our final camp, we ate quickly and climbed into our tents just before it started to snow. We wanted to get a few hours' sleep before we set out for the summit at midnight.

We were so exhausted that we fell asleep straight away and were woken by the guide at midnight saying, 'Excuse me, Mr Matthew and Mrs Matthew. It's time to summit.'

We got up slowly because we were affected by the altitude, and then set off. It was cold but thankfully it had stopped snowing. Matthew carried the camera next to his skin so that it wouldn't freeze. We were ascending through heavy scree, in the dark, to be at the summit in time for sunrise.

I started to struggle as we climbed higher. It was slow going at that altitude, and because we had chosen a faster walk, we hadn't had the time to acclimatise on the way up.

I wasn't talking much, which Matthew says is always a sign that something's up with me, as I'm normally very talkative.

We had been walking for around five hours, and weren't far from the summit when we stopped on the side of the mountain for a break. Matthew and the guide gave me their tea. There was no milk or sugar in it – which would make you vomit at that altitude – but apparently this helps people make it to the top. It wasn't working on me.

'Just leave me here. Just leave me here.'

I wasn't going any further. Matthew and the guide had other ideas, but I was determined.

'You can pick me up on the way down,' I told them.

'Diane, you're not thinking straight,' Matthew said. He reminded me that the way down was on the other side of the mountain. The altitude was affecting my ability to think rationally.

'Really, just leave me here. You can come back and get me. I'll be fine.'

We sat for a while longer. Eventually, Matthew told the guide and me that we would go down from where we were.

'What do you mean?' I wanted Matthew to see the summit. Just because I was giving up didn't mean he should forgo the experience.

'Diane, I'm not going to leave you here, so if we go down, we all go down from here.' I knew he was serious.

That was enough for me. If Matthew needed me to walk so that he could see the summit, then I would push myself. Our guide was assuring us that we didn't have far to go, and sure enough, a short time later, we reached the top.

The air was thin and cold and the sun was coming up. It was a spectacular day, and we could see for miles around us. It was as amazing as I thought it would be. It had been worth it.

We stayed at the top for a while, taking photos and some video that later revealed just how affected by the altitude we both were, and then descended quickly. We slid and jumped down scree slopes, laughing and yelling. As the oxygen started flooding back to our brains, so did our energy levels and enthusiasm. We were feeling invincible, and were euphoric at our achievement.

Peter Dornan's words had been worth listening to. Our version of Kokoda, climbing Mt Kilimanjaro, had been our biggest challenge. Without Matthew, I wouldn't have even tried to do it, and definitely wouldn't have succeeded.

At the time I was convinced that the rest of our lives would be easy in comparison. I had no idea how hard things might become. I had completed the journey to Uhuru Peak on Kilimanjaro because Matthew was with me. He had supported me, and pushed me, because he knew I could do it.

This time, I didn't have Matthew to talk to. He wasn't there to provide advice or suggest alternatives. He had been in an induced coma for a day, and for the first time in our lives together, I was making major decisions without him.

All I could do was hope he would trust me to do the right thing.

*

Overnight, Matthew's condition deteriorated further and his left arm was amputated late on Friday evening in the hope of stemming the infection. It was explained to us that the infection was causing the tissue in Matthew's arms and legs to die. The toxins being generated by muscle death were adding to the stress on his body, which was now trying to fight both the infection and the toxins being released by dead muscles. So amputation would reduce the toxic load on the rest of Matthew's body, and give him a greater chance to fight the original infection, which could be treated with antibiotics.

I stayed close. There are two waiting rooms outside the Mater's ICU. One is a large room including a kitchen, and the other is a small, narrow room that could fit no more than three people comfortably. It's quite dark and quiet, and that smaller room was where I spent the night.

Matthew's mother Christine had slept in the bigger waiting room on a large recliner. The nurses had looked after us well with sheets and pillows but despite that, neither of us had slept well.

The door to the ICU seemed to be busy. Every time I heard it open, I would wonder whether someone was coming to tell me that Matthew had died. I would hold my breath and wait. The footsteps would pass by the room, and then I would try to drift off again.

Dawn came, and no one had come to my door.

The family gathered again. It was our fourth day of waiting. Roy, Rachel, Kate and our great friends Dan and Annette Alexander met Christine and me. Dan was Matthew's best man at our wedding, and we have been friends since university. Christine and I were given coffee, and clean clothes so we could shower. It was comforting to have everyone there.

I then had a fantastic lift when my sister, Jenny, arrived. I hadn't seen her since I sent a text to tell her Matthew was in ICU and her coming to the hospital was important to me. Jenny has a calming influence when she is around. She walked up to me, gave me a big hug and said, 'I just wanted to be here for my little sis.'

Jen coming to the hospital reminded me of our time together with mum and dad, when she was a huge support to me at another really trying time. Mum had lost her battle with bowel cancer three years earlier, and Dad had a massive stroke and died the following month. They had loved Matthew like a son and would have been devastated about what was happening. Emily was born almost exactly a year after they died, and her just being in our lives helped me heal. I did not know it yet, but Emily would play a similar role in helping our family deal with Matthew's illness.

We all visited Matthew. We could see where his arm had been amputated, and also that he was getting worse. The areas of dead black skin on his face, ears and neck were growing. His hands and feet were a deep purple, and it seemed that the only thing keeping him alive was the breathing machine – his chest was heaving with every pump of oxygen.

I noticed that even though Matthew was in a coma, medical staff would talk directly to him about what they were doing. Roy had asked Amod Karnik, one of the senior intensivists, whether he believed Matthew could hear what we were saying while he was in a coma.

'We don't really know, but I like to believe so,' Amod had said. It was a comforting response.

I talked to Matthew a lot on my visits during these early days. While I tried to be brave in front of everyone else, when it was just Matthew and me, I would cry. I told him to fight on – that we needed him, and that I couldn't be without him.

I would normally hold his hand while I was talking, and on this day, I noticed that his hand, the only one he had left, was cold.

Eamonn Maher, a senior ICU nurse on whom we would come to rely greatly, came into the patient waiting area soon after everyone had gathered and told us that the medical team wanted to have a meeting with the family, and a short time later, they joined us in the waiting room. Dan and Annette stayed – we wanted them to be there.

Everyone looked a bit grey. The team lined up along the wall, all standing, while we were seated around the room. I can't remember how many there were – possibly around eight staff. They were almost balanced with family.

Amod started to talk. He had been direct with us the previous evening when he told us that Matthew would probably die during the night, and he was direct again now. I knew Matthew would have appreciated his approach.

'Well, Matthew didn't die last night, but he will.'

The doctors told us about the overnight operation to amputate Matthew's arm, and said it hadn't slowed the speed of the infection.

The team, which included orthopaedic surgeons Brett Collins and Tim McMeniman, told us our only option now to save Matthew was to remove his remaining limbs. They would only be able to do this if CT scans showed that the disease had not entered his lungs or his brain.

'If we are able to take him to surgery, it is highly likely that he will not survive,' Tim said, 'but if we don't, he will definitely die.'

I asked what the chance of survival was.

'It's low,' Tim said.

'Can you give that to me in percentages?' I asked.

'I would say around one per cent,' Tim responded. I liked that I felt he was being honest.

The family asked lots of questions. Would his limbs still need to be amputated even if he did survive? (Yes.) Would he have brain damage? (We don't know.) Then there was silence as we digested everything.

Kate spoke. She seemed to know what the rest of us were thinking.

'Look, we understand the difficult decisions you are having to make in relation to his quality of life,' she said.

'If it was anyone else in this room, we would say let them go. But this is the only person for whom you would do this.'

I saw the surgeons were really listening.

She continued. 'This guy is the most pragmatic, positive and calm person you will ever meet. He's an engineer. For him, nothing is ever so big a problem that you can't find a solution.'

There was a brief silence. I wanted to explain the importance of saving Matthew. I knew that he had only a one per cent chance of making it, and that life would be incredibly hard for him, but I also knew we had to go ahead for the sake of our family. I knew I needed to be able to tell the children that we had taken every opportunity to save Matthew, no matter how small. At that moment, there was only one option, and that was to give him and the doctors a chance.

I looked from Kate to Tim and Brett.

'Yes, and our children need their father. They all need their father, but my boys in particular really need their dad.'

'So you are all in agreement?' Tim looked around the room. So did I. Everyone nodded. There was no doubt in our minds – Matthew would at least want the chance to live. I needed everyone to be positive. I spoke again.

'We need you to have faith in Matthew because we all do. He will be the one per cent.'

No one else spoke for a moment. The medical staff looked at one another.

'Okay then.' Tim McMeniman nodded his head and looked around at the team. A few others also nodded. There seemed to be a collective sigh, but not in a bad way. We were at least going to try.

Tim explained what was going to happen from here. Any further step would depend on the results from the CT scan, so they would prepare him for that, and we would know once that was completed whether the surgery was possible. Even doing the scan was high risk – it would require 8000 images and take a few hours, and the intensivists were very nervous about releasing Matthew for that amount of time. It wasn't going to be plain sailing, but it was progress.

By this stage, Tim seemed positive. 'I think this can really work. I think we can do this.'

I stood up and gave him a hug. I was so grateful to him and the rest of the team for taking such a huge risk with the operation.

'He will be the one per cent,' I told him. We knew that this was as important for the medical team as it was for us. There was a feeling that we were all in this together.

*

We were able to see Matthew prior to his CT scan. There didn't seem to be a lot of time before he was taken downstairs, but after that, time seemed to stand still and hours passed.

My brother, Peter, and his wife, Robyn, joined our group. Peter is a GP and it was comforting to have someone there who could explain some of the medical language and what certain things meant. Peter was able to tell us exactly what they were doing with the scans.

It seemed like forever before a nurse came into the waiting room to tell us everything had gone well. She told us that Matthew was on his way back, and would be proceeding to surgery. There was excitement in her voice – we had some hope.

With that excitement and sense of hope, however, came the realisation that we would have to say goodbye in the event that Matthew didn't make it. I thought of the children. They had only just realised how sick their father was, and here we were asking them to say goodbye. But it had to be done.

I hadn't yet told them that Matthew's left arm had been amputated, and I wasn't intending to that afternoon. I was not even going to tell the boys about the operation – they were simply to know that Matthew was very sick, that he might die that afternoon and that the doctors were doing their best to save him. I felt that talking about the amputations might distract them from the most important thing – that their father was perhaps going to die. I asked Eamonn to prepare Matthew so that the children wouldn't be able to see that an arm had been removed.

Kate and Rachel called their husbands, Jason and Aaron, and asked them to bring in the children – Luke, Ben and Will; Maeve, Joshua, Ethan and Lincoln – and I then called Gwen and asked her to bring in Emily.

I had requested through my aunt Janet Leighton that Father Peter Kennedy administer the last rites to Matthew. We had been close to Father Peter when we were part of his congregation at St Mary's. Matthew had great respect for him and had said he always felt challenged by Father Peter to be a better person.

So we knew he would want Peter, if anyone, to do this job.

*

The surgical team was waiting for us to say our goodbyes before they took Matthew to theatre.

Emily arrived with Gwen and Nicole. They had come together to support me and each other, and had stopped at our friend Lisa's house to get a nice dress in which Emily could farewell her father. Emily was handed to Christine, who held her close; she was surrounded by love and happy to wearing a beautiful dress. Being only two, she was enjoying the cuddles.

Father Peter arrived and we talked about how Matthew was going. I could tell it was challenging for him. He had known Matthew really well and had baptised all our boys. He respected our decision and was there to support us.

The boys had been having a great time with their cousins, and were in party mode. I knew the medical staff were waiting for me to tell my children what was going on so they could take Matthew to surgery.

After letting the boys say hello to everyone and talk about what they had been doing, I called them over to me, and we sat down. Christie Barrett, the ICU social worker, was with us, and had given me great advice on what I needed to think about when talking to them, such as being open and prepared to answer questions. Christie was beside me, and the boys were kneeling around a coffee table in the centre of the room.

They settled, and I started.

'Daddy is really unwell, and he is getting worse. He may have to go to heaven this afternoon.'

They were quiet and listening closely. Luke and Will were looking directly at me, and Ben was looking down.

I was devastated to be having this conversation.

'We are hoping that he won't, and that he'll get better every day, but we have to say goodbye just in case he does.' I stopped, and Luke's eyes welled up before he started to cry. They weren't loud sobs, but I could see he was heartbroken. So was I, but it was important that I continue. Ben kept looking at the floor and Will remained silent.

'There is a chance that Daddy is going to stay here with us and we're hoping like anything that will happen. We will never give up hope.' I then told them we were going to go in and say goodbye. Ben and Will were extremely quiet and nodded that they were okay to come with me, but Luke said he didn't want to come in. I could understand why and tried to give him a hug, but he pulled away. Christine, who has always been particularly special to Luke, also tried to encourage him, but he was firm.

Our friend Dan, who had been in the room while I was talking, sidled up to Luke and put his hand on Luke's shoulder.

'It's all right. He can stay with me,' Dan told us.

Dan then turned to Luke and suggested a game of cricket with a packet of macadamia nuts and some bananas we had in the room. It was completely out of left field, but Luke and Dan proceeded, with Roy, Jason and Aaron, to have a game of cricket in the waiting area, taking turns to bowl and bat while the rest of the family and our friends visited Matthew in small groups to say their farewells. As a distraction strategy, it was working well.

Finally, it was time for the kids and me to visit Matthew.

Dan could see I was ready, and said to Luke, very casually, 'Okay, mate. Let's go and see your dad.'

Luke was hesitant, but agreed. I was so relieved and will be forever grateful to Dan. It reminded me that sometimes men just understand what boys need better than I do and reinforced in my mind why we needed to be doing everything we could to save Matthew.

We assigned each of the children an adult, so it was a large group going in this time. We had to buzz at the ICU door, which was still intimidating even though we had become familiar with it. This time, the wait for a response seemed to take forever; for me, each minute of waiting was a minute in which Luke might change his mind.

Father Peter came in with us, and we started with a prayer for Matthew. I then lifted Ben and Will up to give their father a kiss and say goodbye, but Luke was standing away from the foot of the bed. He didn't want to come close. Eventually, he came over to me and whispered into my ear.

'Can you please give Daddy a kiss and a hug for me?'

'Of course, sweetheart.' And I did.

Emily wanted to climb all over Matthew, and I lifted her over his attachments for a kiss.

'Bye bye, Daddy.' She patted his face with her little hands, and then waved. As we left his bedside, she blew him a kiss as though she was going to see him soon.

Walking away from Matthew's bed that day with our children was one of the hardest things I've ever had to do. But as we walked from ICU into the waiting area, I was instantly reminded that I wasn't alone. Friends and family filled the room – some were quiet, others were still talking. Everyone seemed to have a different way of coping.

Very shortly afterwards, Eamonn knocked on the door of the patient waiting area and told us they would be wheeling Matthew past the waiting room in a minute. We lined the hall, and the doors opened. Matthew, surrounded by medical staff, was wheeled slowly past us. We blew him kisses, every one of the 20 or so of us in tears. It was just after 5 p.m.

Amod Karnik, as he walked past, smiled at us. It was just a little smile, but it was a smile.

'See you tomorrow.'

I had learned that doctors wear a non-committal expression on their faces when they're giving you any kind of news. It's not a criticism – it had just taken me a while to get used to it. So a smile made me instantly hopeful.

Oh my God!

'That means you think he's going to make it!' I felt excited. I could have hugged him.

Amod was calm, but the smile was still there.

'I'll just see you tomorrow.' He patted me on the shoulder before heading off behind Matthew.

I turned to Kate and Rachel, who agreed with me. If Amod thought he would see us tomorrow, there was hope. If Matthew died tonight, there was no way we would still be here in this waiting room. It was a great sign.

While we were all still devastated, our collective mood seemed to lighten for a moment, but then it was time for the children to go home again. Emily, in her beautiful borrowed dress, was going to stay another night at Gwen's house, where they would make her feel special. Luke, Ben and Will were going to continue their party with the cousins and their uncles Aaron and Jason.

Parting from the kids was actually the hardest moment for me. It hadn't been saying goodbye to Matthew, because I hadn't given up hope, and I never really believed Matthew was actually going to die. But it was something I knew we needed to do because there was a really strong chance Matthew might die; it was important that the children had the opportunity to say their farewells.

At that moment, when I was kissing and hugging the children goodbye, I felt I was trying to be all things to all people. I was their mum, but I was also Matthew's wife. I wanted to be there to support them, but I couldn't because I needed to stay close to Matthew. I knew that the kids would have a great night playing, watching movies and being treated with special care. I knew that would be better for them than staying in the sombre environment of the hospital, but I just wanted to hold them and be close.

But you can't do everything on your own and they were with people who loved them. I had to let them go.

It had been such a long day, and there wasn't anything we could do other than sit and wait. We needed to have dinner and Christine suggested it would be good for us to get out of the patient waiting lounge for a couple of hours. I wanted to stay but I also needed to get out, and Kate elected to stay at the hospital so I felt reassured that someone would be there. Our small group walked across the road to a restaurant at the Morrison Hotel on Stanley Street, Woolloongabba. I would be minutes away in the event that I needed to come back.

As it turned out, that was just what we all needed. We were able to regroup and prepare for the long night ahead.

*

Matthew was in surgery for six hours. I thought every hour that passed was a good sign – it meant he was still alive. Eventually, midnight came. A young nurse popped her head into the waiting room. She looked elated.

'They're finishing up now. He'll be on his way up soon,' she told us.

The hours of waiting were over. We were all excited, and I was so proud of Matthew. I knew he was fighting for us. I knew he wanted to be here with us, and he was being so strong. I could not have loved him more at that moment.

It was the beginning of a new struggle. I understood how hard it was going to be and I was up for it.

While the others left to head home for the evening, Christine and I again set up our makeshift beds in the waiting rooms, with the help of the nurses. It was quiet, and I was feeling fragile. I had been in to see Matthew, and the shock of seeing how short his arms and legs actually were was sinking in.

I went into the room where Christine was sleeping and sat down. She was also awake, and I started to cry.

I do now recognise that the doctors who hadn't diagnosed Matthew with a strep infection had let us down. But at the time, I felt responsible that I hadn't done more. I tend to blame myself very easily.

'Christine, I am so sorry that this happened.'

Christine looked surprised. She didn't say anything but just held my hand and let me go on.

'Matthew's your baby,' I told her. 'I get what it is like to have your baby hurt.'

I had started with a few tears, but now found myself sobbing uncontrollably. Christine hugged me, tightly.

'Diane. He might have been my baby, but he was yours twenty years ago. This is not your fault.'

We cried together for a while. It was very comforting to know I had such incredible support from my mother-in-law. It didn't come as a surprise.

CHAPTER 4

LIFE GOES ON

Matthew survived the night, and no one came to knock on my door, although again, I barely slept. When I did rise, I thought about the huge day ahead of me. It was important for the children that I be strong.

It was Sunday 17 June, and the day of the annual school fete. The fete is a huge community event that raises funds for the school. It attracts hundreds of people each year, and has lots of rides, stalls and kids' performances. More importantly, it is the highlight of the school year for the boys. They were so excited – we had bought a package for unlimited rides, and they had been rehearsing their songs and dances for weeks. Each had a role to play and would perform in different events throughout the day.

I would never have cancelled their involvement or my attendance. I was determined that we would all go because I wanted to show the children that just because we were sad didn't mean we couldn't have fun. They had so much to deal with and I didn't want the disappointment of missing the fete to worry them.

I knew Matthew would be in great hands and that there was nothing I could actually do. Christine, Roy, Rachel and Kate would stay at the hospital, and they were going to call me if Matthew deteriorated.

Matthew and I had devoted our lives to our children. We had left having kids until quite late in our marriage because we wanted to have time to ourselves first, but when we decided to bring them into the world, we wanted to make their life on earth a wonderful experience every day, and to help them be really good people.

I was certain that Matthew would support me in making the decision to go, and he would want the children to have a lovely day.

I packed up my makeshift bed and visited Matthew at six-thirty that morning. When I had first seen him after his operation, I had been shocked at how short his stumps were, and I was still a bit shocked when I saw him again. He looked so terrible, and I cried again.

When I left, I knew there was a distinct chance I wouldn't ever see Matthew alive again. He was still fighting for his life, and the infection was still in control of his body. I took a photo of him, aware that it may be my last. I told Matthew to keep fighting, to be strong and to know that we loved him.

Then I kissed him on the head, and walked out the door of ICU.

*

I sent a text to Gwen, Nicole and Lisa to let them know I was coming to the fete, and then went home to shower and to collect the boys' clothes and the costumes they would be wearing during their performances. When I arrived, I found my washing had been done and brought in off the line. Miss Maureen, my wonderful neighbour, had ironed all my clothes, and Lisa had baked all the cakes and slices that Gwen, Nicole and I were supposed to bring for the stalls at the fete.

Then I went to Rachel and Aaron's house to pick up the boys, get them changed and take them directly to the school, where the fete was being held. The boys were excited about the day ahead but their first questions were about Matthew.

I told them that he was doing really well and that we might see him later that afternoon. It was the most beautiful day – cold, but the sun was shining and there wasn't a cloud in the sky. We were looking forward to meeting up with Nicole, Lisa, Gwen and, of course, Emily, who had stayed the night with Gwen.

The girls told me later that they had devised a plan for the day once they knew I would be coming; at the time, I was oblivious. They were each going to take turns to stay with me. They had allocated their husbands, David, Stuart and Anthony, one of my children each – David was responsible for Will, Stuart had Ben, and Anthony was to look after Luke. Mandi and Scott Gosling were also going to keep an eye out for the boys, and my brothers-in-law, Jason and Aaron, brought our nephews and niece, so they would be able to lend a hand too. There was a big team around me.

I needed the support. I was running on pure adrenaline, and the fact that different people at the fete knew different levels of detail, and most knew more than my kids, was a problem that I hadn't thought about. I am a very open person and find it difficult to keep information to myself. So when I first arrived at the school and ran into a few fellow parents, I told them about what had happened to Matthew. Information spread quickly – not through malice or a desire to gossip, but simply because of concern and shock.

The school is very small and community-based. There are around 400 children from roughly 200 families. We had three boys across three grades, and I'm on the school board. We also attended Mass, as did many of the families – so our community was close-knit and it was reasonable to expect that people would be concerned and want to help. As I walked around the school grounds, the news about Matthew was spreading around me.

The problem was that while the children knew that their father was ill, they didn't know about the amputations.

Later, I learned that Gwen spent her first half-hour at the fete trying to track people down to tell them that the boys didn't yet know about the amputations, but she soon realised that the news was moving more quickly than she was. So the girls stepped in to protect me. They fielded questions from everyone who asked how Matthew was, and let them know I was too upset to stop and talk. Normally, I would feel bad about not talking to people – I am usually the last to leave and often late home from school because I've been busy chatting – but my focus was entirely on my children and just making it through the day.

I was grateful for my friends' protection.

First up were the performances. We had to get the children to their classrooms before the fete started and then we sat down near the front of the crowd on the school tennis court. Emily was in her pram, and close friends and family surrounded me. I didn't move or talk to anyone as each of the boys performed on stage with their class – I concentrated on what they were doing. I was so proud of them – it's a big thing for little people to get up in front of a crowd like that.

I sat through all the performances with my glasses on, and I cried quietly at times. The hardest song to listen to was 'Reach for the Stars', which Luke sang as a member of the school choir. This was the only time I really cried heavily, and even if Matthew hadn't had his operation, I probably would have been in tears watching my beautiful boy sing his heart out.

Looking at the children, it would have been difficult to notice that something was wrong in their lives. At one point, Will was doing a little dance and obviously enjoying himself so much that it made me laugh, and I thought, *Wow. He is having so much fun, and is living so*

much in this moment. That made me appreciate what I was doing this
for – to help the kids celebrate what was great in their life, rather than
focus on what was making them sad. I tried not to think too much
about what was going on back at the hospital; I knew they had my
phone number and would call if there was a problem.

As the day progressed, I was able to keep my tears in check. My
ability to live in the moment helped, and I felt happy when I looked
at the boys. They were having a great time – especially Will, who,
under the supervision of David Webb, was on consecutive cans of
Fanta and lemonade.

I didn't let go of my phone all morning, which was unusual for
me, and at lunchtime, I did receive a call from the hospital. My
friends were as tense as I was when I took the call.

It was good news.

'He's stable,' I told everyone. I told the kids their daddy was
going well.

I had an overwhelming feeling of relief.

Knowing that he was still with us and okay at that moment gave
me the confidence to stay a bit longer. I remember thinking throughout the day how wonderful everyone was being, and how lucky
I was to be part of such a caring community – even if I couldn't
express it aloud at the time. I couldn't have done it without the support of my girlfriends and their families, and I knew that everyone
was behind me. It allowed us to have a lovely day and we ended up
being among the last to leave. Gwen stayed with me until I decided
to go, which was when the rides were being packed up.

I knew I was delaying the inevitable – telling the children about
what had happened to Matthew's arms and legs.

Even then, I was scared about revealing the whole truth.

*

After we left the fete, I took the children up to the hospital to see Matthew. They were on a high, perhaps from the sugar in the soft drinks they'd consumed, but also because they had been on so many rides and done such exciting things – their faces were painted, and they had stories to tell about their performances.

I called ahead to tell the ICU staff that I was coming, and I let them know the children still didn't know about the amputations. I asked them to make it appear, for the time being, that Matthew still had arms and legs, as I was yet to explain in detail what had happened to him.

When we walked in, Matthew's appearance hadn't changed. He was still a deep pink colour. His tongue and lips were swollen and scabbed, and he had black streaks, like zebra stripes, across his fore-head. The tip of one of his ears had gone black. He looked hot, and his breathing via the ventilator was laboured. We could see how hard he was still fighting.

The nurses had rolled up towels underneath the bedsheets so it would look like he still had arms and legs, and all we could see was his face.

I asked the boys to talk to Daddy and tell him about their day. It was difficult for them – they were so excited, but they didn't receive any feedback when talking to Matthew. Will was fantastic in sharing the news of his day. He had been photographed by the local newspaper and was eager to tell Matthew that his photo was going to be in the paper. I encouraged them by asking questions and prompting each boy – they talked about everything they had done that day, who they had played with, the rides they had been on, and how much fun they had.

At the end of the day, at around 6 p.m., I took them home. Matthew was still critical, so Christine elected to stay at the hospital once again that evening. It was my first night at home in days.

I knew the time had come to tell the kids in more detail about what had happened. I had a specific reason for wanting to keep information from them up to this point. The children believed in God and heaven. They prayed every night as part of their bedtime routine, and their prayers included my mum and dad, who the kids believed were in heaven with other members of the family who had passed.

They were familiar with the concept of death, and in the event that Matthew did die, I wanted them to think of him in heaven as they had last seen him – with arms and legs.

Later, when I told Matthew about this, his response was typically pragmatic: 'But couldn't you have told them that my arms and legs would meet up with me in heaven?'

Things always seem so much simpler in hindsight.

When I did sit down with them that Sunday evening, I was still reluctant to tell them about the full extent of his amputations. I was still coming to terms with that myself, and I thought it might be too much for them to take in at once.

So I told them that Daddy's hands and feet had been amputated to help save his life.

They had lots of questions, which I answered as best as I could.

Was he still sick? Yes, he was still very, very sick.

Would he still die? Perhaps, but he was fighting as hard as he could.

They had one question they seemed to keep coming back to, which was, 'What happened to his hands and feet?'

I don't think I answered this very well because they kept asking. I was always a bit vague. Again, Matthew had the right answer when they asked him later, which was simply, 'They went into the bin.' Everyone seemed to be okay with that, and stopped asking.

Although we never told the children directly that the limbs would have gone to a rubbish dump, they made the association later in a strange way. Matthew, after he returned home, would sometimes shiver to shake off pain associated with his phantom limbs. The first time he did this in Ben's company, Ben looked up from what he was doing.

'Looks like someone drove over your arms and legs at the dump, Dad,' he said, as casually as anything, before putting his head back down to continue what he was doing.

He makes the same comment to this day if Matthew shivers in his presence.

We laugh about it now – the first time, though, was a moment of revelation. Our children, through this event, were losing some of their childhood.

The thought saddened me then and it saddens me now.

I've learned that it's best to be straight up with the kids because they can handle it. My reluctance at the time was probably because I was struggling to handle it myself, and so I thought they couldn't. The boys accepted everything I did tell them that Sunday evening.

We set up a prayer shrine for Matthew that night. There was a special shelf, on which each of the boys placed something that represented them and their father. It also held letters for each child's name – LBWE – photos of the children, a candle, photos of my parents who were in heaven and two ceramic angel statues. The children seemed to get a lot of solace from the idea that they could pray to God. We would direct our prayers to the shrine each night and a lot of our words were along the lines of, 'Daddy is fighting so hard to stay with us.'

The next morning, we prepared for school as usual. I knew how important it was to keep the routine the same and, most importantly, I knew the boys had beautiful friends at school whom they could talk to about what was happening. It was a deliberate decision on my part to help them deal in their own way with everything that was happening.

That afternoon, Emily and I picked up the boys from school and started to drive to the hospital. The first question from the boys was, 'How is Daddy?'

I told them there was no change, but he was still fighting hard. Will and Ben were keen to tell me about their day at school; Luke was quieter. When we got to the hospital, I parked the car, got out and walked around to speak to Luke, who was still sitting in the car.

'Are you okay?' I asked him.

'Yes. Someone asked me if Daddy had his arms and legs amputated,' Luke told me.

The question had come from a child who just needed to know and there was no malice intended as far as I could determine. Luke and I talked for a while longer, and then I asked him what he would like me to do.

'Can we please get picked up from school at lunchtime?'

'Of course, sweetheart.' If he had asked not to go to school at all, I would have agreed to it. I was only sending the boys to school because I truly believed it was best for them.

We only had a week to go before the end of term. I spoke with the boys' teachers and the school principal, who were supportive, and for the rest of the week I would pick up the children at the lunch bell, and we would go to the hospital for the afternoon.

It turned out to be the only school the boys missed aside from individual sickness during the period Matthew was in intensive care and, later, rehabilitation.

That afternoon, I sat the boys down in the patient waiting area at the hospital before we went in to see Matthew. I pointed on my own limbs where Matthew's arms and legs had been removed. The children accepted this, so when we visited Matthew, we looked at the extent of his amputations.

Christine, Roy, Kate and Rachel were basing themselves at the hospital, and being close to the extended family seemed to give the kids strength. A few days after the children had been told that Matthew had no arms or legs, Kate showed us videos of Nick Vujicic on her iPad. Nick was born without limbs and his motto is 'No arms, No legs, No worries'. It was a significant moment for everyone – Nick is so positive and open about his journey that it made everything seem possible.

We would sit in the patient waiting area looking at Nick Vujicic videos on YouTube, the boys saying, 'Check out this next one – wow, look at this – look, Mummy, he can swim.' They would get so involved that I would have to remind them that it was time to go home. After a dose of watching Nick, Will would walk down the hall into ICU chanting, 'No arms, no legs, no worries; no arms, no legs, no worries.'

Nick Vujicic's message was important because it was all about hope.

The 2012 London Olympic Games were also looming, and Oscar Pistorius's blades were the focus of media attention at the time. Pistorius had gained entry to the able-bodied Olympics, and we could read stories to the boys that suggested people with disabilities might be more 'able' than people without. It may have seemed far-fetched, but it gave the boys, and me, great comfort.

When we were at home, we would lie around in our bedroom, having discussions about disability and what Daddy would and wouldn't be able to do in the future. Each day gave us new ideas and renewed hope. I was always trying to be extremely positive, and I would talk to everyone about the fact that looks aren't important – it's what's inside that makes a person.

Luke obviously absorbed that idea. A few days after the operation, he said to me one afternoon, 'It doesn't matter if Daddy has no arms or legs, Mummy. It's what's inside that counts.'

'Yes, Luke. You're totally right.'

He was eight years old and such a gentle soul. I was so proud of him at that moment.

CHAPTER 5

TOUCH AND GO

Seeing Matthew in the days after his operation was confronting. He didn't look like the Matthew we all knew and loved.

His face remained swollen and distorted, and his tongue was so distended that it hung out of the side of his mouth, pushed in part by the breathing tube attached to the mechanical ventilator that was helping Matthew breath. A portion of his tongue had died as a result of the disease, and large ulcers were developing around his mouth and lips.

We could see that death was still a distinct possibility.

Normally when you're comforting someone, you hold their hand or give them a hug. Matthew had no hands to hold and getting close was impossible. Tubes and wires linked his body to lots of machines, and touching Matthew's head was our only option for personal contact.

When we visited, I would take the children around to the back of the bed and lift them one at a time so they could kiss the back of his head. Emily in particular found this really difficult – she wanted to get up on the bed, but we couldn't let her because she was an active two-year-old, and the risk of her knocking one of the tubes helping keep Matthew alive was very high.

Matthew had always been very affectionate with the kids – he would hug them and swing them around when he came home from work, and he was always letting them climb over him if he was in bed or on the couch. It broke my heart to watch the children struggle to communicate with him. I would watch them every afternoon – our six-, seven- and eight-year-old boys trying to tell their father about their day, getting nothing in return.

We were used to short conversations on the phone when Matthew travelled – 'Hi, Daddy. Yeah, okay. Bye, Daddy.' But this was different.

I would encourage them and prompt them to talk, but I could see it was particularly hard for Ben to find enjoyment in trying to interact with Matthew. I didn't push him – I would talk on his behalf.

So I tried to make the afternoon visits just about being close to Daddy. They didn't have to talk to him. Luke would talk to me, Ben would draw, and Will would sing songs or read his school readers to Matthew. Emily would stroke Matthew's hair, and say, 'Wake up, Daddy. Wake up.'

The medical staff helped with the entertainment – surgical gloves became balloons, nurses would tell jokes, and out in the waiting room, Roy would demonstrate weird and wonderful things to do with cups, serviettes, gloves and straws. So visiting hospital, despite its difficulties, was something to look forward to. It also highlighted a benefit to having four children – the odds were in our favour that if one was ever in a sombre mood, someone else was going to lighten that mood so they would all end up having a bit of fun.

Luke's reaction to Matthew's illness was different to the other kids' – he really understood the gravity of the situation. He would sit quietly in the patient waiting area – so quietly that we would almost forget he was there. We would be having adult conversations about what was happening to Matthew, and he would hear it all, although he never said anything. Initially, I was concerned about how much Luke was hearing and how much he wanted to stay at the hospital, so I would talk indirectly about things, or ask someone to come outside the room with me if we needed to discuss Matthew's condition.

But Luke knew what was happening, and the idea that he wasn't being told about things seemed to cause him more anxiety than hearing the truth. As days passed, I started to understand that Luke needed more information to feel comfortable – he didn't like surprises, and wanted details about what was happening so he could make his own assessments. It wasn't enough for him if I said, 'Everything's good', or 'Everything's tracking in the right direction', especially when he could hear people talking in lowered voices, or see them leaving the room for short periods before coming back in.

Luke became reluctant to leave his father and me. While Will and Ben would accept invitations to sleepovers with the cousins as school holidays loomed, Luke and Emily didn't want to be with anyone but me or the family in the patient waiting room. The nurses were amazing with them. I got a sense that some of them were translating what was happening to Matthew to their own family situation – thinking, *What if this was my wife and kids?* They would tell Luke what was happening and involve him in helping nurse Matthew, giving him tasks such as reading the temperature or passing them equipment.

Everyone on the ward treated Emily like a star. She would wear her princess dresses every day – she would be Snow White one day, and Belle from *Beauty and the Beast* the next – and everyone would make her feel special. They would hear us coming down the long corridor that led to Matthew's bed in ICU – Emily would often run and call out to Matthew: 'Hi, Daddy. I'm here, Daddy.'

If Eamonn was on shift, he would stand back and salute her, saying, 'Hello, Matron, great to see you back again today.' Emily had her own seat beside Matthew's bed. 'Your seat is ready,' the nurses would tell her, and she would sit up beside Matthew. Later, when Matthew had woken and he and I would try to speak, she would interrupt. 'No, no,' she would say to me. 'You can't talk. It's my turn to talk to Daddy.'

At home, Luke took it upon himself to be the male of the house. I overheard him, a few days after Matthew's operation, speaking to Ben and Will while they were all in the bath.

'Now,' said Luke. 'While Daddy's in hospital, there is to be no arguing, and we have to help Mummy.'

The boys agreed. Shortly afterwards, when they had finished their bath, they emerged as though nothing had transpired. I didn't say anything to Luke because I didn't want him to know I had overheard the conversation.

A few days later, we arrived home to a messy kitchen. While the others ran off to do their own things, Luke came up to me.

'Look, Mum. I'll give you thirty minutes of my time to help you clean up the kitchen. It won't take us long if it's the two of us.' He did help, and it is true that because it was the two of us, it didn't seem such a big task.

We became a bit of a team, but I was always conscious that he might be losing his childhood and so was very careful about setting boundaries. I involved him where it seemed appropriate, and spoke with the ICU social worker, Christie Barrett, a lot about how he was going – she was great with both of us, and reassured me that we were doing well.

I still wanted Luke to be my little boy – I wasn't ready for him to be all grown up – and I would talk about this with the family when he wasn't around. One afternoon, I was discussing it with our friend Dan Alexander who was visiting Matthew in ICU, and Dan reminded me about the need for perspective.

'Diane. Think of the childhood he would have lost if Matthew actually died.'

He was right.

*

Matthew's recovery was slow but steady. He was still on life support, which in his case meant he relied on assistance to breathe from a ventilator, and was on full dialysis because of kidney failure. His temperature remained high, and efforts were being made to bring his body temperature down because of concerns about the effect on his brain.

Each morning, I would meet with the head of intensive care, Dr Shane Townsend, and the senior intensivist on duty. My agenda was very simple – I just wanted to know if things were progressing in the right direction. The doctors were being very conservative, while I wanted to take every single thing as a positive sign that Matthew was getting better.

They would never let me get excited because they genuinely didn't know if he was going to pull through. I knew they were trying to manage my expectations – no doubt they would have seen many situations where things were going well, only to be followed by a sudden crash.

Despite their reluctance to let me get excited, I always got a sense that the doctors and nurses were with me on the journey. One of the orthopaedic surgeons involved in Matthew's operations, Dr Tim McMeniman, was amazing – in my mind, he not only helped save Matthew's life, but he was also particularly good at delivering the bad news in a calm, rational way, and his follow-up was always so caring.

On one occasion, I was sitting on my own in the patient waiting area outside ICU. We were having a 'not so good' kind of day.

Tim walked past the room and saw that I was there. He came in, sat down and looked at me. He didn't say anything, but stood up, came over to me and gave me a hug, and then left the room. He may have sensed I was the kind of person who needed that.

I didn't want to dwell on 'what might be' scenarios such as Matthew dying, so I would often seek out happiness, and I knew that the person I would get the most happiness from was Roy, who was usually in the patient waiting area. I would sit down and give Roy the latest update. If it seemed to be even slightly good news, Roy would say, 'That's a great sign, just a great sign. That's fantastic.' We both knew he had no medical background, but he loved all the numbers, and if they were going in the right direction, things were good.

And to put things into perspective, we were coming from a place where the children had said goodbye to their father. From there, it couldn't get any worse unless death actually came calling. So, the fact that we didn't have to stay at the hospital overnight any more was a good sign. The fact that Matthew wasn't going to die in the next hour was a good sign. A drop in temperature of half a degree was a good sign.

It was really important to me that everyone around us was positive. I didn't care if people thought I was in denial about the seriousness of the situation – I knew I wasn't because I was very aware that Matthew could still die at any moment. I just wanted everyone to realise that as soon as we became negative, the trickle-down effect would be huge. I felt that I was the hub of the family, and that if I, or anyone around me, were negative, the kids would pick up on it.

I am good at living in the moment, and encourage the kids to be the same. There was a vending machine on Level 7, beside the lifts, which we would raid if something good happened, like Matthew's temperature coming down. We had never used food as a reward, but in this case, it seemed a simple way to celebrate small wins. Sometimes, when things weren't going well, we didn't visit the machine for a few days; then Matthew would improve, and have a run of small victories. I would be thinking, *Goodness. These kids are going to be as big as houses*, as we retrieved our chocolate or packet of chips for the day.

These good moments were important because Matthew's recovery was very much a case of 'one step forward, two steps backwards', and lots of things were happening. His kidneys were still not working, and he was on full dialysis, although we were reassured when one of the doctors referred to kidneys as being lazy – 'They'll take any excuse for a holiday, and just need to be reminded about what their job actually is.'

The problem was that at the time the dialysis machine was helping to keep his temperature down. Every time Matthew needed a procedure, such as a tracheostomy, he needed to be taken off dialysis, taken to theatre or wherever he needed to go, and then returned and cooled straight away. He had cooling blankets on him, and in the days after his operation, his temperature was still in the high 30s–low 40s. The high temperature was a reminder that despite the amputations, Matthew's body was still fighting infection.

We were looking for ways to reassure the kids, and Rachel found something that worked really well. She bought each child a small Little Miracle puppy. These are soft toys sold by the Mater to raise funds for the Mater Children's Hospital. It was meaningful to the kids because as babies they had been given larger versions of the puppies, which remain special to this day.

Rachel left the puppies on Matthew's bed in ICU one afternoon – one for each child, and different colours so we could tell them all apart. Emily's wore a tiny pink ballerina tutu. Rachel told the children that the toys were a special present from Daddy, and that the puppies should go everywhere with them, including school.

'If you want to talk to Daddy, you can talk to him through your puppy,' she told them.

'Daddy will hear you.'

Ben in particular took this to heart. At the time, he wasn't saying very much and of all our children, he aligned himself with Matthew and relied on being close to him the most. I could tell he was internalising things, and it was difficult to know exactly what he was thinking.

His puppy became his friend, and he took it absolutely everywhere. I suspect he did talk to his father through the puppy, although it was something he kept to himself.

*

While Matthew was in a coma, our life went on as usual, and I wanted it to be that way. Our daily routine was to wake up, have breakfast and get ready to go to school. I would drop the boys at the school gate, head up to the hospital for the morning, then pick the boys up at lunchtime and head back to the hospital. The patient waiting area was usually busy – Christine and Roy would be at the hospital during the day, as would Rachel and her son Lincoln, who was not yet at school. Kate also stayed in Brisbane while Jason and their children returned home.

Life at home was sustained by wonderful friends, family and neighbours. My brother-in-law's parents, Dorothy and Doug Fraser, cleaned the house from top to bottom with Kate one afternoon. This was important because Luke was convinced that the bugs from Matthew's infection were still in his room, which he now didn't like to enter. Nicole, Gwen and Lisa organised a meal roster so I wouldn't have to cook. Families at the school, my mothers' group and other friends contributed, and each day enough food for the following day – morning tea, lunch, afternoon tea, and dinner – would be delivered to Nicole, who placed it in an esky outside the front door of her house. I would drop by, often quite late at night, and pick up the food; all I had to do when we got home was heat the dinner, and fill the kid's lunchboxes while they had a bath before we read stories.

The five of us – four kids and me – would crash together at the end of the day. There was great comfort in us all sleeping in the one room, which we did from the time of Matthew's admission to hospital. The children rotated between the mattresses and sleeping in my bed, and Emily would insist I hold her hand while she went to sleep.

I was conscious that while all of us had had our lives turned upside down, it was probably most confusing for Emily. She was suddenly being passed between different people for babysitting, she wasn't having her day sleep, and I knew that she really didn't know what was happening. Her life was about being at the hospital – she wasn't yet going to kindy, so she didn't interact with children besides her cousins and other kids at the park on Friday afternoons, or Gwen, Nicole or Lisa's kids when she stayed with them.

Emily lived in a mostly adult world. She was a typical two-year-old – delightful most of the time, but able to throw a great tantrum when things didn't go her way. She wanted to cling to me a lot, and when I could have her with me, I was very happy to hold her close.

*

What do you say to someone about what happened to Matthew? How do you tell friends and extended family that you made a decision to remove someone's limbs to save their life? How do you cope with saying the same thing over and over, and when you have to counsel others while you are still dealing with the issues yourself?

In those first days after Matthew's operation, it wasn't something I thought about because I was running around with the kids, living from moment to moment. But Kate, Rachel, Roy and Christine were sitting in the patient waiting area for long periods of time between visits to Matthew, and the need for a considered approach was becoming obvious – people's reactions were very different, ranging mainly from shock to horror. Kate suggested we write a letter explaining what had happened, which we could then send out to close friends, work colleagues and extended family. It was, we thought, a great idea, so Kate went ahead.

Hi there, everyone,

It's now almost a week since our lives changed forever with the hospitalisation of Matthew, and it's at this point that it's worth telling everyone the story, and the reason for this will become clear.

Matthew had been unwell for a couple of weeks, and had been diagnosed with the flu by a number of different doctors, but last Wednesday, he deteriorated very quickly with severe joint pain and fever. Dad and Diane, Matt's wife, brought him to the Mater Hospital in Brisbane, and he was admitted to intensive care where he was subsequently diagnosed with toxic shock syndrome, courtesy of a strep bacteria.

He was at that stage given a 50/50 chance of survival, but he deteriorated very quickly, and he was placed in an induced coma on Thursday morning. He was not expected to make the night on Thursday, but he did, but it was clear that his extremities (arms and legs) were being attacked by the infection. It was identified that his left arm was the major source of the infection, and this was amputated on Friday evening. We were told on Friday night that this had not been enough to stem the infection, and that he would die.

It appears that he had other ideas. On Saturday morning, the doctors and surgical team presented us with

*the only option available to save his life, which was to
complete a full amputation of all his limbs in an effort to
get on top of the infection. It was clear at this point that his
limbs were dying, and this process was contributing to the
toxicity in his body. There was no guarantee that this would
work; in fact, it was likely that he would die regardless, and
very likely that he would actually die on the operating table.
If he did survive the infection without taking this action,
all his limbs were in the process of dying and would need
to be amputated at a later stage regardless. The willingness
of doctors to attempt to save Matthew's life in this way was
dependent upon the results of a CT scan that was required
to determine whether the infection had spread into his lungs
and brain.*

*As a family, we agreed that if the CT scan indicated that
the infection hadn't spread, we would allow the surgeons
to go ahead with the operation in an attempt to save his
life. We agreed that Matthew was in fact the only person
for whom we would make this decision, and that if it had
been anyone else, we would have agreed to let nature
take its course. Those of you who know Matthew well
would understand why. As the father of four very young
children (Emily – 2, Will – 6, Ben – 7, and Luke – 8), he
has been a source of strength and joy to everyone who has
been fortunate enough to be part of his life. An incredibly
optimistic, stable and passionate person, he has always been
the one to encourage, advise and counsel others. As Diane
would say, he's just perfect. He's the only one we think
would be strong enough to cope with what would be asked
of him if he survived.*

*On Saturday afternoon, the family gathered, including
all our children, and we said our goodbyes, which was*

undoubtedly the saddest thing any of us has ever had to do, and we waved him off as he went to theatre not thinking we would ever see him again. The operation was expected to take most of the evening, and would remove all his limbs.

It's amazing what tragedy can do, and the moments of joy that you can find in the process. With little left to do but wait, the mood as the hours went on became somewhat celebratory, and even the nurse who came to advise us that he was on his way back to ICU almost had to contain her delight. And so he returned from theatre and began his fight.

And fight he has continued to do. It's now a week since our journey began, and he has improved steadily every day, to the complete amazement of everyone involved, including the medical staff. His case has been unique from the outset. Prior to his final bout of surgery, Diane asked the medical team to believe in him, because we did, and it has been heartening to see them rally behind Matthew as they've become more confident that he has it in him to survive.

So we're at the stage where Matthew's life support is being withdrawn and he is becoming more independent each day. He is still in an induced coma but his sedation is also being withdrawn. He remains critical, and he's certainly not out of the woods yet, but there's growing hope every day.

For all of us, life won't ever be the same. We don't know how the story is going to unfold, and what Matthew's response will be when he awakes and becomes aware of what has happened to him. What we do know is that we're all very aware of the implications of the decision to operate to save his life, for everyone, but particularly him and his wife, Diane, and their children.

One of the reasons for putting this in writing is so that we don't have to revisit this moment in the future. As time goes on, hopefully, this week will dim into one of those 'can't really remember the details' periods of life. We don't really want to talk about what happened in the past, but about what's ahead. So, in catching up with people, we'll be really happy to talk about how Matthew's doing, but think we would like to leave this past week behind.

Hopefully, the story has a happy ending, and at some point we'll be able to reflect upon the turning point in our lives with a view to what it gave us all. In the meantime, thank you all so much for hanging in there with us, and we will look forward to catching up with you all at some stage.

Lots of love, Kate, on behalf of the extended Ames family.

We were able to adapt the letter to suit our different friendship groups, and Rachel sent it to my contacts. I felt lucky to be surrounded by really caring and capable people in Matthew's family and my own, as well as among my friends, who were able to help manage information.

I was conscious that some people were feeling shut out by my lack of communication at this early stage, but my entire focus was on the children, and simply surviving emotionally. My main concern was making sure that our kids and Matthew's family got through it. Our real friends would understand, and members of my extended family were leaving messages saying they were thinking of me, and that they knew I would get back to them in my own time, which I appreciated.

I only answered one phone call during that time. It was from my wonderful uncle Gary McMahon, whom I love dearly. He called me a day or two after Matthew had his amputations. I had all the kids at home, and they weren't in bed. I went out onto the back verandah to talk, and Gary and I ended up crying on the phone together. After I hung up the phone, I thought, *I can't do this*. It had nothing to do

with Gary – it had been lovely to talk to him – but it had everything
to do with my ability to cope.

I realised then that I actually needed protection from the question,
'How are you?' It would make me cry, and the boys didn't need to
see that. If they saw me cry, they would think something was wrong.
Obviously it was, but I never wanted them to know how bad things
were – I wanted them to remain hopeful and focus on the positives.
Later, I was able to deal with the question, and was very grateful to be
asked, but in those days of waiting for Matthew to wake, I was running on adrenaline and very fragile when I wasn't around others.

From then on, I reverted to text messages. With SMSes, no one
could see my tears, so I would lie in bed once the children were
asleep and catch up on texts until I became too tired. That's when
I would cry, and cry, and cry more. Wherever I got up to with the
texts, I got up to. I was particularly heartened by messages that
didn't need a response, but reminded me that people were thinking
of me. My cousin Richard and his wife, Anita, in Sydney, for example, were really good at sending simple texts like *Thinking of you*, or
Sending a hug your way.

Within the immediate family circle, Matthew's sister Rachel was
especially helpful because she was committed to turning thoughts
into action.

'You can be positive, Diane,' she said one day, 'but that's not
enough.'

If we were having a bad day, she would make sure she diverted
the boys' attention – she would take them for a swim or a sleepover
with her boys, Ethan and Lincoln. It was hard for her – she was the
Acting Chief Executive Officer for AgForce, so a lot of her time in
the waiting room was spent juggling work and my needs. She started
pulling the paperwork together for me so I would be able to organise insurance and medical care, and she updated friends, family and
work colleagues every day.

She said later that she feels a sense of responsibility for Matthew. As part of the group who committed him to this life, she feels she has to do what she can to help.

I know she would have done everything she has anyway, even if she hadn't been in the room when we made the decision.

*

A week after Matthew's operation he had improved to the point that the doctors were considering waking him.

It seemed to be really soon after his amputations, but the operation had worked the way it was supposed to. It was an amazing recovery – the wounds where his limbs had been amputated were healing quickly, and the black spots on his face, head and neck were reducing in size and intensity. His mouth and lips still looked terrible, but the colour in his skin seemed to be returning to normal. I could see how hard he was fighting, and every day he seemed to be winning just that little bit more of the battle.

Matthew was still critically ill, and the doctors told me they were concerned that the sustained high temperatures he had experienced might have caused some residual brain damage. They wanted to check if this was the case, and could only do so by waking him from his coma. We were all desperate for him to wake, and the doctors were just waiting for the right moment. It seemed that every day, Dr Shane Townsend would tell me we were getting closer.

I was so excited at the thought of being able to talk to Matthew, but very nervous about what was to come. Then, on Sunday 24 June 2012, the doctors told me they were planning to wake Matthew the following morning.

None of us knew exactly how he would react, but we all knew he would be waking to a new life.

CHAPTER 6

TELLING
MATTHEW

The surgeons warned me that I might have to tell Matthew more than once about what had happened. It was still a shock when it became obvious he didn't remember what I had told him previously. This happened three times. On each occasion, his reaction was exactly the same. He looked me in the eye and, without crying, he nodded okay.

The first attempt to wake Matthew was only nine days after his operation, on Monday 25 June. Dr Tim McMeniman warned me that Matthew would be angry – it was a common reaction in cases where patients had undergone medical procedures while unaware of what was happening. Those of us who knew Matthew couldn't see him being angry – it just wasn't like him to lose his temper or display anger if the reason for something was rational. We told Tim that, although I know he thought that Matthew would probably not be so calm on this occasion.

I have always been a studious type of person who likes to be prepared. When Matthew and I were students at university, I would only let him talk to me on the phone for 10 minutes because I was such a conscientious student, although he grew to know that once he got me on the phone, it was often easy to extend that time. He was always encouraging me to push myself.

On this occasion, I wanted to be strong for Matthew because he had been so strong for us. Deep down, I knew I had it in me, and I knew Matthew believed I did. But to appear strong, I had to know what I was doing, so I wanted to prepare what I was going to say.

The day before we were expecting to wake Matthew, Eamonn offered to listen to what I was going to tell Matthew when he woke. It was a lovely offer, and I accepted gladly. He took me to the nurse's station, sat a chair down opposite him so I was directly facing him, and said, 'Okay, pretend I'm Matthew. Tell it to me like you would tell it to him.'

And I did. It seemed like forever that Eamonn sat there listening to me, and everyone left us alone as I delivered my speech about what had happened, most of the time crying as I talked. Eamonn didn't interrupt me once.

I finally finished.

'What do you think?'

'Well I only have one comment to make, otherwise it was fantastic,' Eamonn told me. 'You need to reassure him that he's still your man, and that you still find him attractive. He's a bloke. He's going to want to know that.'

'Oh! Okay.' It hadn't even crossed my mind that Matthew would be in any doubt. We laughed. I knew he was right.

I will be forever grateful for Eamonn's time that morning. It meant I was feeling confident when the time came to speak to Matthew. I know Eamonn would say it's all part of the job, but to me, it was so much more.

The next morning, I got a call to say Matthew was waking up, so could I come in straight away. I had just dropped the kids at school, and Roy, Christine and Rachel were already at the hospital waiting for me. I tried to get there as quickly as I could because I knew the doctors wanted me to be the first person Matthew saw, and they only had so much control over the drugs used to wake him up.

Once I arrived, I joined Roy, Christine and Rachel and we walked into ICU. We were supported by Christie Barrett, Chris Smith (the nursing unit manager), Shane Townsend, Amod Karnik and Eamonn. They fanned out around the bed, while I sat on Matthew's right-hand side because all the machines he was attached to were on his left. He had no hand I could hold, so I put my hand on his head, and stroked his hair.

Matthew's eyes were open and he was awake, looking around where he could. He had his breathing tube in, and couldn't move his head, but when I started talking, he looked directly at me and maintained eye contact.

Even though everybody was there, it felt as though it was just the two of us.

'Matthew, it's so great to see you,' I started. 'We have been waiting to say hello.'

I paused for a moment to let it sink in, and continued. 'You have been really unwell, and you've been in hospital for twelve days.'

I could see his eyebrows lift with surprise, as if to say, *Really?*

I walked through exactly what had happened, in sequence. I told him that he had become progressively worse after being admitted to hospital.

'The doctors had to do some operations. The first was to clean the area where you had the rash on your left arm, but you still became worse. You were continuing to deteriorate. Your arm had stopped working and had died, so we had to make the hard decision to amputate your left arm.'

I told him that the doctors and nurses had been doing everything they could to save his life.

'On the Saturday, it looked like we were going to lose you, and the kids came in to say goodbye. We all came in to say goodbye.'

Matthew welled up at that point, knowing that the boys and Emily had had to say farewell to him. I kept going. I was pleased that I could feel myself being strong. I was crying, but the tears were just falling quietly down my face. I was determined to finish.

'The only option to save you was to remove your remaining arm and legs, otherwise you were going to die.'

I was looking for a reaction to that, but Matthew simply nodded. He seemed to accept what I had told him.

At this point, people moved away a bit to give us some space. I continued, telling him that the kids had accepted everything and that we loved him very much and had great hope for the future. I remembered what Eamonn had said, and reassured Matthew of how beautiful I thought he was. Matthew told me later that this was important to him.

The reason I explained everything to Matthew in so much detail was that I wanted him to understand that, medically, we had done everything we could for him; that we were there to support him; that we had been with him as a family the whole time; and that all of us, including his children, had said goodbye to him along the way. I wanted him to understand that his situation had been that dire, so he would understand why his arms and legs had been amputated.

The love I had felt for him the night he survived the operation had never left and was with me at that moment. I told him I thought he was so brave and strong for fighting to stay with us. I told him I could not have loved him any more – to me, he was the ideal husband, the perfect father, trying to be here for the family.

We were all so happy that he was with us. The kids got to say hello, and it happened that both Kate and Ruth, Matthew's aunt, were in Brisbane, so they were also able to see him that afternoon.

While I had never thought the outcome would be any different, it was still nice to be celebrating, even though we knew that there was still a huge battle ahead. Living in the moment, as I tend to do, allows me to just accept what is in front of me right now. And right now, Matthew was alive, he was awake and he was accepting what had happened. Life couldn't be better.

*

Matthew's awakening was short-lived. He suffered internal bleeding within a few hours of being woken, and a day later was re-sedated. His doctors couldn't find the source of the bleeding, and even though it was a small bleed, they had to keep topping up his blood levels with a series of blood transfusions. It seemed to become a frequent event and when doctors told me he was having one, I would think casually, *Oh, okay. Just another transfusion.*

Eventually, they found the source of the bleeding in the small intestine. It was a setback, but in the end, it seemed to sort itself out, and almost a week later, on the first of July, we tried to wake Matthew again. Because Matthew probably wouldn't remember what he had been told the first time he woke, we needed to repeat the same process, exactly. So everyone gathered around again – Roy, Christine, Rachel, Christie Barrett and the medical team. Again, I could feel the support behind me, but this time, everyone hung back at bit more, so it was just Matthew and me at the bed.

The first time around, I had a sense that Matthew fully understood and accepted what I told him. Matthew never surprises me, so I expected this second time to be the same. I stood in exactly the same place, and said exactly the same words. I started the same way, and I cried. Again, Matthew only cried when I talked about the children, and he expressed surprise at how long he had been in hospital. He had the same reactions in the same places. He was as accepting this time as he had been the first, but again, he suffered medical setbacks and had to be re-sedated; this time, however, it was only for two days.

It was particularly hard on the children when Matthew would have to go back to sleep. During the moments when Matthew was awake, they were very excited because they could finally get some feedback – it wasn't a lot because Matthew couldn't talk at first, but it was better than nothing. They could see that Matthew was happy when they walked in the room – he talked with his eyebrows, which would go up and down to express that he could hear them and was excited for them when they were telling him about their day. I had learned to be very open and honest with the boys – when Matthew had to be re-sedated, I would tell them what was happening, and that Daddy was still fighting. They would ask if he was going to die, and I would have to tell them that he still might, although I never really believed this.

On Tuesday 3 July, Matthew was woken from his coma for the last time. It was just 17 days since his limbs had been amputated. He had been in hospital for just under three weeks. This third, and last, awakening was a repeat of the first and second times. Again, I stood in exactly the same spot. I had the same support. Matthew's reaction was the same, again in the same places. This time, though, he stayed awake.

The doctors were amazed at his reaction.

Matthew later told Tim McMeniman that he was pleased that they had done the operation, and Tim told us that this was the greatest relief of his clinical career. We know from emails and conversations we've had with people involved in the operation to remove Matthew's limbs that it was as emotional a time for them as it was for us. Were they doing the right thing? What would Matthew really want? What would he say? While we, his family, knew him well enough to know what he would want, at that stage the doctors and nurses didn't know him as a person. Later, when they did finally get to meet Matthew, many told us that they knew we had made the right decision for him. It was important for us to hear that, and I am so thankful they took a leap of faith and went with us on this journey.

*

I thought I had made it pretty clear to Matthew that he had no arms and legs, and I thought he was really okay with that because at no point did he cry when I told him about his limbs. His only tears, each time he woke, were when he heard that the kids had had to say goodbye.

A few weeks later, however, when Matthew had the breathing tube out and could mouth a few words, he tried to tell me he had no legs.

I was visiting with Emily, and I could see that Matthew was trying to tell me something. I tried to understand what he was saying – going through the alphabet, giving him clues he could nod to, a little like a game of charades. I asked Chloe, his nurse on duty at the time, what she thought he was saying. We would have spent half an hour trying to get the words. Matthew must have been so frustrated, but he just kept slowly mouthing the words. He was trying to raise his head, and his eyebrows were working hard.

We eventually realised Matthew was saying, 'No legs.'

I felt so bad. I had thought he understood that he had no legs, but now felt that maybe we needed to reinforce it. The doctors had told me that we would need to reinforce what I had told him, even if Matthew didn't go back into a coma. I was worried that maybe he was upset that he had no legs, and I carried this concern with me for a while.

Matthew told me later that I had actually forgotten to tell him just where his legs had been amputated. So when he was trying to talk to me, it was because he had realised that perhaps he had absolutely no legs *at all*. He was okay with the fact that he had had amputations – he just couldn't hold up his head to look, and he still had phantom pain telling him he had arms and legs, so he had no sense of where his limbs ended.

He says he was actually thinking, *So when you said I had no legs, you really did mean, NO legs. Okay then. Just getting confirmation.*

We can laugh about it now. Traditionally, I had always been the one who was good with detail. I think Matthew was learning how important detail can be.

*

It was obvious to me that Matthew was 'all there' the first time I talked to him. I knew instantly that he didn't have brain damage – that everything was okay. He looked directly into my eyes. He couldn't say anything, but he could nod just a little bit. It was Matthew, looking at me. We had the connection, and I knew when I told him about what had happened, he got it.

From that point, I never worried about Matthew having any residual brain damage, although I know other members of the family were a bit concerned. When Matthew did eventually start to speak, his speech was very slurred – similar to the way it might have been if he had suffered a stroke. Still, it wasn't a view I shared.

Roy was quite funny – once Matthew could talk, he would test Matthew by stealth, asking him questions that would reveal whether anything was wrong with his memory. Matthew says he knew this was happening, and that he wondered sometimes if actually there was an issue. Until, he says, 'I remembered that my memory was always not that great.' When the doctors tested Matthew, asking him name, address and birthday kind of questions, the only question he failed was what part of the month it was.

'Mid June,' he said. By the time he was permanently awake, though, June had passed him by.

*

Once Matthew was medically stable and conscious, the time came to look forward. He concentrated on getting himself better, while I focused on looking for the best options for his care once he left ICU. Doctors advised us that Matthew would be in rehab for a year, so selecting a hospital was important. I met with Dr Saul Geffen, a senior rehabilitation specialist at the Mater Private Hospital. He came to visit Matthew a few days after he woke – he had only ever worked on one quadruple amputee, as a junior doctor, but was keen to take Matthew on as a patient. He is a forthright character, but it was obvious that he had Matthew's best interests at heart. He was happy to help us explore other rehab options, which I appreciated.

Once it was clear that Matthew would make a medical recovery, Amod Karnik pulled me aside one morning.

'Now, Diane. You need to start planning some things.' I wasn't too sure what he meant.

He suggested I find out what I was covered for with our health fund, among other things. He may have thought I was getting too absorbed in Matthew's day-to-day medical recovery, and I suspect he was right. It was great advice.

I made an appointment with a health fund representative at the BUPA branch in Capalaba Park Shopping Centre. I can't imagine what he thought when I turned up and told him our whole story – my husband got a sore throat and ended up with no arms and legs. It was the first time I had really had to explain to someone else what had happened. He was fantastic – he reviewed our cover, talked through what our options were, and then a few days after our visit, the BUPA Capalaba office sent me 250 dollars' worth of home cleaning vouchers. I was so appreciative; I had thought it would all be much harder.

Matthew was only just awake at this stage, so Luke and I went during the school holidays to investigate rehabilitation options.

At the time, Luke only wanted to be at the hospital. While the other kids were happy enough to have play dates with friends, and sleepovers with Rachel and Aaron and their cousins, or with Roy or Christine, Luke was set on being either with me at home, or at the hospital with Matthew.

Getting Luke to help me with the decision about rehab was a way to involve him in the next part of Matthew's recovery.

Our first stop was the Mater Private Hospital Rehabilitation Unit, on Annerley Road, Woolloongabba, around the corner from the Mater Public Hospital. We made an appointment with the unit's Rehabilitation Coordinator, Deirdre Cooke. She was wonderful. She had set aside the meeting area to meet with us, and from the moment we arrived, treated Luke with a huge amount of respect, which I really appreciated. Deirdre is quite a gentle soul, so she was the perfect person to talk to Luke. She explained what they, as a unit, could do for Matthew, and she was quite specific about how they would manage his case.

'We anticipate we will put him right next to the nurse's station,' she told us, 'and ideally it will be a big room because there'll be so many people visiting him.'

She told us that Matthew would have a nurse assigned to him as his primary care nurse.

Luke and I loved hearing all of this. We knew that Matthew was expected to be in rehab for up to a year, so we wanted to get the decision right.

Deirdre then invited us to tour the facility, and we had the opportunity to visit the gym and the ward. Overall, we would have spent almost two hours at the unit, so we had a very good idea of what to expect. Deirdre suggested we have a family conference to let the rest of the family tour the facility and ask questions.

A couple of days later, Roy, Christine, Rachel, Luke and I met with Deirdre and Dr Saul Geffen. Roy had typed out a page of

questions about rehab procedures, our involvement, and prosthetics. Deirdre and Saul answered all our questions as best they could,
and suggested that, once Matthew was admitted, the Mater rehab
staff have a weekly case conference about him. We would then be
able to meet with Deirdre for a family meeting every week after the
conference. Deirdre also had a doctorate in occupational therapy, a
strong interest in amputee rehabilitation, and maintained an international network. We left feeling confident that Matthew and the
rest of us would get great care.

It was, therefore, something of a shock when we went to the
Princess Alexandra Hospital a few days later. The hospital, known
to Brisbane locals as 'the PA', is located close to the Mater hospitals
on Ipswich Road, Woolloongabba. One of its specialisations is rehabilitation, and it is home to the Queensland Spinal Injuries Unit. It
was initially the obvious choice for Matthew's rehabilitation, but
things didn't seem to be as simple as we expected.

The PA is such a large hospital that it is divided into units, including the spinal unit and trauma unit – and Matthew didn't fit into
either of those categories because his amputations were the result
of an infectious disease. If Matthew were to go to the PA, he would
be placed in the Geriatric and Rehabilitation Unit (GARU). The
profile of GARU was similar to the Mater Private Rehabilitation
Unit – patients were generally older, and weren't the victims of
trauma or spinal accidents.

I had rung the unit, just as I had with the Mater, and explained
that I wanted to come and have a look at what was available for
Matthew. I explained that I was going to bring my eight-year-old
son with me, and made a time to visit. A few days later, we found
our way to the nurse's station and upon introducing ourselves,
which seemed to come as a surprise to the nurse on duty, we were
advised to just 'go and have a look around'.

The nurse pointed to where the rooms were, saying there were four beds to a room, separated by curtains – a typical hospital set-up. Most of the patients are elderly in this particular unit, and we were told that all the patients had to have dinner together each night to further their social engagement.

I asked about the family.

'Could we have takeaway dinner some nights?'

'No, that's not really an option.'

It was very clear that there wouldn't be any special considera-tion made for Matthew's high level of dependency, and Luke and I found the experience daunting and disappointing. No doctor was available to speak with us about Matthew's care, and I got the feel-ing that, in contrast to the Mater, where Matthew was going to have a dedicated nurse, he was going to be just a number at the PA.

The nurse pointed out the gym, but didn't take us in, so we just looked through the window. It didn't seem as big as the Mater gym. The facility might have been amazing – in fact, I'm sure it was. It's just that we didn't know because no one took the time to tell us in detail or explain what the equipment could do.

Luke and I both got a very prickly feeling about the situation, and as soon as we had passed through the doors of the unit on the way out, Luke turned to me.

'Mummy, we cannot let Daddy go there.'

From that point, Luke was adamant that he did not want Matthew to go to the PA, even though we knew it had a great rep-utation as a rehabilitation facility. I totally agreed with him. This wasn't just about meeting physical criteria – it was about finding the right emotional fit, too, for all of us. We knew that Matthew would need his family around to get through the next stage of his recovery, and the kids needed to be able to engage with their father. Before finalising our decision, I also visited Sunnybank Private Hospital, which we had heard was quite good. I went on my own, as Luke was at school, and the staff were lovely, but advised me that Matthew's case was outside their scope – his level of dependency was simply too high for them.

We felt, in the end, that the Mater was the only place that would allow us to be involved as a family in Matthew's recovery, and we were fortunate to have private health cover that would allow us to access the facilities.

We knew it was going to be a big risk for everyone. Saul Geffen had made it clear that Matthew would be a unique patient, and that his case was going to be challenging. But the Mater's motto is 'Exceptional People, Exceptional Care', and we had experienced this first hand. We had been treated as part of the Mater family while Matthew was in ICU. Everybody knew us, and had accommodated us – we would make a huge amount of noise when we visited, we were in and out at all times of the day – but most importantly, seemed to be on the journey with us. We knew they were committed to our care.

So, we decided on the Mater Private Hospital Rehabilitation Unit, and a week later received approval from our health fund.

I know there were people close to us who questioned our decision. Ultimately, the difference came down to a sense of culture rather than medical reputation. The unit would be Matthew's home for the best part of the next year. Matthew's family and I were comfortable, and so were the children because of Luke's involvement. We were able to look forward to the next stage, and we were excited.

Matthew, on the other hand, was just catching up.

PART TWO

MATTHEW

CHAPTER 7

A NEW DAWN

I am inside a helix, being squeezed harder and harder. I'm in pain and can feel myself travelling upwards, and every time I think it's getting better, I feel the pain become more excruciating. Every piece of my body is screaming and I can't breathe. I'm trying to thrash and struggle, but I can't move because the helix is squeezing me. I am dizzy and I desperately want it all to stop. Colours and textures keep changing and I'm confused. I pop through a surface. Everything stops.

It's a dream, but it feels real and I know something is happening to me. At other times, I dream of gliding across the ground, fig trees, international hospitals and alien pods. My body's asleep, but my mind is firing.

Then I wake. It's the third of July, 2012, and I've been asleep the best part of three weeks. I know instantly that I'm happy to be here.

*

I don't remember too much about what exactly Diane told me, but I knew that because it was her telling me, everything would be okay. I know now that it took three attempts, and other people were there, but in the wake-up that eventually counted, I can only remember Diane. I was so happy to see her.

When I woke up, I could remember instantly how sick I had been, so as Diane was telling me what had happened, I was thinking, *Yes, that makes sense. No wonder I was feeling so unwell. Good decision. I would have made the same call.* From the moment Diane told me, I've always been aware that this happened, and of why, so there was never any sense of disbelief. I was just grateful that everyone had faith in me, for me to be at this point.

It was one thing to know that my limbs had been amputated, but it was another to come to terms with the reality of my new body. I didn't know where I was, and I couldn't move or look around. I felt physically trapped – as though I was completely encased in liquid concrete, so that any attempt to move was against an opposing force. It was impossible, so I was initially completely immobile. I felt no pain, but I was exhausted and the feeling of fluid in my lungs, as if I was drowning, was overwhelming.

While I could only see Diane, I was aware of the presence of other people and I could hear machines whirring, and a lot of background noise. I tried to look down at my arms and legs, but they were covered, and I couldn't move my head because of the tube in my throat. My brain was telling me that my limbs were still there, and I had no idea how long my arms or legs were.

I was able to understand what had happened to me and I only had one main thought in response.

I have to get home.

*

I don't know how the children reacted to me the first two times

I woke because I can't remember, but Diane tells me it was similar the third time around.

As they walked in to my cubicle in ICU, I could instantly tell they had a routine. Luke was confident – he came straight in and checked the monitors for vital signs. Emily wanted to scramble up on the bed. She was clearly very happy that I was awake. I was so happy to see them – I could feel my heart racing with excitement.

Once they came into the cubicle area, though, Will and Ben stopped about a metre away from the end of the bed.

I felt heartbroken when I noticed this, and I could feel tears welling at the edges of my eyes before they rolled down my temples to the bed. I could see that they were hesitant. I still couldn't talk or move, so I couldn't say anything to reassure them. Diane tried to encourage them closer to the bed, and they did come a little closer, but I could tell that they were still really reluctant. There was no way to wipe my tears away. I didn't want them to see I was upset.

Diane was so positive. She didn't push them but talked them through the experience, encouraging them to tell me about their day. *My God, I love this woman*, I thought as I watched her teasing details about what they had been doing at school and sport from them.

Then it was time for them to leave. I felt a bit sad as I watched them walk away, but my thoughts progressed from *I have to get home* to something more specific.

I have to find out what I need to do to get better.

*

I needed to understand what was attached to me and what the attachments were doing. As an engineer, I wanted to know how things worked. I remember trying to figure out what the dialysis machine was, and what the breathing machine was. Eventually, I worked out that the attachments were either assisting me or monitoring me – either someone told me directly what a machine was, or I figured out what it was doing by watching and listening to people. I couldn't see much because the machines were behind me.

Each morning, a small conference would be held at the end of my bed, and I would try to overhear what they were saying. Typically, the entourage would include an intensivist, a couple of doctors, registrars, the nursing unit manager, nurse administrator, the nurse assigned to me and, sometimes, the physio – probably a group of around 10 people. I could also hear that the nurses were talking to Luke about what everything was doing, and I felt grateful that they were including him. He would come in and check stuff out (he was obviously used to checking my vital signs because quite often he wouldn't look at me until he had checked my monitors), but sometimes the details weren't explained to me, and I couldn't talk to ask anyone what was happening.

At that stage, I didn't realise that I had lost hearing in one ear as well as sight in one eye, so I wasn't actually aware that I couldn't hear or see a lot of things that were going on. I felt quite isolated, but at the same time I was just happy to be here, so I tried not to wince or make it obvious that I was uncomfortable.

There was a lot of attention being devoted to my mouth, throat and lungs. My lungs burned, and I couldn't get a clear sense of where my mouth was. I felt like I had two sets of teeth, one set behind the other. The signals from my tongue were confused, and I could feel non-existent rubber bands crisscrossing my mouth, constricting my tongue, and everything was numb. I found out later that the disease had killed part of my tongue, close to the back of my mouth. The dead patch is now scar tissue.

My lungs were filling with fluid. With the amount of trauma that had happened in my throat, I was producing a lot of mucus and the flap that closes off my windpipe wasn't working properly, so I had a continuous stream of liquid going down into my lungs. As I was breathing, I would start to gurgle and a nurse would have to put an instrument through the tracheostomy that went down into my lungs and suction them out. It was very uncomfortable, and I had to have that a lot.

I knew I couldn't do anything about the dialysis, but I wanted to work out how to get rid of my attachments and start communicating again. I was desperate to talk to everyone, and I could see that they were desperate to talk to me. They were trying all sorts of ideas, and after a day or two my sister Rachel devised a blinking system, wherein each letter of the alphabet was read out, and I would blink at the one I wanted.

It was a great idea in theory, and I was really keen to try it, but my brain wasn't working fast enough. Rachel would go through the letters, but by the time I processed what letter I wanted, and then blinked, she had progressed by one or two letters. We tried to stick to a rhythm but even that didn't seem to work too well.

Everyone was in on it, including the nurses, and we all gave it a good go. It was a little like playing charades without me being able to prompt for clues. Eventually, we gave up, but it wasn't without everyone trying their hardest to help me. I was thinking, *I'll be talking soon, so don't worry about it too much.*

We then tried a voice box, a Passy-Muir valve that attaches to the tracheostomy. It was extremely exhausting. The boys loved this – I sounded like a robot, and to this day, Ben can do an amazing impersonation of me as I sounded during that phase. I would only be able to get out a few sentences before I felt the need to sleep for a couple of hours. It was lovely to get a few words out, though, like 'I love you' to Diane and the kids, and 'Thank you' to the nurses or doctors. I became really motivated to push to the next step.

The trauma in my throat had generally made the changing of tubes that were associated with my mouth, nose and throat very painful. Medical staff had to change my nasal feeding tube a few times, which was horrible, and at one point they needed to replace my tracheostomy for reasons I can't remember. To allow the doctors to do this, I had to be removed from the oxygen machine and hold my neck back while they removed the tracheostomy tube. I had an overwhelming feeling of drowning as blood and mucus filled my throat.

As the procedure went on, I could feel that whatever the doctors were doing wasn't going well. My nurse that day was May. I loved working with May – she was so kind and careful with me. I could see the fear in her eyes that something wasn't right. It felt like I was drowning, and I mouthed to her, *Please, stop now.* But by then, it was past the point of no return so they had to keep going. They eventually got the tube placed into my throat in time and got me back on the breathing machine. Some time later, when doctors had to go through my nose to look down my windpipe when my voice-box wasn't working properly, I had that 'final-straw thought': *I just don't think I can take anything else being shoved down my nose or my throat.* But it was pointless to complain – everyone was doing the best they could to help me, and it was working. I was slowly getting better each day.

I was determined to simply learn to breathe on my own again sooner rather than later. That would also mean I would be able to eat because while I had the tracheostomy, I was being fed by a tube through my nose.

I devised a plan to get off the tracheostomy, which was actually a really hard thing to do. Doctors told me I needed to breathe humidified air for 24 hours before they would take out the tracheostomy. Breathing was torture – I felt like my chest was being crushed from the outside and I was drowning on the inside. But I had to try. I built up the number of hours I would breathe humidified air each day.

I remember one day I got to 20 hours and I was so exhausted that I had to give up. I was really disappointed in myself, but that was the moment I decided to set 24-hour goals. If I failed today,

I would just try again that little bit harder tomorrow. I tried, then, to celebrate small wins. If I got to 21 hours tomorrow, that would be great.

That approach made things easier – I woke up the next day and decided I would try again for a little bit longer. I did 24 hours that day on humidified air. That was really exciting because it meant they let me breathe without the ventilator for a few hours the following day. I took the same approach with this, and would breathe on my own for longer and longer periods until eventually I was breathing completely on my own. My nurses knew what I was trying to do, and they would work with me. They would ask me what I needed and we worked out ways to communicate. I know now that I probably pushed myself a little too hard on all of this – looking back at photos of myself, I always get shocked.

Wow, I looked really, really sick.

In reality, I knew I was sick. Obviously I was. I was in an ICU unit in a hospital, and I had never actually been admitted to any form of hospital before.

But Diane kept telling me I looked beautiful, and my family told me how great I was looking when they visited, and I was happy to believe them all. I was getting better, and I could feel that. I tried not to focus on how unwell I was at all – I was only looking ahead at where I wanted to go. It made it easier for me to cope.

*

On the highest part of the wall opposite my bed, Dad and Diane had placed photos of my family. I knew instantly who they were when I woke from my induced coma, but I momentarily wondered how they got there, and it was difficult for me to orientate to where they were.

There were photos of the kids, Mum and Dad, Kate and Rachel and their families, and lots of drawings. They were the first thing I looked at when I woke, and the photos gave me strength and comfort throughout the day. There were three photos I came to need emotionally: a collage of photos of our family that I had put together for Diane's birthday a few years earlier; a photo of Emily and me in Fiji; and one of the three boys in their Christmas shirts.

I felt a sense of warmth, and calm would descend over me when I looked up at them. Those photos would remind me: *This is why I am still here.*

There were no windows near my bed, and I had no concept of time. My brain was playing tricks on me, and I often felt very disoriented. One night, I thought I was in one big room with lots of patients in their beds, and I was calling out but no one could hear me. At another stage, I thought I was in a hotel overlooking the river underneath the Story Bridge. My dreams continued once I had woken, and to this day I can still picture many of them as clearly as if they had occurred last night.

My bed in ICU was directly in front of the main nursing station, so there was a sense of busyness around me. I found it difficult to sleep – the incessant beeping and general noise was at times overwhelming. I could hear people gurgling and spluttering in the beds beside me – all sorts of bodily noises, not that I ever held that against anyone because I'm sure they could hear mine. On the upside, I got to watch a whole lot of things going on, and later when I could talk, life was quite social with my bed in that position.

The nurse on duty looking after me would sit at a small lectern-style table a few metres from my bed. Because I had an infectious disease, he or she would be covered in protective gear, such as an apron and gloves. The nurses seemed to make a lot of notes, and I was amazed at how much paperwork there was. The ability to focus so much of their attention on one patient was incredible. Everyone else wandered in and out; various specialists – the speech pathologist, dietician and physiotherapist, for example – attended to me during the day, but a nurse was there all the time and I formed great relationships with some of them, especially once I could talk.

They seemed to know when I might need someone to talk to. They told me that they didn't normally get to know their patients, let alone include a patient in the coffee round, as happened a few weeks into my stay. The nurses tended to focus on the immediate task at hand. They told me what they were doing while they were doing it, but not too much more than that, although they all grew to know that I really liked to understand the details of what was going on.

I was amazed at how busy you could be while lying flat on your back. I would have physio on my chest in the mornings, and various appointments throughout the day. By the evening I was often completely exhausted.

I was under the care of four intensivists while I was in ICU, each with their own approach: Shane Townsend, John Morgan, Amod Karnik and Jeff Presneill. Every one played their role. My family remember Amod as being particularly compassionate, even when he had to be blunt about my condition. Shane would talk regularly with Diane, so she formed a great relationship with him, and John Morgan was particularly good at explaining things to me, involving me in my own care, which I appreciated. Jeff was into figures. I called him 'Mr Chart Man'. He loved his charts, and I enjoyed his visits because he would pull up the computer and show me the trend of my kidney concentration levels. He worried about the trends and whether I was getting better. It seemed to me that everyone worked really well together as a team.

From talking to my family, I know that some of the medical staff possibly doubted the decision made to save me. But if they did, they didn't show it to me and all of them, in their own way, were responsible for helping to save my life.

I knew that they had taken a great risk in operating on me, so my respect for them, and the way everyone was dealing with me and my family, was immeasurable.

*

I wasn't hungry, but had a desperate desire to taste food and drink. A few times a day, I would watch the trolley go past with food and drinks on it that I couldn't have. On one particular occasion, the trolley came past with reconstituted orange juice on it. The juice was in those little triangular sachets off which you cut the corners – I remembered them from when I was little and living in North Queensland.

I was in the central area of the ICU, so couldn't miss the trolley as it came by. For some reason, this trolley seemed to go more slowly than usual – as though in slow motion – and then it just kept going past my bed and around a corner until it disappeared. *My goodness, I want that juice*, I thought. I would have given my right arm for just a small taste of that orange juice, reconstituted or not. Unfortunately I had no arms to give, so I just had to watch it roll on by.

At that stage, my feeding tube was continually scraping against my oesophagus. It was uncomfortable, and making me cough. I pleaded with the staff to take it out. One day, after my tracheostomy had been removed, they did, and I was so happy. Then I remember thinking, *Oh, crap. That means I've got to eat.*

It felt like a long process to start to eat again. My epiglottis wasn't working properly, so normal fluid and food could go straight into my lungs. I started on thickened water, which I never knew existed, and puréed food, which was just disgusting – like spam put through a blender. I was also still learning to speak properly, and was having all sorts of issues with my tongue, which seemed to have forgotten how to work properly. This also affected my ability to eat.

My speech pathologist, Andrea Whitehead, spent some time working out what consistency of food I could tolerate. At one stage we did a barium swallow, which examines the upper gastrointestinal tract. I had to swallow barium sulphate and then got to watch my insides in real time as I swallowed, which was pretty cool.

I was trying my hardest to work out how I was going to get off the puréed food. I didn't have too much of an appetite, but was doing the exercises Andrea had given me to try to get the back of my throat working again. She was fantastic, and would bring in different things for me to have a crack at. I told her I was a little bit sick of lime. It seemed there was lime flavour in everything, and I asked her if she could make it a bit more interesting.

'What do you like?' she asked.

'Chocolate.' I didn't have to think about that response.

The next day, Andrea brought in a packet of Maltesers. *Oh, wow. Great*, I thought. She put one on my tongue so I could try to roll it around inside my mouth, and I managed that, but it was pretty hard. My tongue wasn't working well enough to be able to put things in the right place within my mouth, and a lot of my mouth was still numb. But we were feeling positive – I had managed to move the chocolate ball around my mouth and it had dissolved so I could swallow it. It also tasted different to what I had imagined. Apparently your tastebuds change every six weeks or so. I used to be able to eat a whole box in one sitting, but on this occasion, one was enough – it was so rich.

The next day, Andrea brought in a Caramello Koala. *Wow. Even better*, I thought. *This gig is pretty good, I'm enjoying this*. It was another one of those 'great in theory' moments, though. We thought the koala was soft and would dissolve pretty quickly. The caramel, however, got stuck on my teeth and I couldn't do anything about it because my mouth nerves weren't working. I couldn't chew properly or fast enough to catch the chocolate, so it began to spread very quickly throughout my mouth. I started coughing and spluttering – choking – on that chocolate koala. Andrea had to scoop some of it out and I had to spit the rest out as best I could.

It was a little bit scary, but ultimately worth it – Caramello Koala is Caramello Koala, in any form. It tasted fantastic.

A few weeks later, we were progressing well and I was moving on to solid food, but I was getting pretty sick of the same thing over and over again. It helped that a good friend of Rachel's was Sally McCray, who happened to be the director of nutrition and dietetics at the Mater. I didn't know that Rachel had been in contact with Sally, and had mentioned that I was keen to try something new.

One afternoon, a dietician came to see me.

'We're looking at your diet, Matthew. What would you like to eat?' she asked.

My nurse that day, Eamonn Maher, was with me. Eamonn and I had developed a wonderful relationship and I had come to rely on him a lot. I knew that he had been amazing with Diane and the kids, and now he was like a confidant – in on my plans, and ready to do absolutely anything he could to help me.

We talked about what might be more interesting for a weekend breakfast.

'Avocado and poached eggs on toast,' I told the dietician. It was one of the ideas Eamonn and I had come up with when we were discussing what might taste great.

I was supposed to be on a low-potassium diet, and avocadoes are very high in potassium. Sally told us later that when they got that request, they had to rejig my entire diet for the rest of the day so I could have that for breakfast. But they did allow it, and I was so grateful. Again, it was harder work to eat than I remember avocado and eggs on toast ever being, but small things made big moments, and that was one of them.

*

Diane's visits with Luke, Ben, Will and Emily became part of my daily routine. Luke was always interested in how I was progressing medically, while we had to make sure Emily didn't pull out any of my tubes. She wasn't fazed by anything much, and she liked to come up onto the bed with me. I had a wedge to keep me slightly rolled onto one side and Emily's position was between the wedge and the bed rails. She would always come and lie next to me, which was lovely. At one point, while lying on the bed, she decided that she needed to teach me to walk again.

'Look, Daddy. Daddy, I show you how to walk.'

She lifted herself up, propped herself up on her knees and shuffled forward to the end of the bed, then turned around to look at me. She was so proud of herself.

Diane and I laughed. If only it was so simple – but I was glad that for her, it seemed to be that easy.

Eamonn wanted to get me to do as many normal things as I could, and include the kids in those occasions. My hair was getting pretty dirty, so he planned a hair wash that involved the kids. It was, as usual, a significant logistical exercise. We waited for the kids to come in before the bed was tipped backwards, and Eamonn placed a sheet of plastic underneath my head. He got a bucket, gloves and sponges for Will, Luke and Emily, who all wanted to help with the shampooing and rinsing.

It was nice to feel their physical presence again, particularly Will, who had been so reluctant to touch me up to that point. Ben was still reluctant to touch me, which made me a little bit sad, so he was sitting on a chair, out of the way. I wasn't overly concerned, though. Ben and I had always had a special connection, and I thought he would do things in his own time.

He had grabbed a piece of paper and begun drawing as soon as everyone else had started working on me. He didn't look up, concentrating on his picture, which was an intricate and colourful dragon.

Once we were finished, Ben came over to the side of the bed. He was very proud to show me his drawing and described in detail the dragon he had drawn for me. It was nice to know that he had his own way of connecting with me.

Later, when Diane was at home with the kids, she asked Ben about the afternoon's activities.

'Ben, why didn't you want to help wash Dad's hair?'

The reply was classic Ben.

'Because he's been in hospital so long, he's probably got nits.'

*

I started to feel a desperate need to go outside. I remember Eamonn and May working really hard to make sure I got outside on one particular day. Photos remind me it was the ninth of July, only six days after I had been woken from the coma. I was still on oxygen and hooked up to monitoring equipment, and it seemed like it took them hours to get ready, just to take me outside for a short period.

The destination was a concrete balcony just outside intensive care. Everyone was worried that it was going to rain, but I didn't care. Fortunately Eamonn and May were happy to work with me, and it was beautiful to feel the wind on my face, and just that little bit of rain, which did eventuate, too. I felt very lucky, sitting with Diane and Emily, who were rugged up against the winter breeze while I was bare-chested and happy to feel cool.

Not long after, when I was taken off the oxygen and was feeling a bit stronger, we decided to go out underneath the fig trees in the grounds of the Mater. That became part of the daily routine. I would go outside for an hour or so, and I think by doing so I scared some of the new mothers. To get to the trees, I needed to be pushed across the bridge between hospital buildings and taken down in the Mater Mothers' Hospital lift. I would then roll along in front of all these expectant and new mothers on my way out of the building. On one occasion, I thought, *Everybody's happy and going home with a newborn baby, and here am I with no limbs being wheeled through the foyer every day in a big blue chair*. I felt like I was raining on their parade for a moment or so.

Whichever nurse was working with me that day would come with me, and Diane would often come and sit with us outside as well because at that time she was visiting twice a day – once with Emily and later in the afternoon with the boys.

Sometimes, the wardies would bring down my lunch, so we would all eat outside. The days were spectacular – the sky blue and cloudless, and the air crisp with cold. I would enjoy the breeze while the poor nurses would sit there freezing, and it reminded me of the lengths they often went to help me.

Temperature control was an issue, as my body was unable to regulate itself. It was a reminder of what we take for granted – you need skin for temperature regulation, and without arms and legs, I didn't have much skin. One day I went a little over the edge. When I got back to my bed, I started to vomit. The medical staff thought it was a bladder infection, which I also had at the time, but I think I pushed it a bit too hard, being cold for too long. It was probably a bit of both.

It was fantastic to feel a little bit normal again. I always liked being outside, so I was doing something I wanted to do, supported as always by the nurses. I had my first coffee since being admitted to hospital under those fig trees. I was so desperately looking forward to it, but as with my experience with chocolate, my taste-buds had obviously adjusted to life without coffee. The first cup, sipped through a straw from a takeaway container, was awful. My memory of what coffee tasted like was different to the reality. I persevered – pretty soon after that, I was included in the coffee rounds for the nurses, and we would grab coffees before heading outside (or they would!).

One afternoon, Diane, Emily and I were having some time together under the trees. Diane and I were talking, and Emily was just enjoying running around on the grass. She would run across to the edge of the grass, turn around and run back, and land at the chair I was sitting in. It was so simple, and so normal, but I remember thinking, *It is so nice to be alive to see her play*, and it was even more special because Diane was by my side, as usual.

It was another of those small things that made for big moments, and those moments all added up.

One of these was being able to watch the third State of Origin rugby match. I had been in a coma for the second game, and I mentioned to Dad that it would be really nice to watch the game. So Dad brought Luke into ICU, and we had a boys' night in. Dad sat on one side of the bed with Luke on the other. I think I missed a lot of the game because I slept between tries, only being woken by the roar of the crowd and Luke and Dad's excited cries. In a strange kind of way, we were doing exactly what we would have been doing if I was at home – sitting there having a bit of fun, getting excited about the footy.

It was enough to remind me that every day that passed I was a day closer to going home.

CHAPTER 8

THE STARTING POINT

I have only had a couple of fully measurable down days since I had my limbs amputated, and both of them were associated with specific events. The first was while I was in ICU, when Dr Saul Geffen from the Mater Private Hospital Rehabilitation Unit came to see me. I had briefly met him previously, but this was the first time he had really sat down and talked in detail about me as a patient. He told me lots of things in that meeting. He was trying to explain what my prospects were.

'Matt, if you are going to walk, you realise you're going to walk like a penguin.'

I frowned, I think, but didn't respond. It was the first time any-one had given it to me straight about what things were going to be like.

I think this was the beginning of the 'what life is going to be like' phase. I had been so focused on simply getting through each day that I hadn't really thought too much past that. It was a great introduction to Saul. He's direct, which is something that I learned to appreciate about him – it meant I knew what I was likely to be in for. I also learned that he appreciated directness in others, so I was able to be as open with him as he was with me, and that became the basis of a great relationship.

But at that moment, hearing that I would walk, or waddle, like a fat little black bird that has to launch itself from side to side to propel itself forward set me back mentally.

This was the first time I had been prompted to think ahead about what life was really going to be like, and that was hard. *I am not going to be able to walk like I used to. I won't be able to do things I want to do.* I had been so caught up in existing when I was in ICU, just getting through each day, that I hadn't been ready to face anything more than that. I didn't have the energy either. But this time, I had no escape. It was something that had to be confronted.

I found that it was better to focus on acceptance and choose what I was then going to do. I was going to let myself be sad for a little while, but then look for opportunities to see if I could prove the doctors wrong.

So in this case, my sadness lasted only for a day or so.

My family sensed I was a little down in the dumps at the time, and I was extremely lucky to have so many people around me who were able to recognise that. I think the nurses also helped, by letting Diane know how I was travelling. Somebody must have said something to somebody else, and I suddenly noticed everybody turning up a lot more over those few days. Rachel, Diane, Mum and Dad visited even more than usual. It made a difference.

One of Rachel's friends again stepped in to help – Louise Lanigan, the salary cap manager for national rugby league team the Brisbane Broncos. Rachel had told Louise about what happened to me, and had asked if there was a chance of a visit from a Bronco to help improve my spirits. Louise sent word on to Broncos management, and Shane Webcke and Allan Langer were keen to help.

Shane and Allan visited me independently in ICU, and Darren Lockyer also visited later while I was in rehab. When I first heard about Shane's visit, I was really excited but my biggest issue was actually working out what to wear. I almost couldn't believe I was worrying about my wardrobe.

At one point I was trying to convince Rachel that it would be okay if I didn't wear a t-shirt. Anyone who knows Rachel would know that there was a risk she would be 'not happy' with the idea that I was bare-chested for a visit. She had originally brought in a range of t-shirts with motivational statements on them, having ordered them off the internet, but they were proving too hot for me to wear. So Rachel then brought in some athletic training singlets, which are breathable, and I elected to wear one of those – we were both happy with that option.

Dad ended up with my motivational t-shirts – it's why you see him regularly getting about in slogans like 'Attitude is everything' and 'Never ever ever give up'. And while I don't know that I'm what Nike had in mind as a poster boy, their singlets are fantastically comfortable, so I'm sporting the 'Just do it' slogan. Dad and I are pretty good for motivation, between his t-shirt and my singlet collection.

Looking forward to a visit gave me something other than walking like a penguin to think about. Allan Langer's visit was particularly important because the kids got to meet him after they had finished school for the day. Diane was also excited – so much so that she introduced Will to Allan by saying, 'This is Will, and Will's teacher has a crush on you.' We all laughed – it definitely broke the ice.

Allan's visit seemed significant because afterwards Ben cuddled me for the first time since my surgery. Diane and I had been watching the children closely for signs that they were having problems dealing with what had happened to me, and Ben was probably our biggest worry because he was clearly internalising things.

I have no idea if the two events are linked. Diane is convinced that they are, but Ben might have just been ready. Now, why he might have been ready then, I don't know, and he probably doesn't either. It would be nice to think that seeing others think of me as special, or feeling comfortable touching me, in some kind of way helped him feel comfortable doing the same. Ben would have seen Allan shake my stump and hold my shoulder – that might have been enough for him.

Whatever it was, it was good to have Ben back. I had really missed him.

Allan and Shane's visits also helped because it showed me there was a positive side to what had happened. In an everyday scenario, I wouldn't get the opportunity to meet people like them. They made me feel special, and I was humbled that people who would obviously be quite busy would take the time to come and see me.

I didn't realise it then, but it would be the first of many meetings with amazing people – people with disabilities; professional athletes, including Paralympians; heroes from the community – every one of whom has inspired me in some way.

So I found it hard to stay down for long. I knew that prolonged sadness would have an impact on those around me that I love, and would change the nature of our relationships. I learned that I wanted more than anything to continue to be close to my family in particular, and that this required me to always make the genuine effort to look on the brighter side of any situation. There are a hundred reasons every day for me to push through the mental barriers that could hold me back, and those barriers are present all the time. I have learned that although I automatically seem to orient to being positive, I do have to be wary of those moments when I have multiple challenges that overwhelm me. It's those moments where I have to consciously manage my thoughts, and being married to someone with the positive disposition of Diane makes this easier.

As for now, I would be very happy to walk like a penguin. I know now that any form of walking would be just great.

*

At around six weeks into my recovery, while I was still in ICU, Diane decided we should have a 'date night'. I knew that it was going to happen, but I didn't realise Diane was taking the term 'date' literally. I still have the image of Diane pushing aside the curtains that surrounded my bed, saying, 'Hi honey,' with this huge smile, and wearing a beautiful long burgundy dress. Her hair had been done, but she was a little like me – she had a few bandages and bandaids on her chest and across her nose because she had been to the doctor to get some moles removed that day. We made a great pair.

Diane had organised some different options for drinks – a few alcoholic and a few non-alcoholic – and food. I was starting to eat more normally, so she had brought me a cheeseburger – I had been craving one for weeks.

Eamonn had borrowed a big-screen television and put it at the end of the bed, and Diane brought in some DVDs. The nurses propped up my bed so it looked a bit like a large chair, and Diane sat in the big Regency care chair that I normally used for going outside – that way, we were able to 'hold arms'.

Eamonn had told everyone to stay away from the curtains, which he had drawn around me so we could have some privacy, and Diane had brought in *The Girl With the Dragon Tattoo*, which has some pretty graphic sex scenes. Because I'm now partially deaf, the volume was up really loud – you would have heard all these sex noises coming out of this intensive care bed. I was pretty confident people would know that it wasn't Diane and me.

It was so nice to do something with Diane, just the two of us, again. I had been really missing her company and we hadn't had any chance to be together just hanging out as a couple. On most of Diane's visits to hospital she was accompanied by at least one child – most often Emily, who would rarely sit still or let us have uninterrupted conversations.

I was asked once whether our date night was one of the moments when I thought things would be okay. I was surprised at the question. It hadn't occurred to me that people would have doubted my happiness to be here.

Even though I always thought things would be okay, Diane making the effort to remind me that she thought I was beautiful and special was incredible. I'm never in any doubt how much I love her, but there are moments like that when it blows me away.

*

Learning to breathe, eat and speak again was one set of challenges; learning to move again was another level of challenge altogether. The feeling of being encased in liquid concrete never left me, and I still have it to this day. I can only imagine that it's because I've lost the length that gave my limbs the impetus to move. So now, when I try to move, I have to propel myself from my core, rather than rely on parts of my body being pulled along by momentum.

The short length of my stumps became really obvious to me when I got itchy because I tended to get itchiest around my face – my ears, nose and head. When I realised that I couldn't scratch myself, I remember thinking, *If only I could scratch the corner of my eye!* Now, I find that quite easy – in fact, I can touch most of my head with the end of my stump – but at the time, I couldn't lift either of my arms high enough, or push my shoulders in far enough to move my stumps to where I needed them to go.

So I learned to have great respect for that extra inch, and after some time thinking about things, decided very early on in my recovery that I suffered from 'stump envy'. Everyone kept showing me videos of different people who had had amputations – I watched them closely, and examined how they moved. I realised that in quite a number of instances, my stumps simply weren't long enough to allow me to do the things they were doing. I still watched what they did and tried to learn as much as I could, but it drove me to get a bit of a focus. I would look for people who had no knees and no elbows, and I found there weren't a lot of amputees like that around.

I also learned that the shape of the end of the stump is really important. I had the chance to meet other amputees and I watched how they moved. Some were able to type on their iPhones because their stump was so pointy; others could effectively dress themselves because their arms were long and they had wrists that could still rotate. The value of joints, and the importance of what one elbow and one knee could do, became obvious. For example, I watched people who were bilateral leg amputees, and noticed that if they had at least one knee, they seemed to be able to balance reasonably well, and mobilise themselves with that longer leg.

I really wanted those extra inches. Saul reminded me soon after I met him about the importance of doing exercises so that I maximised the range in my short arms. I simply had to use what I had, and it was becoming very clear that I didn't have a lot. It was imperative that I got the most out of what was left of my limbs. Ideally, I would be able to oppose myself, as in when you might put your hands together and press. If I could press the ends of my stumps together, I would be able to stretch and strengthen my limbs, but it became evident that it just wasn't going to be possible. So I needed to start moving, despite the difficulties involved. I had to learn how to move, and people had to learn with me because no one at the Mater had ever worked with such a short-limbed multiple amputee before.

Physiotherapy was my key to movement, and it was going to have to be a journey of discovery. I had never been to a physiotherapist in my life before, and I would not even have been able to tell you what one did. I can tell you now – they're important.

My introduction to physio started on the day I woke up in ICU. Initially, I worked with Felicity Prebble and Matt Hutchins, the physiotherapists for ICU. Both would come to my bed while I was immobilised and work on my chest to clear the fluid from my lungs. This involved beating their hands up and down on the front of my chest. It felt and sounded like someone playing bongo drums on my chest.

Matt was the one who got me out of bed and sat me up for the first time. He got me moving a little bit to start with – trying to lift my neck and my stumps off the bed – and then he got me sitting up. He had to lift me to start with, and I would then have to try to sit there by myself for as long as I could. I was extremely light-headed the first few times I sat up, almost passing out each time. I know everyone was expecting me to sit up and fall straight over, but I did manage to last about 40 seconds on my first attempt before I lost balance. I was pretty impressed with myself. I've always been com-petitive at heart – this was a new type of competition.

I remember looking down at my leg stumps when I first sat up. They were moving all the time, jerking all over the place as I was try-ing to find my balance. Now, when I sit up, my legs are really stable. It's taken almost two years, and three five-hour sessions per week in rehab to get to that point. I have developed a deep respect for the 'core' of my body. It really is amazing what the muscles in your torso can do.

I became quite fascinated by what was going on with my body, so I was really keen to work with Matt to see what we could make it do. Matt would spend an hour a day with me while I was in ICU. He was fantastic – he was so committed to helping me, and he would do anything to facilitate progress, no matter how small. He got me really thinking about movement generally. I know he was questioned about how much time he was spending with me – in the very early stages in ICU he largely devoted his time to trying to prompt my muscles to remember what to do, as they had severe atrophy. (In simple terms, atrophy is when muscles waste away if you don't move them enough.)

At one point, he rolled me over onto my stomach, and got me to try to turn my head. At the time I couldn't lie on my stomach, lift my head and turn it. So if I was on my stomach, I was literally flat on my face unless someone turned my head for me. And once there I was stuck, and couldn't move anywhere else. I knew I had a long way to go!

Very soon after I woke from my coma, I also met Jacqui O'Sullivan (then Jacqui Wright), who was the physiotherapist from the Mater Private Hospital Rehabilitation Unit. We met in unusual circumstances, when she and fellow physio Jane Nielsen, also her best friend, accidentally plastered my testicles while casting a mould for my stumps.

Saul had sent Jacqui and Jane over to ICU with Nisha Sharma, a registrar, with instructions to create plaster moulds of my stumps. The idea was to make a protective cover for my stumps at a very early stage so they couldn't be damaged before the time came for prosthetics. None of us was convinced it was a great idea, but we were happy to give it a go. I was still a bit sedated and in something of a drug haze, so I didn't really understand what was going on, but to cast the mould, Jane and Jacqui had to use plaster of Paris and a lot of bandages.

There I was, flat on my back, with my stumps being plastered up. My stumps are so short that it was impossible to do this without involving testicles and pubic hair. Jane and Jacqui were trying not to be embarrassed. They were so lovely, and kept apologising because plaster was going absolutely everywhere. Fortunately, I was drugged up on so much pain relief I can't recall getting the plaster off.

To lighten the mood, they tried to tell me about what had happened in the world while I was in a coma, like who had won the State of Origin, and who was in charge of the country. It was all small talk, but it made for a bit of fun, and overall, I remember us laughing a lot.

We had to go through the procedure a few more times, and I remember thinking it was kind of a crazy idea: *I can't move, so how am I going to damage my stumps?* In retrospect, I don't know that it needed to be done, but it was part of the process, and marked the beginning of a really great relationship with Jacqui that has continued to this day.

*

At first, my only visitors after I came out of the induced coma were close family, and for the rest of my time in ICU visitors were restricted to family and a couple of very close friends and colleagues. I didn't appreciate then just how good it was that this part of my recovery was mainly family time.

I was just trying to get myself better, and doing everything I could to move in that direction. I had been stripped bare in every sense – emotionally and physically – and I needed my family to get me through that tough time. They would support me, but they would also be honest with me – they challenged me to get better, and wouldn't accept anything other than progress. At the same time, they would be happy to just come and sit by the bed, or in the waiting room outside ICU. We didn't have to talk, and I didn't have to generate effort to be sociable if I was really exhausted.

I didn't really have the energy for other visitors, but it was nice to know everyone else was supporting me, and I hoped they would understand, which they were assuring the rest of the family they did. I was always aware of the overwhelming level of support surrounding us, but I needed to be able to concentrate on worrying about myself, Diane and the kids.

I got to see other sides of my family. My brother-in-law Aaron, who's often quite quiet when he's with the rest of us, would visit me at lunchtimes, and as a radiographer, was able to give me a medical perspective on things. He proved to be a great ally and confidant. My sisters and mother, who could descend into world war–style conflict at the drop of an eyelash, all seemed to hold up white flags, and peace descended as they rallied in support of Diane. It was nothing short of amazing. Dad was Dad, as enthusiastic and positive as ever, and Jason, my other brother-in-law, took on helping Diane with the boys when he moved to Brisbane ahead of Kate and his own children. He would take Luke to cricket practice every Wednesday and help run the other boys around when he could.

Our concerns about the impact on the children decreased over time. Diane and I would talk about how they were going when we could but those opportunities were rare because the kids were usually with her when she visited me. So I tried to take notice of how they seemed to be going when they were with me.

I could see that Luke's interest in my care seemed to give him comfort and a sense of purpose when he visited me each afternoon. Will and Ben became more comfortable during their visits as my ability to interact increased. Will would bring in his Grade 1 readers, and he would sit up on the bed and read to me: 'The – dog – was – h-h-h-h-hung-g-g-ry.' He did this even while I had the tracheostomy down my throat and couldn't respond. It was challenging to sit through, but I wasn't going anywhere, and it was nice to be part of their daily life. Ben was particularly good at writing poems, so he would also read to me, and draw. Emily was Emily – she would often just lie on my bed and watch whatever was going on.

A few weeks after I woke from the coma, Diane asked the ICU social worker, Christie Barrett, to take the kids aside independently one afternoon to assess how they were doing. Christie came back to say that they were, given the circumstances, doing just fine. They seemed happy enough, weren't missing school or any of their other activities, and were coping with the rush in the afternoons, which included having afternoon tea in the car between school and the hospital.

Knowing that they were okay for the moment was a relief. I was so proud of Diane. Others might have questioned her approach of keeping to routine, but it seemed to be working. Diane and I took the opportunity whenever we could to talk about how we were all handling the changes in our lives. I was astounded at the level of support that Diane was receiving from the people around her, and that was a relief. Diane would always tell me that she was fine, but I knew her well enough to know that she was extremely stretched. But I also knew she was comforted in the knowledge that the kids and I were going well. Diane says that after Christie's assessment of the kids, she really did appreciate just how resilient children could be, and we were both really happy to know that ours were coping.

We seemed, as a family, to be going well.

*

My recovery while I was in ICU was pretty rapid – probably too fast at times. At one point doctors were really worried about my kidneys, which were proving stubborn. The kidneys must have overhead some threats because just when it was looking like I might have permanent damage, which would have meant ongoing dialysis, they kicked in.

Every now and then I would think about work, and one of the rare outside visitors I had in ICU was my boss from Origin Energy, Paul Zealand. Paul had been instrumental in my career success and had been a bit of a mentor for me, particularly when I was first appointed to a corporate role running a large business. It was an exciting time for me, and Paul helped me through that and was very supportive.

It was nice to see him. He is always extremely positive, and if he was shocked by my appearance, he didn't show it. He said he thought I would look a lot worse than I did. He gave me an update on how everything was going at work. I really hadn't thought much about it, amazingly. It had been so important before this happened. I knew I had been replaced, and had realised that would be necessary. But I was keen to hear how people were coping – I had been close to my work team, and I was very grateful for the support they and Origin had offered me. I appreciated Paul's visit.

Everyone around me was starting to plan ahead, and while I was focused on learning to move, Diane was exploring options for rehabilitation hospitals, lifts and car modifications.

It's funny the things that worry you. Here I was, with no arms and legs, worried about where Diane was planning to put the lift in the house. We knew we would have to start planning sooner rather than later because of the time it would take to install. We don't argue about much, but we were having a few debates about details – where the lift would go, and what type of lift it would be. As two engineers, our arguments have always been very civil and logically based. We're very respectful of one another's opinions. We never yell, and have lots of long discussions on particular points, and have always been good at resolving issues. On this occasion, I wasn't sure about where Diane wanted to put the lift, off the side of the house outside the lounge room. Diane was concerned with functionality – she just wanted to be able to get me upstairs – but I was worried about the impact installing a lift would have on the design of the house. At one stage, we were looking at a hydraulic tower hanging off the side of the house, but I would have needed to pull open a door to get into it. We had reached a bit of a stalemate because other options were looking too expensive. Diane was in a hurry to get a solution, and I was more concerned about taking a considered longer-term view, knowing we would be in the house forever.

At the time we were having our debates about the lift, our good friends Brigid and Andrew Kudzius contacted Diane to ask if they could help. Brigid had been the MC at our wedding, and we had forgotten that Andrew happened to work for Schindler, a commercial lift company. Diane asked Andrew to visit the house and provide some advice, and he came back with a list of possible lifts that we could afford. It was a great help because one of the lifts was commercial standard – the doors didn't require anyone to pull them open, and it catered for the weight of my chair and others at the same time.

So we agreed on a lift and where to put it in the house, and Diane started the ball rolling to get it installed.

It was another step forward for me mentally on the road to going home. I wanted to go home to the house we had built, and with a lift we would be able to stay there.

*

It was a nervous time for me when my stay in ICU came to an end. I had been there for eight weeks, three of which while in a coma. I had reached the stage where I was machine free and medically stable. I still, however, had specific sites of infection on my body. One was at the top of my left buttock, there were several down the side of my right leg stump and another on my head. They were reminders that the game wasn't over. I was a candidate for the hospital ward, but I also really needed to start at rehab. It was obvious that there were, as in most things to do with my care, a lot of logistics to sort out.

Senior intensivist Dr John Morgan said at one point, 'We've worked too bloody hard on you to let you loose in the ward, so we are going to hold you here until we find the right spot for you.'

This isn't a reflection on anything other than the team's concern about the level of care required, given my dependency, and their intense desire for me to continue to improve. At the time I needed to be hoisted for showers, and fed every meal. I was aware that there was a bit of to-ing and fro-ing happening, and at some stages, it really wasn't clear where I would be going.

I wanted to go, and I knew everyone wanted that for me – they could tell I was ready for the next step. Every day, doctors would talk with me about my departure date.

Then, finally, one morning I woke up and there was a note taped to the top of the curtains, which was effectively our wall in ICU.

The note said: 'Congratulations. Wednesday will be your transfer day.'

It was exciting but a bit daunting as well, particularly when I had been lucky enough to have one-on-one nursing care in ICU. Diane and I, and the rest of the family, had developed a great relationship with the ICU staff. We had a small farewell party, and there were a few tears. Mum and Dad came but Diane wasn't there. She was really focused on making sure everything was as normal as possible for the kids and was the parent volunteer on a school excursion with Luke.

This was the first time I had been out of the hospital grounds and I distinctly remember lying horizontal in the back of the ambulance transferring me to the rehab unit (which was only a couple of hundred metres away), looking up at the sky and thinking, *This is wonderful – just to be out, just that little bit of freedom.*

There was a sense of entering the unknown, but I also knew I wanted to come back. To one day be able to walk back through those big white doors that mark the entrance to ICU.

This was, in a way, the starting point. I was in control now. It was up to me.

CHAPTER 9

THE FOG LIFTS

The Mater Private Hospital Rehabilitation Unit in Annerley Road, South Brisbane is based within the Mater hospitals complex. According to senior staff, it had never received a patient as dependent as me before. The majority of the patients were older than me, recovering from strokes, knee and hip replacements, and other similar conditions. I was going to be a nursing challenge.

When I got there, I found extra staff had been hired purely to look after me, which was lovely. I did feel special, with a nurse sitting outside my room at night watching me sleep, but I wanted to be as low maintenance as possible. I talked with Lara Aitken, the nurse unit manager, and as my needs became more evident, we transitioned to normal staffing levels.

This was to be my new home away from home, possibly for up to a year, although I was pretty determined that I would be home much sooner. I had my own, quite large room on the fourth floor. The room had a large window, which meant I could look outside, and beside my bed was a cupboard that housed a pull-down double bed, so members of the family might be able to stay. I remember first arriving in the room from intensive care and being overwhelmed with joy when I could see outside from the window. I always enjoyed the outdoors and it was a link to getting better again. Just as Diane had been told when she visited the unit to check out rehab options, I was assigned a nurse whom I would share with one other patient. One of these nurses was Janice Kruesmann, who worked with me four days a week.

From the day of my admission, there was a routine to follow, and this meant life was very busy.

At first, I would wake up, be fed breakfast, and then showered. I would be taken to the gym where I would work for a few hours, be fed lunch, and then either go to sleep due to exhaustion or go back to the gym. If I went to the gym, I would then get back to my room in time for dinner and visits from family and friends. The morning was a really busy time for the nurses because everyone needed to be showered, and as I was such a heavy load and needed more intensive care, I usually had to wait until everyone else had finished before I could shower. This meant I would then be late for gym. I also found that I was actually falling asleep after lunch, and I would still be sweaty from the first session. I wouldn't get the opportunity for another shower until the following day.

I asked for the routine to be changed. With my new timetable, I would head to the gym early in the morning, meaning I could work out for a little longer. I would then be showered before lunch, after which I would sleep. This seemed to work much better. I also had to see specialists – I still needed speech therapy, had to meet with the dietician to help me put on a bit of weight (but not too much) and had weekly sessions with a psychologist, who assured me I was going well.

My focus, though, was on progress so I would be able to use

prosthetics. First would come my arms, and then my legs, although there was doubt about whether I would be able to wear prosthetics on my right leg. I couldn't think about that – we wouldn't know until we knew for sure, and the only way to do that was to get to the point where I could wear prosthetics on that leg. It was a step-by-step process.

The first challenge was simply to get moving. I had learned that the feeling of being encased in concrete was not temporary. It was a permanent state of being. I can only describe it to someone who has limbs by asking them to lie on their side on the ground, making sure their arm is trapped under their body weight, and then asking them to move. I have limited muscles I can call upon to move anything. It's exhausting.

Initially, I had very limited range in my arms and no capacity to roll, so we needed to work on bed mobility. I worked closely with my occupational therapist, Nick Flynn, and physiotherapist Jacqui O'Sullivan. Nick would help with equipment to support me – 'gearing me up' – and Jacqui would figure out exercises to help. Neither Nick nor Jacqui had ever worked with a quadruple amputee before, and I obviously hadn't been in this position either, so we worked as a team. Nick and Jacqui would listen to me, and we would figure out how I might do something.

It's fair to say that YouTube played a large part in my recovery. Kate had introduced the kids to Nick Vujicic via YouTube only a few days after they had learned about my limbs being amputated, while I was still in a coma. Nick's motto of 'No Arms, No Legs, No Worries', gave the children and Diane great comfort. When I finally came out of my coma, I had to catch up on what everyone thought I would be able to do. While I was in ICU, the kids would come in with their daily Nick update and excitedly show me new videos they had found of him. 'Look,' they would say, 'look at what Nick can do.'

On one level, it was very helpful and inspirational, but at that time, I wasn't really ready for it, and couldn't process it. I would think, *Yeah, that's cool, but he's had thirty years to learn how to do that. Give me a couple of weeks at least.* I was a little frustrated, but I never said anything – it was great to know people were looking out for me.

As time passed, though, referring to Nick's videos became much more helpful, especially when it came to practical things like teaching myself how to flip over. I would watch the videos to see how he moved. There was one in particular that Jacqui and I looked at to learn how he sat up.

'Matt, if you do it that way, you'll hurt your neck,' Jacqui told me.

We had a talk about it and decided that we wouldn't do it that way because it was very risky in my case. These were the types of judgements we would make. If it was really important for me to do things a particular way, we would persevere, but I also knew that in the longer term, we were aiming for prosthetics, which influenced how hard I would push myself in a particular direction.

Sometimes the videos would help, but they weren't always enough. For example, I watched a video to learn how to flip myself over. It was really helpful and it worked, except I missed the bit about getting back onto my back. I was elated about flipping myself over for the first time, but that emotion was immediately followed by the realisation that I hadn't thought about getting back again! So I was stuck on my stomach like a turtle, unable to move or flip over. I just laughed and thought, *Probably better plan ahead a bit better next time.* Anyway, it was just another step and gave me my next goal to aim towards.

Saul Geffen gave me a bit of advice early on. He came in and, without warning (which was his usual style), said, 'You know, Matthew, if you get hurt, it's your fault.'

I was left searching for words for a moment.

'Okay.' I paused. 'Thanks.'

He went on.

'You know how you need to be moved. You need to take control of the risks that you will face. Everyone is there to help you, so you must tell them exactly what you need.

'Check that the wheelchair brakes are on, or ask people to check for you if you can't or don't know. Make sure things are oriented the right way, tell people where to hold you. It's totally up to you.'

I took the advice as it was intended. It proved helpful. While I knew it anyway, it reinforced the idea that sometimes you just have to be a bit assertive to make sure you stay safe and get what you need to do so. I had to be confident in letting people know what I wanted or needed.

I was always optimistic about what I could achieve, and that worked in my favour. Sometimes, though, I pushed things a little too far, and learning about what my body could and couldn't do was part of the recovery process.

*

Jacqui and I were trying to see how far I could lean forward on an angle without falling forward. It was in the very early stages of rehab, and Jacqui was trying to build up my core strength and my balance. We were in the gym, and she was doing perturbations. These were little pushes to disturb my balance so my core had to find its centre of gravity in response. It was going well, and I was staying upright after each push. Jacqui was sitting behind me, which we had decided was best because my biggest risk generally was falling directly backwards. My leg stumps, while really short, are in front of me and the theory was that they would prevent me from falling forward.

Then Jacqui gave me a slightly more forceful push that I couldn't control. The next thing you know, I've face planted onto the physio bed.

As I fell forward, I thought, *Hmmm, I don't know what I can do here.* I managed to turn my head slightly sideways to avoid breaking my nose. I landed on my cheek.

I was fine, but Jacqui burst into tears. She was saying, 'Matthew, I'm so sorry. I'm so sorry.'

I laughed. I reassured her that I was fine, which I was.

We learned a lot from that, in particular that it was best for Jacqui to sit at my side so she could catch me if I fell either directly to the front or the back. It could have been much worse – I could have been on the edge of the bed, in which case I would have landed on my head upside down. That risk wasn't there, though, because Jacqui had positioned me in the right spot. I was on a soft bed, in the right position – I was safe.

As a safety professional, having done quite a lot of risk management in my career, I found it really interesting that I was now applying risk management to my own health and safety in an environment where everything I did would involve more risk than a normal person would take. With every movement, I was thinking, *What can go wrong? How can I prevent it?* But I also knew it was imperative that I did take calculated risks because otherwise I wouldn't improve.

There is no manual for rehabilitating someone like me.

Most of my work with the allied health professionals involved in my care was done on a trial and error basis. We would set a specific goal and work towards that. It meant that I was given a lot of opportunity to contribute ideas, and I really enjoyed the collaborative process. Obviously, the medical staff had their professional knowledge, and I had a working knowledge of my body, what I thought it could and couldn't do, and ideas about keeping myself safe. We would have an idea, try it, and if it didn't work, we would try something else. I would give feedback, and depending on how things were going, we would adjust a little, or change direction completely.

I also needed to find a way to manage my weight. A few kilos could significantly impact my ability to balance and move, so I needed to find some way to 'exercise'. At one point, Jacqui and I decided we should work with a trampoline. My ability to get aerobic exercise is compromised because I don't have any large muscles – most people would use their legs to get most of their aerobic workout. So we were trying to explore different ways of improving my general fitness. We found that the trampoline was one of the few things I could do that actually got my heart rate up again. Any other form of exercise was extremely difficult because of that feeling of being encased in concrete – I got fatigued before I even started. I have such limited leverage, and the force needed to move my body is therefore so much greater. I also don't have the muscles. Sitting up normally, for example, requires leverage by quadriceps muscles at the front of your legs. I don't have any of that – I have these tiny little muscles at the top of my femur to move my leg and body with no assistance from the major muscles that used to be there.

I got the idea for the trampoline thanks to YouTube footage of some returned servicemen at the Walter Reed Rehabilitation Center in the US. I watched amputees using the trampoline for exercise – they were jumping up and down, which I tried to do. I found it really difficult because I kept on moving one way, and I would eventually end up on the edge of the trampoline. However, I worked out that I could stay centred on the trampoline if I spun around at the same time as I jumped.

My balance by this stage was very good. It felt great to be bouncing, although painful, but that was a usual state for me. I was wearing a helmet just in case I fell off, but that hadn't happened so I started pushing myself to go a bit faster and higher.

On one occasion, as I swung around, I noticed that Jacqui was looking really uncomfortable.

'Jacqui, are you okay?' I asked.

'I just really need to go to the toilet,' she said.

'You go. I'll be fine,' I assured her. We both knew there were other physiotherapists in the gym working close by, so I wouldn't be alone. So Jacqui got up and left, and I kept jumping.

I think my mind wandered, and I really didn't appreciate at the time how hard I needed to concentrate. My jumps ventured closer to the side of the trampoline, and eventually on to a hard edge that then seemed to flip me. I keeled over sideways towards the wall beside the trampoline; my head whacked, and then slid down, the wall, while my bottom stayed wedged on the trampoline. I ended up jammed between the wall and the trampoline, bottom in the air, head on the floor.

Karl, another physio, ran over to me and helped me up, but I was laughing. Jacqui saw me keel over on her way back from the toilet, and I think Karl gave her a dirty look, as if to say, *What the hell were you doing leaving Matthew?* But I was fine – as Saul had advised, I had taken control. It was a momentary lapse that had some consequences, mainly embarrassment on my part.

That helmet came in really handy.

*

I had always been aware that if I started to compare myself to others, there would always be someone who seemed to be better or worse off, and in rehab I was able to meet a lot of people who had been dealt a rough hand in life. It became evident how different people chose to respond to what happened to them, and one day I found myself pondering the fact that the pool of people worse off than me was now smaller.

I had befriended a couple of other patients in rehab – Peter and

Kevin. Peter was a bit older than me, and had suffered a fairly major stroke. He had worked for a large energy company, like me, and subsequently lost his job, although he has since recovered pretty well. Kevin had a brain tumour, which he has now had for 10 years, and had also suffered a stroke. I found Kevin quite difficult to understand at first, but the three of us were very similar in our positive attitude and determination, and we became gym mates. I valued their friendship greatly.

I heard that one lunchtime Kevin had been sitting at the same table as a patient who had broken a joint. This patient was forever complaining about his lot in life. A broken joint might be painful, but generally, you can expect that you're going to get better. At one point, this patient was talking again about how dreadful everything was for him, and he announced to the table, 'This is the worst thing that could have ever happened to anyone.' He was sitting next to Kevin, who had been through hell and back and was still smiling.

Kevin was really struggling with learning how to talk again, but one of the first words that came out of his mouth, under his breath in response, was, 'Wanker.'

Peter and I were talking about this incident one day, and joked about forming a Shit Happens Club. It was a light-hearted moment. We had been dealt a really poor hand, and we were working hard to just get on with it.

I knew some people loved it when I came into the gym because it made them realise how lucky they were. They told me directly, and I understood exactly where they were coming from. I would have been the same. I in turn learned a lot from hearing about other people who were encountering obstacles. It reminded me that I'm not a terminal case – I still have life ahead of me no matter how difficult that might be, so as far as I'm concerned, I'm lucky.

I tried to focus every day on how to improve and make the most of what I had, on what was unique, what I could learn that was new, and what was better about life now.

*

As I began to get better physically, I also started to reconnect with friends and colleagues. Word about my circumstances had spread in some circles, so by the time I got to rehab, people were keen to come and visit. I wanted to see people too. Rachel, who had been managing communication with friends in conjunction with Kate, started to manage visit requests, which had been building. We found that some friends had been out of the loop – they had perhaps been away with work or travelling – so for them, the shock was still very current, while others had become used to the idea.

I was conscious that some of my friends were very nervous about seeing me in my new state. It seemed reasonable to me that they were thinking that way. It's exactly what I would have been thinking. Kate and Rachel would talk to friends about what to expect, and in some cases, send photos so they knew what I looked like.

I understood how hard it must have been for visitors and I tried to make them feel comfortable around me. I was always genuinely happy to have visitors, and was actually surprised that people thought I would be anything other than positive and happy when they came to visit – I knew it would make it hard for them to relate to me if I wasn't. I didn't want that because I was keen to have conversations about what was going on in the outside world. Some people cried when they first saw me, which was just fine. Others, I suspect, cried when they left the room. That was okay. I was crying a bit too. It was normal.

I was grateful to the many people who made regular visits to see me to provide support and relieve the boredom, including family, members of the school community, close friends and colleagues. It became particularly important as the kids' school term got underway. I was conscious that Diane coming up twice a day wasn't going to be sustainable, so we had a difficult conversation about reducing the amount of visiting for the family. This was really hard for me, because I wanted Diane to continue to visit. In an ideal world, I would have had Diane with me all day. In turn, Diane didn't want to cut down on her visits, and she resisted the idea when I suggested to her that she and the children only visit occasionally during the week. Diane told me she was fine and coping, but I could see how tired she was getting from all the running around she was doing.

I had recently started to go home on weekends, so really, we were only talking about reducing our contact during the week. I ended up having to insist that this was the best for everyone, which was tough but it was the right decision in the end. Visits from Diane and the kids then became less frequent but special. Everyone would come in twice per week after school, and every now and then, Diane would make a special visit in with Emily during the day.

Some friends and members of the family developed a regular routine. Mum was a constant. During my time in ICU, she had started to come in every evening to feed me once I started to eat. When a nurse was feeding me, I knew they would have other things to do, so I would eat quickly. With Mum, I could take my time, and we could talk between mouthfuls. Mum continued the daily dinner visits when I went to rehab. It was really good having a visitor I didn't feel I needed to talk to. She was great that way. If she came into my room and I was asleep, she would just sit and read rather than waking me and I would often wake to find her there. It was usually just her and me, and it was often when I was feeling quite exhausted. Sometimes Dad would come up if Mum couldn't, and sometimes they would come together. Their visits were particularly important given that I was seeing less of Diane and the children.

I would normally have talked about my concerns and issues in detail with Diane, but during this time, the kids were always present, and I was very conscious of what I said in front of them. So Mum was probably the person who saw me at my most vulnerable, and I was able to confide in her. I really looked forward to seeing her each day. We talked a lot, and I think she saw me cry the most. Because Mum was usually there in the evenings, she got to meet lots of my friends and colleagues she probably never would have had the opportunity to meet otherwise.

Like Martyn Robotham, a great friend who had been away when I had my operation, and so was completely blindsided by the news. He was initially very nervous about coming to see me for the first time, but ended up visiting every Thursday night. His wife, Steph, also became a regular visitor despite her initial trepidation at coming to see me. I really looked forward to their visits. They were always so positive, and never questioned anything I thought I might be able to do. I think if I told Martyn I wanted to climb Mt Everest, he would help me find a way to do it – he made me feel like there were no limits to what I could achieve and I loved that.

Other regulars included members of our families, and some colleagues of mine, including Graeme Bartrim, Rob Ully, Rosahlena Robinson and Fiona Allen, who would fill me in on what was going on at work. Some of the sports dads including Dion McCabe and Andrew Oberthur would visit regularly to keep me up to date on what was happening in the world of kids' sport.

Visitors would often come around six in the evening on their way home from work. I really enjoyed hearing about life outside – talking to people about what was going on with them helped me look outwards. Life goes on, and while I know some people felt guilty that they were having a good time and things were going well, I never saw it as a relative thing. I was simply happy to hear their news.

I had more visits from my boss, Paul Zealand, and my personal assistant, Sandra Schulte, also came to see me. I can't imagine how hard it must have been for her the first time she visited. I was off work for literally a couple of days, and the next time she saw me, I was limbless in a hospital bed. It was fantastic to see her.

Mum says she was often comforted when she left in the evenings knowing I was in good company.

*

A month or so into rehab, I decided to see whether we could manage a sleepover with the children. It wasn't originally in the plan, but I thought we may as well use the double bed in my room that retracted into the wall. One day, I asked my nurse, Janice, if the children could have a sleepover. She in turn asked Saul, who said, 'Sure. This place needs a bit of younger blood to liven it up.'

The first sleepover occurred during the September school holidays and was with all three boys. Diane brought in an extra mattress, so two boys slept on the bed, and one was on the mattress on the floor. I informed the day staff and the nurses that this was going to happen, but they hadn't told the nurse unit manager. When the afternoon staff came on that day, the kids were there, and Diane had left.

A nurse came in to tell me that the nurse unit manager wanted to know who was looking after the kids while they were having the sleepover.

I looked around, turned to the nurse and responded, 'Me.' It hadn't occurred to me that there was any other option. 'They're good kids. They'll be okay.'

I got a sense that the nurse thought, *You've got to be kidding. You're looking after three kids, and you can't move?* Happily, the nurse decided not to argue with me and went away to check with the nurse unit manager, who agreed that the boys could stay. They had a great time – it was the perfect holiday. To lie in bed and watch movies all day was their idea of heaven. It was a big adventure – using a hospital toilet and shower, eating hospital food, coming to the gym with me.

The sleepovers became a regular feature of my time in rehab. The boys were on a roster – Luke, Ben, Will and then Diane slotted in every fourth week. Because two children could sleep in the bed in my room, each boy got to invite a brother. Diane would drop them off on Friday nights, they would take part in my physio sessions on Saturday mornings, and we would catch a taxi home after that. I would then catch a taxi back to rehab on Sunday evening.

Emily also had her chance for a sleepover on the odd occasion. The first time she came with Diane, she was pretty excited. She had a shower in the bathroom and had her dinner. Diane dressed her in her nightie, and she climbed up onto my bed. I found a little girl's movie for her to watch, and she cuddled up into my shoulder where she fell asleep an hour or so later. Once she was asleep, Diane moved her into the sleepover bed. We suspect Emily was convinced that Diane wasn't there – that it was just her and me. Moments like that were really important. At the time, Emily was only two and a half. This was all she knew of life. I was grateful to be part of it, even if we were cuddling up in a room in a rehabilitation hospital.

The Mater had promised the family could be involved in my rehabilitation, and the staff kept that promise. The boys got to know the nurses, kitchen staff, wardies, cleaners and doctors, but mostly, they got to know Jacqui and the staff at the rehab gym. The boys in particular had a lot of energy, and playing with them became part of my gym routine. We would play soccer, have races, do some stretching, or I would be their transport – one day I was their 'skateboard', and they got on my back to ride me.

I was always a bit concerned that they would wipe out some of the other patients in their enthusiasm – one of the hip-replacement patients doing a slow walk around the centre, for example.

That never happened, and the other patients were always very accommodating to the rowdy little crew that accompanied me.

At one point Jacqui organised a mini Olympics for us as the London 2012 games had just finished and the boys were still infected with Games fever.

The boys had to do the same exercises as me, without using their arms and legs. For one exercise, they had to sit on their bottoms and keep their legs up in the air. I could do this for long periods by that stage because I don't have all the weight that goes with arms and legs, and I had built up my core strength. The boys are quite competitive, so they were pretty impressed that I could beat them.

The events included a bottom running race, which involved quite a bit of cheating, and a game of soccer, for which the boys kept modifying the rules to make it easier for me. Emily got involved too, and Jacqui got some medals made up for them. Everyone had a lot of fun.

*

Once I got moving, the time came to get my new arms. I was excited because I thought they would be able to give me some independence, so getting prepared for them gave me a sense of moving forward. Saul had told me that prosthetic arms were difficult and in my case probably wouldn't work. I had to find out for myself.

The first step was to get a cast taken for moulds so the sockets would be the exact shape of my shoulders. It's quite a primitive process, and the measuring stage involved lots of bandages and plaster. My prosthetist, David Sweet, was assisted by Emily, who wanted to help put the bandages over my arms. She was having a great time, and wasn't very happy when she had to leave with Diane to pick up the boys from school. She obviously thought she was running the show.

'I not go,' she told Diane. 'I not finish Daddy's arms.'

We were both happy active kids.

For our first date
we went to the
Engineering Ball,
and within two
weeks we knew
we would marry.

We were great lovers of the outdoors and adventure travel in our first 10 years together.

In Aguas Calientes, Peru.

Doing a 100-metre free abseil in New Zealand.

Climbing Mt Kilimanjaro in 2002 was an enormous challenge. We were convinced that the rest of our lives would be easy in comparison.

I'd always taken on too much and been too busy. At one stage in my life, I had a new baby, a renovation and a new job, all at the same time.

Our future dream home (2000).

Renovation well underway in 2004, with newborn Luke. We would add a lift in 2013 so we could all keep living there.

After three boys — Luke, Ben and Will — Emily arrived and our family was complete.
(*Courtesy Eye On Eye Photography*)

The extended Ames family in November 2010. L–R: Aaron and Rachel, Roy and Christine, Jason and Kate at the back and us on the end. In the front: Lincoln, Ethan, Maeve, Ben, Luke with Emily, Will and Joshua.

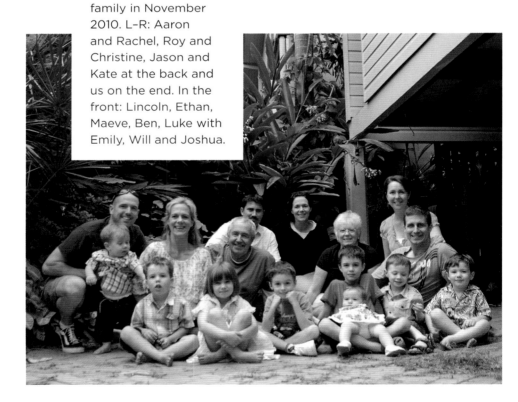

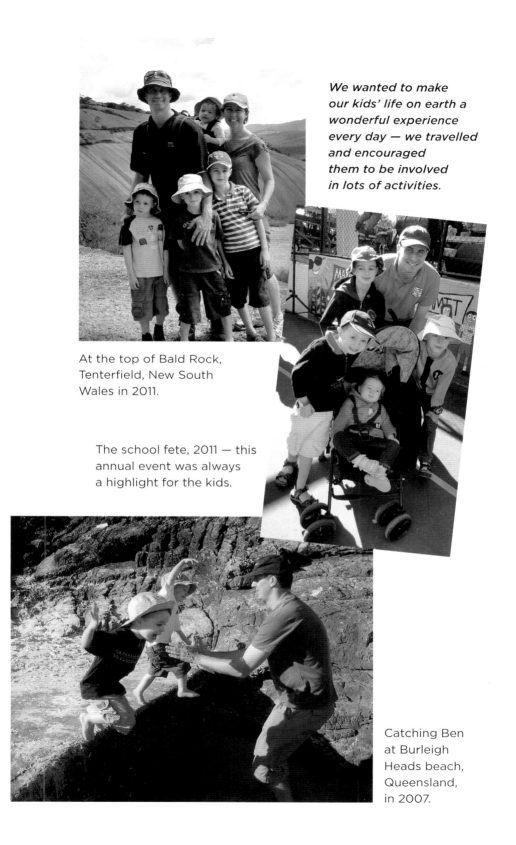

We wanted to make our kids' life on earth a wonderful experience every day — we travelled and encouraged them to be involved in lots of activities.

At the top of Bald Rock, Tenterfield, New South Wales in 2011.

The school fete, 2011 — this annual event was always a highlight for the kids.

Catching Ben at Burleigh Heads beach, Queensland, in 2007.

Our perfect family life was irrevocably changed on 16 June 2012 when my limbs were amputated.

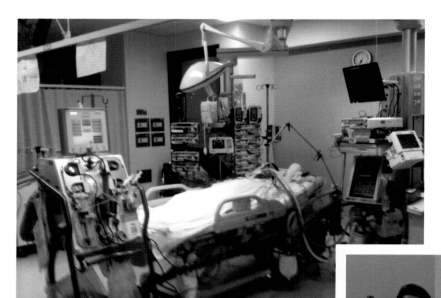

The morning after my surgery, the day of the school fete.

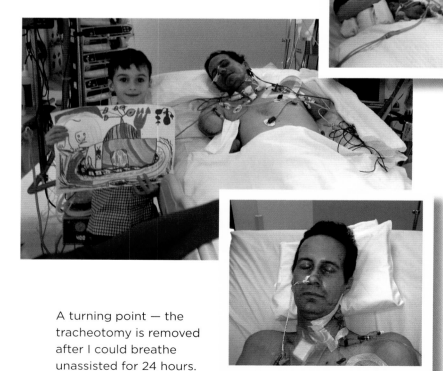

A turning point — the tracheotomy is removed after I could breathe unassisted for 24 hours.

ICU became our second home. Our whole family was involved in my recovery.

Rachel kept my spirits up by bringing me motivational t-shirts.

Date night in ICU, about six weeks after the operation.

Six days after I was woken from the coma, I was allowed to go outside — it was a huge relief to feel fresh air. I would spend a lot of time under the fig trees in the grounds of the Mater with Mum and Dad.

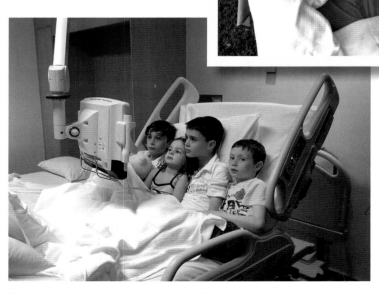

The kids having a sleepover in rehab.

When I got my prosthetic arm, I managed to write 'I love you' to Diane in the best handwriting my sisters tell me they've ever seen from me.

One of my first goals was to make it home for Luke's ninth birthday in August. The party had to come outside and downstairs to me because there was no wheelchair access.

'Help' came in many forms in the gym at rehab.

Comparing leg length with Luke.

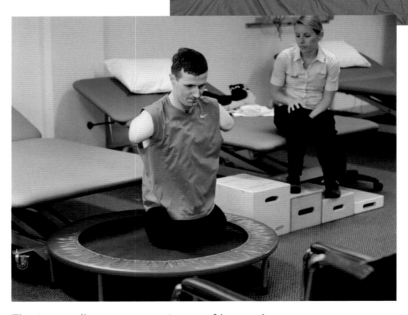

The trampoline was a great way of improving my general fitness as long as Jacqui kept a close eye on me — it was easy to lose my balance.

I became
motorised
transport
for the kids,
especially
Emily who
often hitched
a ride to rehab
with my arms
hanging on
the back.

The rehab stairs
became known as
Mount Matthew.
Climbing them was
something I felt I
needed to do before
I went home.

There was quite an audience in rehab when I took my first steps. It felt like wearing stilts in gumboots.

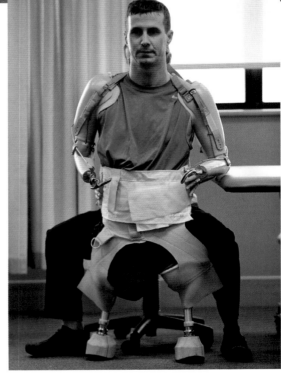

My challenge was to walk further each day, building up to walking without support. Jacqui is supporting me here.

(*Courtesy Alex Garipoli,* Sunday Night, *Seven Network*)

We've learnt that actions based on pure goodwill and generosity of spirit make a really big difference.

The Renovating Matthew Ball was held in September 2013, and we were blown away by the support. (*Courtesy David de Groot Photography*)

My dear friends Nicole Webb, Lisa Moroney and Gwen Lea, who, with their families, continue to be there for us.

While we were in Sydney for the 2013 Pride of Australia awards, we visited Luna Park. It was great for the kids but every ride was a no-go zone for someone with no limbs.

We met the Australian cricket team after the first Ashes test in 2013 — that would not have been possible in our old life!

At the school sports day I was assigned tunnel ball. I don't have arms and legs, but I do have a big voice when I need it.

The theme of renovation and rebuilding stuff has been with me for most of my life but I never envisaged bolts and nuts sticking out of my arms and legs.

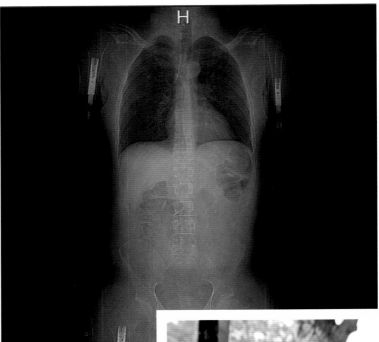

The osseointegration surgery is complete.
(*Courtesy Qscan*)

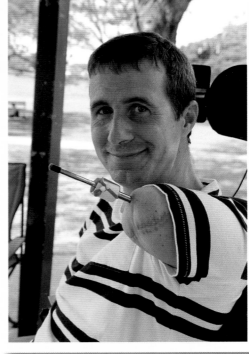

Dad's invention: in May 2014, he extended my bolt to enable me to do more.

A few weeks later, all the kids were in the gym with me when my first arm arrived. It was an exciting day because it promised hope for independence.

The prosthetic arm I received that day is essentially built from polycarbonate with an elbow and wrist joint, and a metal hook that acts as a 'hand'. The arm is fitted to my stump with a socket, and is operated by a cable that is attached to my body by a harness placed across my back. To move my hook or flex my elbow I had to move my shoulder and I could alternate between using the hook or elbow by pulling a tag located on my shoulder with my mouth. Initially, I had one arm, which was then connected to the second a few weeks later. Straps and buckles were everywhere, and the arms were heavier and more difficult to use than I expected.

I spent the first afternoon with my arm in training – learning how to use it, and what I could do with it. The first thing I did was scratch my eyelid. It was nice to be able to do that. I picked up blocks and moved them around with the hook, and David told me he was impressed by how quickly I seemed to be taking things in.

I even managed to write 'I love you' to Diane in the best handwriting my sisters tell me they've ever seen from me.

We were really excited by the possibilities, and the more I thought about the path ahead, the harder I wanted to work to get to the end.

CHAPTER 10

LOWS AND HIGHS

I learned early on that to know my limits, I needed to find my boundaries. To do that, I had to test myself. Sometimes I made great progress; on other occasions I had to completely reassess what I was doing. I worked out that I needed to set goals.

I wanted to go home for Luke's ninth birthday.

When Diane had asked him what he wanted for his present, his response was, 'I want Daddy to come home.' She told him that it would be unlikely, but started working in the background to see if we could make it happen.

Diane decided to hold a very small party for the family and a couple of close friends. Gayle Schabe offered to cater and organise kids and games, so Diane only had to worry about me and the children.

I had been in rehab for just over a week at this stage, and I knew it was going to be a challenge. The medical team was nervous, and visited the house to see whether it was suitable for me in a manual wheelchair. I was allowed to be away from the hospital for no longer than two hours, and it would be the first time I had actually been in any form of wheelchair because prior to this I had always been moved in a specially designed Regency chair on wheels. I would be travelling with a vest that secured me to the back of the wheelchair to make sure I didn't fall out.

While it was very cold and crisp outside, my body was still unable to regulate its temperature, so I was constantly hot and sweating profusely.

Aaron and Rachel came to rehab to pick me up, and Rachel travelled back to the house with me in a taxi. She asked me how I was feeling, and I told her I was a little worried about how it would all go. Before leaving the secure and safe environment of the rehab unit, I had been through my internal checklist to make sure I had what I needed. It was a bit of a test to see if I could do it, although I never really had any great doubts that I would be okay. This would be my first time home since I was admitted to hospital, and I was very excited.

When I arrived at the house, there was a small welcoming party on the front driveway, but because the children didn't know I was coming home, we had to sneak down a side path around to the backyard, hopefully unseen.

Diane greeted me as I was pushed along the path at the side of the house.

'Hi, honey. Welcome home,' she said as she leaned down to embrace me.

It was a hugely emotional moment for both of us. Diane hugged me tightly for a while, and after pulling back, had to wipe away both our tears before we ventured on to where the children would be able to see us. I was finally home, if only for a few hours.

I couldn't go inside because at the time there was no access, so the party had to come outside and downstairs to me. It was the most beautiful winter's day, so I was very happy to be outside. Aaron parked me under our back verandah, and Diane called the children downstairs. I remember Luke's face when he saw that I was home – his smile spread across his face as he descended the stairs. It was one of the rare moments where I really struggled to keep myself together.

I look at photos of that day now and wonder how I managed to do it. I looked emaciated. I still had a wound on the side of my head, and in a video taken on the day, my speech is still quite hard to understand.

At the time, though, I thought I was doing so well.

*

It was fortuitous that I ended up at the Mater rehab facility because my medical issues were ongoing and I received regular visits from the Mater Adult Hospital staff. Some visited me socially, to see how I was going, but others came to provide medical advice on my residual issues.

Two weeks after Luke's birthday, just as I was discovering the joy of moving again, doctors found I had a detached retina in my right eye. While I had been in ICU, I had developed a really bad candida infection in that eye, due to my low immunity. At one point, I had needed an injection of antifungal medicine directly into my eyeball – to this day it's one of the most painful experiences I've ever had.

The candida infection caused a retinal tear as it healed, and the eye had been constantly blurry since. I quite quickly lost about a third of my vision, but I didn't really notice because, in a way, it seemed normal. It was only when I closed my good eye that I could tell there was a problem, and the only time I closed my good eye was when the doctor asked me to.

Finding out about the detached retina and facing the prospect of lying completely still for a week really threw me.

I had woken up with no limbs, partially blind in one eye and profoundly deaf in one ear. I didn't really have much left. I had my brain, despite the high temperatures it had been subjected to while I was in the coma, and I still had the ability to communicate. I was aware of how special this was – it meant I could maintain relationships with those who were important to me. Just the idea that I could lose my vision concerned me because I didn't want to lose anything I had left.

The doctors moved rapidly once they diagnosed the detached retina, and I was operated on the following day. So I didn't have too much time to digest what was happening. I felt okay immediately after the surgery, which had been conducted on a Sunday, but on the following Monday and Tuesday I felt quite down. In the short time I had been in rehab, I had experienced rapid improvement in being able to move, and I was really upset at the impact being immobile again was going to have on my recovery. I was wondering, *Am I going to be able to attain my goals? How often is this sort of thing going to happen? How much of this can I really take?*

This was my second period of depression, and I soon got sick of myself.

I told myself on the Monday night to get over it, but I wasn't really ready and found I couldn't really shake the feeling of sadness. By Tuesday afternoon, I was a bit stronger. Thinking about what I would be able to do as soon as I was able to move again also helped, and Jacqui and I talked about what we would be doing as soon as I got back into the gym once this was over. That made me feel much better and helped me to look past the immediate setback.

I was lucky that I have the disposition to respond positively to this type of approach – self talk, focusing on the future – when I was feeling overwhelmed. I said to myself that evening, *Enough's enough. It really is only a week of sitting around doing nothing in the scheme of things. We'll start again tomorrow.* I woke up the next day feeling better, and that was it.

Jonathan Brown, captain of the AFL's Brisbane Lions, visited me while I was feeling very blue during those couple of days. He knows my brother-in-law Aaron, and had offered to drop in to say hello. He stayed for an hour, and brought some socks for the boys. I appreciated the visit, but I felt really sorry for him because it must have been hard to try to make conversation with me. Aaron reassures me that Jonathan didn't actually realise I was having a bad day.

I am not someone who tends to get depressed, but I can see now how you don't really treat those people who are trying to help you very well when you are down. You're not in the headspace to respond to efforts to cheer you up. I realise now that those efforts were important. I'm sure people felt like they weren't making a difference at the time, but they were.

Ironically enough, I had always had a fear of my retina detaching. I always knew that the one thing I didn't want lose was my eyesight. It was one of the reasons I never wanted to bungee jump, which Diane convinced me to do while we were in Africa. It was the trip in which we climbed Mt Kilimanjaro. We were on the bus coming into Victoria Falls, and Diane had turned to me and announced that she was going to go bungee jumping. My internal reaction was, *Oh, crap.* After all the crazy, adrenaline-charged things I had convinced her to do over the years, I couldn't let Diane bungee jump and not have a go.

I reluctantly agreed that we could do a tandem jump, together. Once we arrived, we tried to register for a tandem jump but we were a couple of kilos over the weight limit. So, it was going to be solo jumps for us.

When we went up to jump, I was thinking, *I can't go first.* I wasn't chivalrous at all, and declared, 'I don't want to do this, Diane. You can go before me.'

Diane has an amazing ability to trust others, whereas traditionally I am more comfortable trusting my own ability. I'm really happy to take risks and go climbing and whitewater rafting because I feel that I can get myself out of trouble. The difference between Diane and me can be explained this way: if we went whitewater rafting, I would take comfort from the fact that I had a paddle; Diane would take comfort from the fact that there was a guide at the back with a paddle.

So when it came to bungee jumping, Diane had trust in the rope, and that everyone involved knew what they were doing. On the other hand, I couldn't trust in myself because it wasn't up to me. I had to rely on everybody else.

I was running through everything that could go wrong, and asking myself, *Why are were bungee jumping in Africa rather than New Zealand?* As I was doing this, Diane just waltzed up to the edge of the bridge and threw herself off.

Oh, crap.

It took me a while to get up to the edge.

As I started to go over, I said to myself, *Nooo*, but it was too late. I screamed my lungs out all the way down. I'm convinced that as I was hanging upside down waiting to be pulled back up, the clamps around my ankles were loosening. It probably wasn't enough to be a problem, but it was enough to freak me out.

My retina didn't detach that day. Possibly, it was always going to be just a matter of time.

*

I had lots of other medical issues in addition to my eye, including ongoing soreness in my right leg that was concerning me. Saul Geffen recommended an MRI, which showed a problem with the hip joint that appeared to be the result of the initial infection. The infection had an impact on my entire body, but some parts were affected worse than others. While it had been obvious that the infection went to the ends of my extremities – being my hands and feet – I also learned that some parts of the hip had been affected. This is because the blood supply to the bone of my leg ends up in the ball of the hip, and the infection had caused blood vessels to die. As a result, parts of the bone in the ball of my hip are potentially weaker. The condition is called avascular necrosis, or AVN. As a precaution, I was told not to do any weight-bearing exercise and that in the worst-case scenario, I wouldn't be able to get prosthetics for my legs. It was a huge, but fairly short-lived, blow.

My orthopaedic surgeon Dr Tim McMeniman reviewed the scans and reassured me that while his initial reaction was not good, as the inflammation area was sizeable, he thought we could afford to wait and see how the hip progressed. He thought prosthetics were still an option, and his worst-case scenario was that I might need a hip replacement. It was, for me, better than the prospect of not walking.

In addition to the hip soreness, I was also still finding it hard to regulate my temperature. So I was still getting hot and sweating profusely – all the time. Saul assigned me a specialist general physician, who would advise on systemic care and management, and ensure my kidneys were working as they should. The biggest worry for me was the number of wounds on my body that continued to be difficult to treat: I still had lesions on my head, buttock and thigh that were residual wounds from the original disease. They were all as problematic as one another, but my head wound was the most visible. I needed to wear a large bandage across the back right side of my head.

Associate Professor Joe McCormack, an infectious diseases specialist who had treated me while I was in ICU, paid me a visit. Joe was always very reassuring, and he had the most wonderful manner. I know the rest of the family felt good that someone was still paying close attention to the residual wound. Joe continued to provide advice on treating the head wound in association with a specialist wound-care nurse. Every few days the wound would be cleaned and re-covered. It seemed to me that they were trying everything to help it to heal.

Of all the things that had happened to me, this wound in particular worried me. I thought it made me look sick. You can have no arms and legs and be healthy, so the wound was a daily reminder that I wasn't yet well. I thought I might go bald one day, but I didn't expect it to be like this – the hair where the wound was located has never regrown.

The rest of the hair on my head was impacting on the wound treatment; it was difficult to keep the bandages in place as they were partly attached to the hair. This made it harder for the wound to heal because the bandages were then rubbing against it, rather than lying close to the skin.

I was desperate to get rid of the final infection sites. The only way to make the wound easier to manage was to drastically cut my hair, and it would look silly to have one spot that was shorter than the rest.

My brother-in-law Aaron offered to be my hairdresser. He visited on a Friday lunchtime when we knew Diane wasn't going to be there, and brought his clippers. I didn't want Diane there because I was worried she might object to me getting my hair cut that short. I had learned the hard way that very short hair wasn't her favourite look for me after I volunteered to get my head shaved one year at work to raise money for the Leukaemia Foundation. It was the only time I had ever had my hair cut that short. She couldn't speak to me for ten minutes after she opened the front door due to the surprise. Of course, as soon as she found out why, she was accepting of my new look. I was sure she would be the same this time, but Aaron was in on the secret for the time being.

'How do you want to do this?' he asked.

'Let's just cut it all off.'

'Okay then,' said Aaron.

He proceeded to shave my head. It was a number one buzz cut all over. It felt great.

Soon after that, I had to attend a rehearsal for Luke's first communion.

My new haircut made my hair and wound treatment easier to manage, but it had also exposed the wound more obviously. I was really self-conscious about the bandages on my head, but at one point, I thought, *You're worried about the bandages that make your head look a little bit funny?* When you have no arms and legs, it seems kind of trivial.

*

It's a short walk from the Mater hospitals complex in Raymond Terrace, South Brisbane to the South Bank precinct along the southern bank of the Brisbane River.

I had been exploring the area around the hospital, trialling new wheelchairs, and I was keen to get down to South Bank a bit more, to be outside and get a sense of the life that was going on around me.

My first trip with the family was on Father's Day, Sunday 2 September. Diane and the children, Mum and Dad, and our family friends Peter and Claire Malyon collected me, and we proceeded to one of the many playgrounds along the Brisbane River esplanade. This was my first significant outing since the visit home for Luke's birthday three weeks earlier. By now, I had been in rehab for almost a month.

While I was very excited to get outside and see the world again, I was concerned about my wheelchair. I was a bit apprehensive, thinking, *How am I going to get around the footpaths? Am I going to get stuck? Will I be able to control the wheelchair enough so*

I don't run into people? Those thoughts weren't uppermost in my mind, though. I was too motivated by the idea of being able to spend time with the family in a non-hospital environment.

My wheelchair was controlled by a chin pad, and I was still getting used to it. Every time we went over a bump, I would accidently change direction, and when we got to the playground area where we were going to sit, I had to negotiate soft grass and sand. *I hope I don't get bogged*, I thought.

Diane reassured me by telling me how proud she was that I was pushing through the boundaries that could have stopped me going outside – fear of people staring, of my wheelchair not working, of us not having a good time. Knowing I had that support, as always, made me even more determined to push aside any doubts about the occasion so we could enjoy the moment.

I parked myself under a cabana that overlooks the water. It was right next to the playground, so the kids were able to play and come back to us for the huge amount of food prepared by Claire and Mum. It was different to my visit home. This occasion felt almost normal. We were doing what we might have done previously with the people with whom we would have done it.

As I was sitting there, though, I was reminded of the difference when a young boy came up to me. He looked me up and down, paused, and then looked me in the eye.

'What happened?'

I love that kids are so direct. At that point, however, I hadn't yet thought about how best to answer that question. *How do I describe in a short sentence what has happened to me?* I'm better at answering those kinds of questions now, but the only thing I could think of at the time wasn't that complicated.

'Sharks.'

I was trying to be funny.

The little boy looked at me in shock and ran off. Perhaps it didn't work. I hope I didn't cause any long-term issues with swimming at the beach for him!

Diane says she didn't notice people staring at me. She says it's because she lives in the moment and is always trying to count four children at any one time. I noticed a few people would look at me when I was out, but it didn't worry me. Of course people were going to look. I would have stared at me too. That particular day, I noticed that kids didn't look away – if I smiled, they would smile back and that would make me feel great.

So it was another successful step, and I gained confidence. We would be able to do this again.

A week later, we had a second outing with a few more members of the family, including Diane's Aunty Jan who had been with the family in ICU, Jan's daughter Debbie and son-in-law Sal. This time we were also joined by Rachel and Aaron and their children, and again, had a lovely afternoon. Once we knew we could do it, outings to South Bank with Aunty Jan and others became a regular occurrence.

From then on, Diane and I took the children to South Bank almost every Tuesday afternoon during the school term. We would get takeaway pizza from Amici's, a restaurant in Little Stanley Street, and sit at the playground, where the children could play. It was something we all looked forward to. For me, it felt like things were slowly becoming more normal.

*

We found we needed to find ways to turn possible low points into opportunities.

As the September school holidays approached, Diane and I were reminded of 'what couldn't have been'. For two years, we had been planning to go to Disneyland during the holidays with our very close friends Gayle and David Schabe, who have two daughters of similar ages to our boys.

I had reviewed the Disneyland guidebook, so I had a plan, and we had booked flights and accommodation. The boys had picked out what rides they wanted to go on, and aside from being packed, we had been ready to go.

Diane was trying to figure out how I might still be able to go, but the logistics were looking pretty impossible. She was also considering taking the boys and going without me. She felt the kids had gone through a big ordeal as a result of my illness, and it was beginning to seem highly unlikely that we as a family would ever get to Disneyland.

Our travel agent and friend James Hermiston saw Diane each week at soccer training, and would every now and then ask what we were planning to do. Diane says that she usually sidestepped the issue because she didn't want to have to make the call to cancel the trip. Instead, she was exploring all options. She talked to the boys about taking just the three of them.

'But, Mummy, we can't go without Emily,' Luke told her.

Diane wasn't sure how she would cope with four kids, including one two-year-old, on a plane to the US. It's very like Diane, though, that she would even contemplate it.

I was sure that Diane could make whatever we decided work, but I was also clear about what I wanted.

'This was meant to be a family holiday, and I still want it to be a family holiday,' I told Diane.

It possibly sounded like I was being a bit selfish, but I was holding on to the Disneyland trip as a future goal. I was convinced we would be able to go as a family at a later date and if Diane took the children alone, even if it was to cheer them up, it wouldn't be that family holiday.

So, we made the call to first delay, and then cancel the trip. I know it was particularly hard for Diane because she is so committed to delivering on promises, and we had promised this trip to the children. But we had travel insurance, so we knew it wouldn't be a complete loss – the door remained open for us to go some other time.

I remember Saul saying, 'No shit, Sherlock,' when I told him I didn't think we would be able to go, a week or so before we finally cancelled.

Unlike him, I was initially with Diane in thinking that if we got the logistics right, it just might work. As I have learned, Saul is usually right, but I appreciated that he didn't stop me from at least trying to get to the point of departure.

The Schabes went on their holiday, and Gayle collected information on disabled access for us. Her feedback was positive, and when she returned she had lots to say about what rides would be best for me. So Disneyland is still on the bucket list. It isn't going anywhere.

We were sad for the boys, but Diane organised an alternative holiday at the Diana Plaza Hotel, a small hotel on Annerley Road in Brisbane, across the road from the rehab unit. My aunt, Ruth, was planning to visit from New Zealand, so Diane booked two rooms. Ruth would stay for three days, and Diane and the kids would stay for a week. It would be the holiday they could have without really going on holiday. Our own house was only 10 minutes away.

The new plan meant that when Diane broke the news to the boys about cancelling Disneyland, there was an upside: 'Hey, kids. We're not going to Disneyland, but guess what – we are going to the Hotel Diana!'

The kids were probably as excited about going to the Hotel Diana as they would have been about going to Disneyland, particularly when they heard that the hotel had a spa and that the two rooms Diane had booked were adjoining, with a door between them. It was a huge adventure. We made the most of the opportunity for sleepovers, trips to South Bank and exploring new places to eat. Diane was able to escape the routine of running around between school, kindy and hospitals. We had a lot of fun. I even had a sleepover in the hotel, which the kids thought was fantastic. I did too, and we coped well.

*

Part of the Disneyland plan had been to celebrate Diane's fortieth birthday in Las Vegas. I still wanted to celebrate Diane's birthday in a special way, but was very much restricted by life in rehab, and the fact that it was difficult to make phone calls or send emails. I hadn't yet mastered the art of using technology with my new body.

Diane hadn't had too many sleepovers while I was in rehabilitation because of competition with the boys, but the date night tradition we started in ICU continued once I started to make good progress in my recovery. Every fourth Friday night, Diane's cousins would babysit the children, and Diane would come into rehab for a date, but she would always go home.

For her birthday, I wanted to take Diane to dinner, and to have her stay the night – I wanted it to be just the two of us for longer than a few hours.

It meant I had to do some planning, which, other than for travel, doesn't come naturally to me. In my old life I always tended to leave things to the last minute, but it's difficult to sustain that as someone with a disability – I have to really think ahead, about everything.

I knew Diane had no expectations, which was probably a good starting point in the event that I managed to fail. Everyone in my circle at rehab ended up being in on the plan. My physio Jacqui's mother had a friend who happened to work for the Pandora jewellery company, so I organised a charm for a bracelet of Diane's that we added to on major occasions. Mary and Bila, ward support staff members with whom I got on well, offered to get flowers, and ended up finding some champagne and chocolates. My great friend Steph Robotham made an amazing cake, and Mum and Dad had the children for the evening.

The nurses spread roses around my bed and poured champagne into two glasses, ready for Diane's arrival. When she arrived, she seemed very happy, but that's a usual state for Diane. I loved that she just loved me anyway, but it felt good to be able to make her feel special for once – she was always so good at sending the love my way.

I took Diane to a restaurant at South Bank, overlooking the Brisbane River. We ordered olives, which probably wasn't a great idea – Diane not only had to feed them to me, but then also retrieve the pips from my mouth! I still had a bandage on my head, and we were eating al fresco at the front of the restaurant because the wheelchair wouldn't allow us to go any further inside. I wondered what the many people who were passing by must have thought.

I was conscious that even though I had organised it, Diane had to do all the work. It played on my mind then as much as it does now. It's one of the things that push me towards independence.

It was a perfect night and it was just like a normal date night for us. Even then, we found we didn't focus on my disability when we were together. Obviously we talked about how we were feeling about things generally, but there was so much more to talk about, including what our kids, friends, and family were up to. Diane said it felt like we were the only people in the restaurant – it was so good to have time together. The weather was just right – warm enough for Diane to enjoy it but cool enough for me. The city lights across the river and the early evening sky were beautiful.

It wasn't Disneyland or Las Vegas, but it was special. It was another reminder that we were going to be okay, and that life could go on.

CHAPTER 11

WHEELS IN MOTION

I recognised the importance of a motorised wheelchair for mobility, but I didn't realise there was so much involved and that I would learn a lot about wheelchairs, and even more about myself, in the process of getting up and rolling.

First, we had to consider what I needed when buying a wheelchair, and soon it became evident that I would have to trial different models. I had very specific needs – for example, it was very difficult to get on and off a wheelchair without hands with which to manoeuvre myself.

I needed a chair with nothing on its sides that could impede my ability to shuffle into or off the seat. The seat needed to be adjustable so I could be at the same level as whatever I was trying to get on or off because I didn't want to use a hoist to transfer myself from one place to another. Steering the chair was also problematic – with no arms, I had a similar profile to a quadriplegic. A chair driven by chin control seemed at first to be the most obvious option.

Prior to being able to get out and about in wheelchairs with my family, I had many outings with my occupational therapist, Nick Flynn, to trial the chairs. Nick and I would head out along Annerley Road, and sometimes along Stanley Street in front of the Mater hospitals, and down Grey Street to South Bank. At the time, there was a huge construction project going on at the front of the hospital, so it was always an adventure getting around.

For the first time in my life, I noticed that footpaths aren't as smooth as they look. I also noticed how many shops had very small steps that prevented me from getting inside. If I wanted to buy something, I would frequently have to stay on the footpath outside the shop while someone went in to buy whatever it was we might have wanted, such as a coffee.

These outings opened up a new world for me. I was able to get outside, and explore the local neighbourhood of Woolloongabba and South Brisbane. It's an inner-city area, which means it's busy with people and traffic. I needed to negotiate, and survive, footpaths, pedestrians and cyclists, and some crazy people and their driving.

It didn't take me long to have my first run-in with traffic.

*

Everyone tells me that they have never heard me yell, and I don't recall having ever really yelled in my life until the day I was almost run over in one of my trial wheelchairs.

Nick and I had been on a reconnaissance visit to South Bank – this was before the first family trip to South Bank – and I wanted to make sure I would be able to handle it.

At the time I was still subject to contact precautions for infectious diseases, because of the residual wound on my head and upper buttock. So Nick, who always took this quite seriously when working with me, was wearing a plastic apron and gloves. He looked a little like a chef. I, on the other hand, was still wearing a large dressing on the back of my head.

We made quite a team – me in my bandages sitting in a chin-controlled wheelchair with someone covered in white plastic alongside.

We were returning from our outing, and I was feeling good. I was getting better with the chair, and was confident that I would be able to go out with the family without too many issues. Nick and I were crossing Raymond Terrace, a road that separates the Mater hospitals, as we made our way back to the rehab unit. The road is really a lane, and is spanned by a bridge that enables people to walk between the Mater Adult and Children's hospitals.

As Nick and I were crossing, a car came flying around the corner and screeched to a halt, literally a metre or so from me. I stopped abruptly because I looked up, making my chin pop out of the cradle that drives the wheelchair. The driver started to yell at me through the windows of her car, while at the same time beeping her horn.

Our light had been green. I know it must have been because there was no way Nick would have let me cross on any other colour – he always followed the rules. He is dedicated to his job, and was always concerned about my safety.

I was instantly furious, and started yelling back from the wheelchair. This meant I was stuck in the middle of the road because while I was yelling, I wasn't moving – I needed my chin to drive the chair forward. I literally couldn't talk and drive at the same time. So the driver was yelling at me and beeping her horn; I was yelling back at her, waving my stumps in the air from my stationary wheelchair. In the meantime, Nick was trying desperately to break us up.

Eventually I did calm down and put my chin back in so we could get off the road. I was still trying to talk, though, which was affecting my steering.

Here I am, I thought. *I have, to this point, survived everything thrown at me, and now I almost get run over at a road crossing. You have got to be kidding.*

We returned in one piece to the unit. It would have been a sight.

Someone at some stage in my recovery did jokingly suggest that I try to get hit by a car, because I would be covered by funding from third party insurance and therefore able to access more care. Perhaps there was a conspiracy, but having had that close call, I knew for certain I wasn't keen on the idea!

*

A few chairs later, I settled on a model with a seat that could lower itself to the floor. This meant that I could simply get on the chair from the ground, and raise myself to whatever level I needed. Getting out of the chair onto different surfaces and at different heights would also be easier. It was a huge step forward, because it made me more mobile and flexible about where I could go.

One of the challenges with this particular chair was being able to steer it, but it's amazing what solutions you can come up with. One day Bob, the chair salesperson, and I were discussing the problem of having no arms and only a short stump, when Bob suggested one of those plungers you use to clear a blocked drain or toilet as an option for steering. Upside down, it would fit my stump perfectly, and the rubber is soft and flexible so it wouldn't hurt me.

So the lever to control the chair was replaced by an upside-down plunger, which cost a few dollars from a hardware store. Attaching this to a $26 000 wheelchair seemed somewhat incongruous, but it worked. My new chair – financed thanks to fundraising by my colleagues at Origin Energy – was ready to go.

The kids were excited. They got to choose the colour, and Diane was worried they would choose green, which she doesn't like, or pink, which would be Emily's choice. I managed to steer their ideas so they picked bright Ferrari red, with which we were all happy. There's a spot where the kids can stand without the risk of the chair breaking or me falling over. The chair can also spin almost on the spot, and can travel at around 8 kilometres an hour.

I became motorised transport for bags, and the kids.

That wheelchair is part of me. Where I go, it goes too. With me in it, it weighs 200 kilograms. We've learned a few things, such as the fact that Qantas is the only airline that will take a chair as heavy as mine. We found out the hard way that we can't travel with anyone else.

At one stage in my rehab I visited doctors in Melbourne. We flew to Melbourne on Qantas but were returning to Brisbane with Tiger Airways because they were the cheapest. I made phone calls and reviewed online policies to make sure that they could carry me. It all appeared to be fine until we got to the airport and I wasn't able to meet their request to break the chair into 30-kilogram sections. They were very apologetic and booked me a flight with Virgin, who advised I couldn't fly with them either as my chair was too heavy. Eventually, the Tiger staff arranged for me to fly with Qantas, and we got home. So now we know.

Fortunately, Qantas has been fantastic – and they don't really need to be, as I don't have a choice of who to fly with. They not only have the equipment, but the way they deal with my special needs is also compassionate and respectful. In a sometimes difficult life, these things make a difference.

*

We also learned the hard way that the wheelchair needed to be charged regularly. It was another event that occurred in the middle of a road.

The Friday afternoon tradition of a few of the kids' friends and their mothers going to the park down the road from our house after school had continued while I was in hospital. After I moved to rehab, I became a regular attendee. Diane would come for a visit and then take me with her to pick up the boys. We would all head to the park for a few hours before I went back to hospital with a couple of the boys for the night.

The park sessions were new to me – when I was working, I would be coming home from my travels on a Friday evening so I only ever heard about the park from the kids at the end of the day. It was normally a 'girls' thing, but once I started turning up, a lot of the other dads started to join us. First David Webb, who lived across the road with Nicole and was usually working from home on Friday; then Anthony Lea, Gwen's husband, and Stuart Harland, Lisa's husband, would drop around after work. We made quite a crowd in this tiny little park with one covered bench.

The first time I attended a park session, I took the boys down on my own while Diane did some things at home before she joined us. Nicole saw us as we wheeled and walked past, and called out to see if I would like a coffee – to which I replied, 'Absolutely.' So she made me a coffee and she and David joined us with their children. When it came time to go home, I wheeled back up the street, and David walked with me to make sure I could get up the very steep hill to our house. I managed it well, so didn't need his help that day.

The following week was a different story.

I was, once again, wheeling with the boys on our return from the park. It was getting dark, as we had left it until quite late to leave, and we had negotiated one block's worth of footpath as we made our way up the hill towards home. I was crossing a very narrow street, and as I came to the middle of the road, my wheelchair came to a complete stop. I had run out of battery, and was stuck fast – in the dark, on an intersection.

Now I know why these things have hazard lights. However, I couldn't turn them on, because the battery was flat.

My thoughts were jumping about, but I was mainly thinking, *This is not good.* While the wheelchair can be pushed manually, it is far too heavy for the boys to move. I told the boys to get off the road so they would be safe.

I thought it might help if I turned the power on and off. Maybe I would get a small surge of energy when turning the chair back on, and it would be enough to get me to the other side and off the road. I did that, and got a tiny bit more power, but as soon as I started up the hill, the chair cut out again. I tried yet again, thinking that maybe if I reversed down the hill, momentum might help. It did and I had just enough power to get off the road.

Luke and Ben went to get Gwen and Diane, who had remained at the park to pack up and collect gear. Diane came to find me, while Gwen went across the road to get David from his and Nicole's house, but she couldn't raise anyone because by that stage, they were all upstairs and having showers. In the meantime, Will and I waited in the dark.

Soon enough, Diane pulled over to the side of the road in the car, wound down the window and asked what had happened.

'Daddy's broken down,' Will told her.

'I'll get someone to push you up the hill,' Diane said. I don't know where we were going to get that person from, but fortunately we then remembered the car.

We had only just had the car modified, which had taken around six weeks, and we still weren't used to what it could do for us. The car was the reason I could now come to the park on Friday afternoons, and we had only had it back for a week.

'Oh! That's right,' Diane said. 'We can get the chair into the car.'

She backed the car into the street I had been trying to cross. Rather than someone having to push the chair and me a few hundred metres up the very steep hill to the house, we simply needed a push up the ramp into the back of the car. Gwen went to try to raise

David again, and he appeared a few minutes later. By now, a small crowd had gathered around the car.

As it happened, I tried once more to turn on the chair, and had just enough power to get myself into the car. Once we were home a minute later, I managed to back out and roll into the house, where the chair was hooked up to recharge.

I had always been the sort of person who would only fill the car with petrol once the petrol light came on. I learned that I couldn't afford to take that kind of risk any more – electrical items seem to hold their charge well to start with, but then it seems to disappear very quickly.

After that experience, Diane and I made sure the wheelchair was charged up every night. Luke would check on us just to make sure.

*

The wheelchair was just one of my tickets to independence.

There was a lot of excitement about assistive technologies among those around me. Diane and Dad became regular visitors at LifeTec in Newmarket, Brisbane, which I came to refer to as the 'disabled lolly shop'. Every time they came back, they would be raving about all these things that were available to me, and I later also became a regular visitor with Nick, my occupational therapist. We would make appointments with the LifeTec occupational therapists to review items that could possibly help me.

LifeTec provides an amazing service. It's a not-for-profit organisation that provides advice about assistive technology. The staff are occupational therapists and other specialists, and they help review products and educate people on how to use them. Some of the products are so specialised, and produced in such low volume, that they are extremely expensive and hard to acquire. To have what is essentially a shopfront for these products is fantastic.

For example, when Diane and I were trying to work out what

I really needed to help with independence at home, we knew that one of our biggest challenges was eating. At dinnertime when we were together, Diane would feed me first, so I would eat with the children, and then she would eat while I rounded up the kids for a bath and their bedtime routine. It always worried me that Diane was having to put everyone else first, and dinnertimes were an occasion where it was really visible to me, even though she never complained – it was just the reality for us at the time. However, I saw it as a barrier to us being a normal family, and something we needed to find a solution for.

Deirdre Cooke from the Mater rehab unit told us about the Neater Eater, a device made in England that would possibly enable me to feed myself, using levers to which I could attach cutlery. In theory, I could then scoop food out of a bowl fitted to its base. The cost of the Neater Eater was in excess of $3000, which seemed ridiculously expensive. I really wanted to make sure it would work for me before we considered buying it, and to find out whether there were other options.

We contacted the distributor in Sydney, who then sent a Neater Eater to LifeTec here in Brisbane. The staff set it up on a table where I was then able to try it out. The LifeTec therapists ran me through the options, and while I still can't work out how there's 3000 dollars' worth of value in a few levers, a base and a heavy bowl, we decided it would make a difference to us. We knew we were getting independent advice – they weren't trying to sell us anything.

Fortunately, Diane was able to access funds through a grant from Carers Australia, which helped.

The first night of being able to eat on my own was liberating, to say the least. Not only was I able to feed myself, but I was also able to feed Emily ice cream, so she was pretty excited. Diane was able to sit down with all of us at the dinner table and eat at the same time.

It's a bit like the idea that you can build a house easily if you have the right tools. Independence is based on the same principle.

*

Dad's a chemical engineer by profession, and an inventor by nature. He's designed some pretty amazing stuff, such as vacuum pans that are used in sugar mills around the world, and wastewater treatment systems that make some of the cleanest water in existence. He finds solutions to problems. While he couldn't put new arms and legs on me, he was determined from the beginning to help me find ways to do things. I'm sure he could relate to my frustration – sitting still isn't something Dad and I do easily.

In coming up with ideas, Dad is an extreme optimist. Some of his ideas are out there, but I always have to keep an open mind because part of an idea might, or more likely, will, work.

Dad's ideas helped me look for things that would help in my case. I would go on to research something he suggested or talked about – it was a case of taking his ideas and making them practical. For example, I wanted to use my iPad so I could start communicating with people, but the iPad stylus was too short for me to use with my mouth. Dad rigged up a longer stick that had foil on the end, which worked until we found a company in the US who agreed, after many discussions with Rachel, to ship a long stylus with a mouthguard to Australia.

Aside from the wheelchair and being able to eat independently, communication was one of my biggest challenges.

Diane had heard about voice recognition technology while sitting around in the patient waiting area, when I was still in a coma. Soon afterwards, she spent a morning investigating the best voice activation options, and had come back with an iPhone. The boys thought it was fantastic. Siri, Apple's voice recognition system, would try to answer their questions, such as, 'How much wood does a woodchuck chuck?'

The problem with Siri is that I need to be able to press the home button to activate the software. Obviously, that's impossible for me.

Dad acquired a battery with an actuated button, and he rigged up a system so the actuator would hit the button. It required me to press a button placed in the bed, which would in turn press the phone's home button to activate Siri, so I could make a phone call. It was great. But it meant that I was always searching for the button in my bed, and I wasn't able to end the call – the caller at the other end would have to hang up.

We then talked to LifeTec staff, who suggested a hands-free car kit. It was a really simple solution. Mum went to Dick Smith and bought one that could do everything Dad's system could do plus more, for around $120.

Dad then had to come in and collect the actuator system he'd spent ages working on – I felt really bad for him. It was so thoughtful of him to try to solve my problem – his devices were definitely made with love. It's through this process of trial and error that I have discovered what I really need.

We did find out later that Siri can be helpful in interesting ways.

One day Luke asked it if his father, Matthew Ames, was a quadruple amputee. Sure enough, Siri replied in the affirmative. Luke was so excited.

The idea of needing a phone to confirm that made us laugh.

As if there was any doubt.

*

Shortly after I started rehabilitation, the 2012 London Paralympics were on.

Everyone around me was looking to the future. Dad was finding all this research into prosthetics, and there were lots of discussions about technology and disability. Oscar Pistorius's performance at the London Olympics had raised the profile of disabled athletes and questions about disability in general. The kids were fascinated, and it seemed to give them hope that there was possibly an exciting future ahead; they decided that they were looking forward to going to Rio in 2016.

Everyone, including me, was watching the Paralympics with a view to seeing what sport I might be eligible to compete in.

I loved how positive everyone was being even if I wasn't quite ready to engage with the possibility. At that stage, just getting home would have been the equivalent of winning a gold medal at the Paralympics, but it was really nice to know that everybody was so confident. Certainly, future opportunities were in the back of my mind. Competitive sport is a slightly lower priority, though, when you're simply trying to learn how to move and speak again.

My life was basically about 'how'. How do I do this, how do I do that? And actually, as time progressed, it became more about 'can' – how *can* I do something? Often, I and those around me started with a baseline knowledge of zero. Thinking about possibilities was the only way to start.

I was learning that success in my new life is all about logistics. My brain had always been busy, but it was now full of 'what ifs'. I was always thinking ahead, and things that hadn't worried me before became important.

For example, now that I had established that I could go out and get around in my wheelchair, how could I get on a bus? I tried this for the first time with Mum, who was going to lunch with some girlfriends at Woolloongabba shopping village in South Brisbane. It's a one-stop bus ride from the Mater. I was keen to get out, so we decided Mum would take me with her and we could see how it went.

My first impression of the buses in Brisbane was that they are actually very well set up for wheelchairs. The front of the bus can be lowered, and the driver puts out a ramp that's easy to negotiate.

Once I was on the bus, however, I couldn't lock myself down, so my wheelchair was sliding on the floor when the bus went around a corner. But it was okay – it was only one stop. I had a lovely cup of coffee with a group of Mum's friends before it was time to return to the hospital. I wasn't quite ready to risk sliding around the bus again, though, so Mum and I tackled the footpaths to get back to the Mater.

So I knew I could catch a bus, technically, but being able to get on the bus doesn't solve the problem of being able to pay for the bus, and even if I do have the wallet, how do I get the money out? Nothing ever seemed to be that simple.

When the summer storms started to roll in at the end of the first year in rehab, I was introduced to the complications of life without power while I was spending weekends at home. I can't go to sleep if my bed's not flat, and without power, I can't flatten it. I can't charge my wheelchair, open doors, or get down or up stairs because the lift won't work. Life without power in any circumstances is inconvenient; in my new life, it effectively means I could be bedridden.

I also learned that everything in my life is interrelated, and one tiny change can make a huge difference. For example, if something is put in front of me, distance is important. If it is even a couple of centimetres too far away for me to lean forward and access, it's completely useless – it doesn't matter how good it is. A few centimetres closer, and I might be able to use it really well. A straw in a cup of coffee is great – but if that cup of coffee is too far away for me to drink it even with the straw, it's agonising. While my balance is good now, there's still always the risk of tipping forward and not being able to save myself.

Another thing that became really important for me was that things were put back in the same place. I became reliant on being able to describe things to people, rather than show them. A nurse might ask me where a shirt was, or Luke might ask me about my arm prosthetics if he couldn't see where they were located. If I didn't know where things were, then I couldn't describe where to get something when I was trying to help later. I felt useless if I wasn't able to help or direct people when asked, and I became frustrated, although I wouldn't show it.

So I remembered Saul's words about being in control. I learned that I had to be very clear and direct about where people should put things, which made it much easier for everyone later. It also saved time – we weren't spending five minutes looking for some piece of equipment before going to the gym, for example.

I didn't want to have to search mentally for things, because as time was progressing, I was starting to worry about not feeling clear in my head.

CHAPTER 12

DRESS REHEARSAL

I became conscious that I felt hazy and tired all the time. I would wake in the mornings to find I felt like I had been in the boxing ring with Muhammad Ali – exhausted before the day began.

It wasn't getting any better, and I didn't like it. I could feel the need to be more aware of everything that was going on around me, and I wanted to be more in control. I was struggling to concentrate, and incidents like falling on the trampoline were reminders that I really needed to be able to focus for longer periods. I could also hear that my speech was still impaired – I was still slurring, and my speech was slow.

I wanted the clarity I remembered back.

I was on drugs for pain management, including nerve blockers and a form of anxiety suppressant used in my case to treat phantom pain, which, in simple terms, is nerve pain that occurs when the brain is not receiving signals it expects from missing limbs. At best, it is a pins-and-needles sensation; at worst it feels like my limbs are on fire – a sharp, burning feeling that can be incredibly intense. I asked to be taken off everything. At that stage, around October 2012, I was no longer taking antibiotics for the infection, and I was looking at going home for a short period over Christmas. I wanted to be as normal as possible.

I felt I was ready to see how I managed being drug-free.

The two drugs I was taking to help with phantom pains were Amitriptyline and Gabapentin. The doctors suggested that the Amitriptyline was probably responsible for the sluggishness, so I came off that first.

Almost immediately, I felt much better. My head was clearer and I felt more alert than I had since I woke up from the coma.

I still had a pins and needles sensation in my arms, but it wasn't particularly painful. My theory was that any drug that prevents phantom pain would have to work on the brain, and my brain was the only thing I had left – I didn't want to be taking something that would prevent it operating at its maximum capability. I figured there would have to be a side effect to taking the drugs over a long period of time.

So I came off the Gabapentin as well. Because I hadn't been off it before, I actually had no idea what the phantom pain would truly be like. The effect was gradual – the pins and needles slowly became a burning sensation, as though my arms were on fire. This was the sensation that other amputees I had met had described to me. It was intense, and very painful. So, clearly, the drug had been doing something.

The phantom pain in my legs hasn't ever been unbearable so that wasn't really something I was taking into consideration. I did, however, have to decide whether or not the pain in my arms was sufficient to warrant going back on the medication. I decided to try to remain drug-free, although I have since periodically gone back onto the Gabapentin. Going on and off it doesn't seem to make as much difference as it used to because it takes a while to build up efficacy, and by the time it kicks in I don't tend to need it because the arm pains have settled down.

The only times I have used it have been when undergoing further surgery – I found that the phantom pain got worse when other parts of my body were in pain. It was as though my arms were in sympathy with whatever else was hurting, but they didn't just join the pain party – they exceeded it. I used my arm pain as the benchmark. If the pain anywhere else was less than that, I would decide it wasn't that bad, and deal with it. Generally I did this by distracting myself and trying to ignore it. I reminded myself that I actually find some comfort in the pain, and still do to this day. It sounds strange, but it's a way for me to hold on to the memory of what my hands felt like, and it's something I'm not ready to let go of yet. If it gets too bad, I'll try meditation. I periodically have phantom pain in my legs, but it's always been constant in my arms. If the real pain at any time has exceeded the sensation of phantom pain in my arms, I have asked for painkillers or suggested to doctors that there is something wrong.

So my arms do hurt, a lot, and most of the time.

But I know now that I made the right call about taking myself off the drugs. On a later rehabilitation trip to Melbourne, I learned that giving my brain something to look at so that it thinks I have an arm and a hand settles the phantom pain. I had heard about mirror box therapy in rehab and had tried it with my occupational therapist, Nick. Mirror box therapy uses a mirror to trick the brain into thinking there are two limbs instead of one. In my case, because we didn't have the first limb to mirror, we had to be inventive. Research had indicated that where people were able to get visual feedback, alarm signals in the brain were quietened, so we had to trick my brain into thinking I had at least one arm and a hand.

On this occasion in Melbourne, a very realistic prosthetic hand had been delivered to the Epworth Hawthorn centre, the

rehabilitation unit I was attending. The hand was intended for someone else, but as I was there while it was waiting to be collected, my
physio decided to run an experiment to determine whether a theory
about brain association and phantom pain was applicable to me.

She put the hand on a table directly in front of me and put a
towel over my arm so I couldn't see that I didn't have an elbow. She
then oriented the hand so that it looked like it could be mine peep-
ing out from under the towel.

Just looking at the hand and watching the physio brush it with
a paintbrush settled the phantom pain. It took around half an hour
for the pain to really settle, and when the hand was taken away, the
pain returned rapidly, back to full strength in around five minutes. It
was almost unbelievable.

It's tempting to get fake hands and sit them in front of me, but
unless I am going to sit and stare at my hands all day, it won't work.
It might be effective, but it's certainly not practical. It's really a matter of waiting until I have prosthetics realistic enough to make my
brain think that they're my hands.

The experiment was, however, a reminder of how powerful the
brain is, and how embedded the pathways within it actually are. I'm
told that if you're born without limbs you don't have phantom pain,
so the theory is that this type of pain is associated with nerve memory.

The relief from the pain when my brain saw those hands and
thought they belonged to me told me that there was an end point to
the pain, or at least the prospect of significant reduction. I was comforted that I was on the right path.

Now, when people talk or I think about the phantom pain, I just
remember: *The best long-term, drug-free solution for me is to get
the prosthetics on.* And those prosthetics have to be realistic enough
to make my brain think that they're my hands.

*

I was happy to be off the drugs and dealing with the pain myself, but I knew that there was some concern about my mental health and ability to cope. Saul spoke with me about his expectation that I would struggle mentally at some point, and I got a sense as I worked towards going home for a few weeks over the summer holidays that I was entering a danger period.

I didn't dwell on this, however. I was more concerned with practical considerations. There were two things I wanted and needed to do before I went home: climb some stairs, and learn to use the arms I had been given earlier in rehab.

There was a set of stairs in the rehab gym that became my focus. They were not overly tall – around five steps in total, with handrails on either side. They became important to me because by that stage I had seen many people go through rehab with orthopaedic issues, and the stairs seemed to be the key that unlocked the door home. If someone could do the stairs, they were typically considered to be well enough to leave rehab. Even if the stairs and going home were unrelated in my case, I figured that when I could do the stairs, I too would be ready to be discharged for a while.

I was thinking ahead: *The lift's not going to be there. We've got stairs. Wouldn't it be great if I could get up stairs?*

I went to the gym on a Monday morning, looked at the stairs, turned to Jacqui and announced my goal.

'Jacqui, by Friday afternoon I want to be at the top of those stairs.'

She looked at me blankly, as though she was thinking, *You've got to be kidding*, but she checked herself.

'Okay. So let's think about how we're going to do it.'

I was looking at the sharp edges of the stairs, and thinking, *I have a very high risk of rolling over here, and yes, there's soft covering over the stairs, but what else can I do to reduce the risk?* We got a helmet and rolled out a yoga mat to soften my potential fall.

We started that afternoon. The first couple of days involved a lot of trial and error. My legs were so short that the fundamental question was how to propel myself up the stairs. I needed my arms to help, but they are so short that I wondered how I was going to lift the bottom half of my body. I would make it up one step, and then I would be so fatigued that I would just lie there for a while. It was very painful because to get up I needed to push down on the ends of my leg and arm stumps, where there isn't a lot of soft tissue between my skin and the bone.

It was excruciating.

I did more each day. At the beginning of the week, Jacqui would stick her knee under my bottom to give me initial leverage. I didn't have my arm prosthetics, so we put a block on the stair above the one I was trying to climb, where my arm stumps could rest. I could then put my weight into the block, and pull one leg up, then the other. Every day, we did a bit more, and on that Friday afternoon, after 15 minutes of climbing, I made it to the top of the stairs. I was so excited, and felt a great sense of achievement – I think because it had been so painful, and I had kept going. I also thought, *Wow. I am so ready to go home.*

Saul later wrote 'Mount Matthew' on the side of the stairs. I also later climbed them with my prosthetic arms, and found it was much easier because they gave me a bit more leverage. Jacqui has since told me that a single below-knee amputee she was working with specifically asked if he could climb 'Mount Matthew' prior to leaving – apparently my efforts had been inspiring!

In retrospect, it was possibly a totally pointless exercise. I have never climbed the stairs at home – I contemplated it once, but realised it would take me around two hours to get to the top – and can't imagine that I will ever climb any other form of stairs without prosthetics. But it gave me confidence that I could achieve a goal, and at least I know that I can get down the stairs if I ever need it – if there's a fire in the house, for example.

It was good to know I could do it. But it's a bit like climbing Mt Kilimanjaro – having done it once, I can't see that I'll ever want to do it again.

*

I was struggling with my arms. I was trying very hard to make them do as much as I wanted them to do. They were heavy and uncomfortable, and the hooks needed to be oriented the right way in the first place if I were to pick up something.

I watched others using them to see how they did it – a bilateral amputee would walk up to a table and whack the hooks on the corner to hit the button that enables the hooks to rotate. This is fine if you've got legs and can walk up to a table. I was stuck in a wheelchair contorting myself in all kinds of ways, trying to whack the button that released the hooks.

On one occasion, both the hooks on my arms were turned in the wrong direction. Diane and I were at a shopping centre, and we were getting in a lift. I wanted to press the lift buttons to see if I could do it on my own, but needed to orient one hook so I could.

'Diane, don't help me,' I said. She agreed to stand back.

I whacked the button on my arm to try to straighten the hook.

Again. And again.

It took me about five minutes of solid whacking to get the hooks in the right spot to be able to press the button to get the lift. I was exhausted.

It occurred to me that it would be easier to lean down and press the button with my nose. Which I did. It took a couple of seconds as opposed to five minutes.

Despite the difficulties, I was determined to persevere. I thought it was my fault that the arms were clunky. Perhaps I wasn't learning how to use them very well. My shirts got messy from trying to feed myself; food would drop from the hook after a long struggle to get it in close proximity to my mouth. Furniture got bent as I tried to use the buttons on the arms, and get around corners.

I am a mechanically minded person, so I understood how they worked, and what I had to do to get them to work. I'm also, I think, a fairly quick learner. But I was finding that the arms were useful tools for moving a block from one spot to another (roughly), and that was about all. They were good for stabilising me in the gym, eating grapes and strawberries, and not much else.

As the summer school holidays loomed, I was facing the reality that I couldn't do much more with the arms than I could without them. Saul had been right when he said they probably wouldn't work for me. Nonetheless, I was determined to continue to try. We were about to go on holiday – I would see if things were different outside hospital.

*

My final weeks of rehab for the year were spent grieving a little in anticipation of a holiday.

For the last few years, we had spent the first week of school holidays at Caloundra with friends. We would rent an apartment at Kings Beach, and spend the time swimming, making sandcastles and walking along the boardwalk.

I was determined to go again, as planned, this year. We had already cancelled Disneyland on the children, and I didn't want to cancel this as well. Diane wasn't overly keen. She had spent a lot of time getting the house ready for me to come home, and we had both spent time working out how we would manage things.

But the holiday was important to me. I thought it might give the kids a sense of normality – it would reassure them that even though this had happened to me, life would go on and we would do the things we always did. I was ever the optimist.

Deep down, however, I knew that personally, the prospect of the holiday at Caloundra was a double-edged sword.

On the one hand, we would be proving to the kids that we could do it despite my disability; on the other, it would highlight just what I couldn't do any more, and I was acutely aware of this. Holidays had always been my chance to do the exciting things with the kids because during the term and while I was working, I was often travelling or working late.

The reality of the limitations of my arms was hitting me hard, and I was thinking how I wasn't going to be able to do the things I usually did with the kids. I had been talking to the psychologist every week, and he would usually comment on how well he thought I was coping generally. After our last session before I left rehab, however, he prescribed antidepressants. I discovered this when they were handed to me at my discharge.

I remember being a little indignant that he thought I needed medication and had prescribed them without discussing it with me first. I looked at the pills and thought, *I won't need them.*

I was confident that I didn't need drugs, just time with the family. I did take the antidepressants with me though, just in case.

I gave them to Diane, and said, 'I don't think I need these, but I may not be the best judge of myself in this situation. If you think I need them, just say the word, and I'll take them.'

She agreed that I didn't need them yet, but was happy to take the drugs with us just in case.

We went to Caloundra directly from the hospital, and it was a great feeling being able to discharge myself for five weeks over the Christmas period with the blessing of Saul and the rehab team. It was going to be a dress rehearsal for our future life.

We needed some help to get all our extra gear up to Caloundra. We had so much stuff, and after the modifications to our Kia, we couldn't fit any luggage into the car aside from a few bags. So Mum and Dad offered to follow us up with a trailer full of gear, including the commode for the shower and a wheelchair ramp. Originally, the plan was that Mum would stay for the weekend, but we soon realised that we had bitten off more than we could chew. We asked if she could stay for the week, and she agreed. Dad was doing a few projects and would come up between meetings, so they ended up being part of our holiday, much to the delight of the kids.

Just getting our heads around having a holiday with some-one who has a disability was a challenge. We had stayed in the apartment before, but we had no idea whether the bathroom was wheelchair accessible. Diane had asked the hotel whether we could get the wheelchair into the room, and they said yes, but actually we couldn't – we needed a ramp to get into it. We learned then that there are different levels of wheelchair accessibility. Having a shower was difficult, but we managed thanks to a great carer who came for two hours each morning to assist me with getting ready.

I noticed that Diane had to do everything on the holiday. That worried me, and we talked a lot about how we could make things easier for her. She never complained, though – it's not in Diane's nature to ever talk negatively about anything.

I wanted to swim, but as soon as I got in the water, it became clear that drowning was a risk because I couldn't right myself if I was face down. My lower body was buoyant and I wasn't strong enough to counter that with my upper body. Dad bought weights and a lifejacket, and that worked well, but I still needed to be held while in the pool. So every time I was in the water, Diane couldn't be with the kids because she needed to be with me.

Mum is a reluctant swimmer if the weather is under 35 degrees Celsius. I think it was probably her idea of a nightmare to spend as much time in the water as she did, but she was a great help. The kids particularly enjoyed being allowed so much time in the heated spa.

Our apartment opened onto the pool deck. I remember peo-ple's reactions the first time I shuffled out on my legs into the pool area. You could have heard a pin drop. They seemed to get used to the sight over the next few days, though. To get out of the water, Diane would physically have to launch me onto a mat we had laid beside the pool. I would land on my stomach and then roll over, and I remember thinking, *So this is what it feels like to be beached like a whale.*

We wanted to go to the beach, but needed to work out how to get there. Someone had mentioned that you could get a beach-friendly wheelchair, and Diane rang around but couldn't get one. She then visited the Caloundra Surf Life Saving Club at Kings Beach. They told her they didn't have a wheelchair, but they could get me to the beach, and arranged a time the following day for us to visit.

We arrived the next morning. The weather over the previous days had been quite ordinary, but this day was absolutely beautiful, and the beach was extremely crowded. The lifesavers were wonderful. I parked my wheelchair in the club building, and they transferred me onto the back of the dune buggy. They didn't have a seatbelt, so Dad climbed into the back and put his arms around me so I wouldn't tip out while we were driving on the sand.

I was wearing a sunshirt and what I call my slidey pants – lycra skins that have been sewn up on the ends, with padding inserted at the seams for comfort. They had been custom-made by Gayle, a volunteer who assists the occupational therapists at the hospital, and I used to wear them in the gym while walking. I had been wearing the pants in the pool, and thought they would be good for the beach, where I would be walking on sand.

We found a spot, and the lifesavers left us, saying, 'Just wave when you need to come back.'

We settled in, and were joined by Kim Ibbott, one of our neighbours who was also on holiday with us, and her children. Kim is a musculoskeletal physiotherapist and a good friend. Our children have known one another since they were very young, so it was lovely to be able to spend time with them.

Kim had approached the surf lifesavers when she arrived at the beach.

'I'm looking for a friend of mine,' she said. The lifesaver looked at her, and then around at the literally hundreds of people on the beach, which isn't overly large. I suspect he was thinking, *Seriously? Here we go.*

Kim continued.

'He has no arms and legs . . .'

'Oh, yes.' There was instant recognition in the lifesaver's eyes. 'I can help you.' He laughed, and pointed directly to where I was.

It's a positive – I'm quite easy to spot in a crowd.

The boys were having fun making huge sandcastles. They had already, by this point, buried me in sand, thinking it was hilarious that they had made me a human statue with no legs. 'Bury the legs' was a game we usually played at the beach, and it took no time at all to bury mine.

As the morning progressed, I knew I wanted to get in the water.

Before my amputations, Diane would normally, and very happily, sit on the beach with the younger children while I took the others out into the surf, which was often very cold. I would encourage the boys to jump over waves, and we would boogie board and splash around.

I wanted to encourage them to get into the surf again.

'Luke, do you want to go for a swim?'

'No thanks, Daddy.'

'What? What about you, Ben?'

'No thanks, Daddy.'

'Will?'

'No thanks, Daddy.'

I didn't know whether it was because they really were too busy building sandcastles, or because they thought I couldn't go in.

Kim then asked the boys if they would go down to the water

with her, and they again said no. I decided I would have to give the surf a go. I knew they needed a bit of encouragement, and in this instance, the only way to encourage them was do it myself. I could then say, 'Look, *I* did it.'

I looked at the kids, shuffled the sand away from my stumps, and started off towards the water's edge.

'Okay, well I'm going down to the water. Come on, I'll lead the way.'

I shuffled to the water, leaving behind me a noticeable snail trail the width of my body. Everyone soon followed – Kim, Diane and all the kids, and Mum and Dad.

I got into the water, which was a bit rough, and the boys joined me. Soon after, Kim suggested I have a go on the boogie board, which seemed like a good idea to me. Kim and Diane loaded me onto the board, where I lay face up, with my legs closest to the beach. They then took me a bit further out and turned me around, so my head was beachside.

Lying in this position, I could see the waves coming towards me, which was pretty daunting. We weren't too deep, but then they let me go, staying close while I attempted to surf in to where the kids and Mum and Dad were standing. I thought I was going to slide off, so I wasn't feeling overly comfortable, but I went back for a few goes. I only managed to get to the beach once.

I don't know whether I enjoyed it because it was actually fun, or whether it just felt good to do something different. But I did enjoy it.

After a few hours, the time came to head back. We had been in the sun for a while, and I was tired and getting cold, as were the kids.

Given the number of people on the beach, we suspected we might have difficulty catching the lifesavers' attention, but within seconds of Diane turning around and waving towards the lifesaving tower, they were on their feet and coming over to collect us.

They had possibly been keeping an eye out in the expectation that this limbless guy on a boogie board might need their assistance. Fortunately for all of us, I had survived my surfing session.

Getting wet served its purpose. Will and Luke had a go. Ben stayed making sandcastles, but that's not unusual for him, and Kim later took them all for another swim in the pool after we returned to the apartment.

We couldn't have done without Kim's help. During our stay, she would visit our apartment, collect some children and take them for a swim with her kids.

By the end of the holiday, Diane and I worked out that we had done everything we had the year before, just a little bit differently. I was able to say, 'Great. I did get to the beach. I did get to play cricket.' We went for walks along the boardwalk. I went swimming, or floating, with the kids.

So after an enjoyable week in the sun, we collected our things. It was time to spend some time at home.

*

My visits home to this point had been generally restricted to Saturday evenings because the facilities in the house were limited. I would shower after rehab on Saturday, come home, and then wait until I got back to rehab on Sunday evening to have another shower.

This longer period at home was a chance to assess what we might need when I returned permanently.

Diane had arranged for a carer to come for two hours every morning, and that seemed to work well. It did mean I was being woken at 6.30 a.m. while the rest of the house slept, but that was a small price to pay for assistance. And by the time everyone else had finished breakfast, I was clean-shaven, showered and ready for the day.

We were living in the downstairs area of the house, which consists of three bedrooms belonging to the boys, a small living area and a bathroom that is fortunately fairly large. Diane and I slept in Luke's room, and the children slept on beds and mattresses in Will and Ben's rooms. There was no consistency in who slept where or with whom; even Diane had to swap out for the boys sometimes. We had two single beds pushed together – my bed was one we had bought specially. The kids loved it – they could lie on it and use buttons to move the different halves of the bed up and down. The cousins would come over and squeals of laughter could be heard from the room as children piled onto the bed and started 'sailing in stormy seas'.

Luke seemed to take some comfort from me returning to his room. When I had first become unwell I had slept in his bed, out of the way of the family, and he afterwards associated his room with me getting sick. Seeing Diane and I happily sleeping in there seemed to help him relax.

I could access the house via a ramp that Diane had organised – it doubled as a great skating ramp for Ben and a stage for Emily's impromptu singing or dancing performances. The kids often found interesting things to do with equipment lying around the house.

Despite having conquered the stairs at rehab, trying to get up the stairs in our house wasn't an option. It would have taken me a couple of hours, at least, to get to the top, and then once upstairs, there was no safe way of coming down. The stairs are wooden, and encased in glass on one side. The floor on the lower storey of the house is covered in glossy ceramic tiles, which make for ease of shuffling, but wouldn't have been nice to meet at the end of a long fall.

So my life was contained within a few small rooms, plus a back patio area with an outdoor setting where we would have our meals. Cabin fever set in quickly, so I was keen to get out and about whenever we could. The longest period I had spent at home prior to this was three weeks when Emily was a baby. Any other extended periods had been associated with a project such as renovating the house.

At the time, I had to use a transfer board to move from the chair to the sofa. By the end of the day, I would often be sore from sitting down in the wheelchair all day, so we set up a gym mat on the floor beside the lounge. I could lie down and stretch on the mat.

We were looking for a way of moving me between the two rooms without having to use the chair, because it was so difficult for me to get back up on to it from the floor. It was a lot of effort and really hard on Diane's back because she would have to help lift me.

A garage trolley from Supercheap Auto seemed like a good idea. We all took a trip out there one day, and brought the trolley home for a test drive.

It worked well. I could get onto and off the trolley using a bath lifter that we had at home, and I would lie along the trolley on my back, facing the ceiling. The trolley rolls pretty smoothly on the tiles we have downstairs, and the kids pretty quickly worked out, as they do, how to have a lot of fun with it. We would often 'surf' the hall-way – me on the trolley, one boy on my stomach, another sitting with their legs across me, and one pushing. We would get to the end, spin around and head in the other direction.

I never fell off or ran into the wall – they always took great care of me.

While there was a lot that I couldn't do, there was a lot I could, such as read, watch movies and play games in between Christmas catch-ups with people we hadn't seen for a while.

It was a different, and probably more sedate, way of connecting than we were used to, but it was connection nonetheless.

Emily in particular was still exploring what had happened to me. One evening I was putting her to bed. It was hard to hold a book and read to her, so I had started a thing we called the 'Princess Emily' stories.

In lieu of reading a book, I would make up a fairytale with a Princess Emily in it. Princess Emily lived in a castle, and my Emily would close her eyes and listen. We wouldn't get far into the story, though, before Emily would dictate what needed to happen. It was always related to things she was scared of – dogs, jumping castles, whatever it happened to be on the day.

This particular evening I finished the story, and Emily turned to me.

'So you have short arms and legs?' she asked. We had been having regular conversations about what had happened to my arms and legs, but this seemed to come somewhat out of the blue.

'Yes, Emily, I do. And you have bigger arms and legs, and yours will keep growing. You're going to get really big one day.'

Emily turned to me, looked at my arm stumps and then my leg stumps.

'So, Daddy, when are yours going to grow?'

How I wished it could be that simple.

CHAPTER 13

THE ROAD HOME

I didn't end up needing the antidepressants while I was away from rehab. Being busy and surrounded by my family and really positive friends had been enough, and before I knew it, the time had come to go back into hospital.

It was 17 January 2013. Five weeks at home had given me an idea of what life could be like, and we were all feeling pretty good about our 'new normal', as Diane would call it.

However, I knew how hard it was for Diane, and I wasn't yet ready to impose myself on her and the kids during the busy time when school started again. Diane and I had another conversation about visiting, and keeping that to a minimum so the kids could get into a routine. It was a new school year, so they were all going into new grades, and making new friends. I again reassured Diane that she didn't need to visit every day to support me – I was going to be busy.

While on holiday and at home, I had come to the conclusion that the arms really weren't going to work for me. They largely hung, unused, over the back of my wheelchair. I could do just a little bit more when I had them on, but there was a lot I couldn't do, like roll around and cuddle the kids. They certainly weren't enabling me to do the things that are important to me.

They didn't give me any more independence – I still couldn't feed myself, I couldn't go to the toilet on my own and I couldn't take my clothes on and off. Those are the things that would make it worthwhile to wear them. So I knew I needed to look for other options for my arms, but in the meantime, the focus for the next stage of rehab would be my legs.

While I was at home, I had visited my prosthetist, David Sweet, to first get moulds made of my stumps, and then get fitted for the new legs. Luke came along and recorded the visit, after which he sent an email to the family so they could understand what had happened:

> Today we are at Goodwill Orthopaedics, Brisbane. The ladies at the reception welcomed us with tea, coffee and biscuits. Matthew's legs are about half a metre long from the top of the sockets to the heel. They start by lying him down and testing the legs into his stumps. Then they put a rubber socket around the two legs and put the leg on. Next the Goodwill Orthopaedics make shore (sic) that the legs are all right so they stand him up with two men each side so Matthew doesn't topple over wile (sic) one checks the legs are perfect. Meanwhile Diane is taking photos. Matthew wants to lean backwards so they spin the feet 180% to the right (a special feature that only his ankle can do. Don't try this at home.) Then they went away to get a new fitting for the leg and put it on. Next the Goodwill Orthopaedics go and take off a bit of Matthew's leg. They took off a bit of his leg so he can take his first step, and then he took his first step.
>   Luke

I returned to rehab a few days after the fitting with only one aim – to get up and walking again. I thought I would be home for good in around eight weeks. Others thought I was being optimistic, but I needed to have a goal.

I wanted to be home for my fortieth birthday, which was at the end of March.

A few days after my re-admission to rehab, I was able to stand and take my first steps. Most of the family came for the occasion, so I was surrounded by a support crew that included my kids and my niece and nephews. The gym was empty except for us, and the parallel bars had been lowered so I could hook my stumps over the bars for support.

I was originally just supposed to see how I felt while I stood with the new legs, but I wanted to see if I could walk a few steps. I found I was able to shuffle forward a few feet, which I hadn't expected to be able to do so quickly. It felt like wearing stilts in gumboots. I was wobbling all over the place.

Diane had kept my shoes, and at the time I had thought that was a bit silly. Now I realised that they were useful. The shoes were placed on the ends of the prosthetics, albeit on backwards to balance me and make it easier to walk forward.

It was strange to see some form of feet below me but it felt really, really great to be upright.

Just as we were about to get excited and celebrate, Emily, who was toilet training at the time, decided to wee on the gym floor.

Exhilaration was replaced with reality very quickly.

*

It was back to routine in rehab. My challenge was to walk further each day, building up to walking without support. I set a goal of walking on my own within a month.

Jacqui or Diane would sit on a mobile stool beside me and,

initially, they would hold my arms. I was very unsteady – my short little legs would wobble almost uncontrollably underneath me. I'm a believer in the value of 'functional rehab' – the idea that you move for a reason, to achieve something you're trying to do, and move a little bit more each time. I was happy to just walk while being supported, with the goal of getting a little bit further every day.

I had been walking for a week when Jacqui, who had been quietly guiding me from the stool, suddenly announced that I was going to be on my own.

'You know what? I think I'm going to let go of you.'

I had a brain explosion. *You have got to be kidding me! How in the world am I going to do this?*

But I trusted Jacqui. I knew she wouldn't be letting go of me if she really thought I would fall. My next thought was, *Oh well. She'll catch me.*

And I did it. I walked, or more accurately, wobbled, a few steps on my own. I was amazed. Being with someone I trusted, accepting the risk and pushing myself, knowing that someone was there to catch me if I fell, meant that I exceeded my own expectations. It was a really great moment, and I found it hard to keep myself together.

I fairly quickly built up to being able to do laps around the gym on my own with Jacqui or Diane following closely behind me on the stool. I wore a walking belt that had loops that they could grab quickly if they needed to, which was often. It was great. As I walked around, I would say hello to the other patients, and I met some interesting people. I got close to a few in addition to the Shit Happens Club members, including some Sisters of Mercy who were fellow patients while I was there.

Everyone in rehab seemed to be a character – we all had a story, some more unusual than others. I really enjoyed being able to be a bit more mobile and move around to meet people. Some I only met once or twice, but others were longer-term patients like me.

I was still working on other areas, like increasing my shoulder range. I would hang from the ceiling using stirrups tucked into my underarms, and the physios would give me regular massages and get me to do lots of stretching.

I had developed a close relationship with Saul Geffen, my rehabilitation specialist, and as time progressed, my appreciation of his approach grew. I knew that it was not in his interests to let me fail and that he would not accept anything but the best for me because I was such a special case for him and his staff. He actively sought external advice or knowledge on my behalf, and I knew the advice he gave me was given in good faith, even if it was delivered with the grace of a sledgehammer at times.

Saul challenged me, but always included me. He was good for me because he wasn't afraid of conflict. I tend to avoid it, and I could see that his strength in this area would make for a good partnership.

Saul was very honest and I learned that there were things he didn't know, like aspects of technology that might assist me. When he didn't know something, he would work with me to learn more. He's the first to admit that when I started to look for solutions other than socket-based prosthetics for my arms, he wasn't convinced that I was going to get a satisfactory outcome. At the time of writing, I don't know whether he'll be right or wrong, but I do know that he's supported me despite his personal concerns.

This has been the general pattern of our dealings: Saul would give me a frank overview of what things would be like, and what the limitations might be at first; I would try for myself, and usually find that Saul was right; and I would then be driven to work out whether there were other options. The input of others was critical in working out what options were available to me.

It was becoming important to me to engage with other people who were disabled, even if I still didn't think of myself as having a disability. Quite early on in my recovery, I had met a fellow quadruple amputee, Brigitte Wruck, who was really generous with her time and advice. Diane and I had also sought assistance from the Queensland Artificial Limb Service, Amputees and Families Support Group Queensland and Limbs 4 Life, which is based in Victoria, and through those organisations we were introduced to people and ideas that gave us great hope for the future.

My first sense of possibilities and of being part of a wider community came when several Paralympic athletes visited me in rehab, thanks to some organisation by our neighbour Kim, the same Kim who we had holidayed with at Caloundra. The group comprised Cameron Carr and Chris Bond from the wheelchair rugby team, and powerlifters David Williams and Scott Upston. I was very honoured that they would take the time to see me.

I was in awe of their achievements. I now knew firsthand how difficult it is for someone with a disability to simply get out the door, let alone compete at the highest level, but they made me feel very comfortable, like just another bloke. I remember limbs being pulled off and passed around, and they shared a great deal of knowledge with me – showing me different liners and sockets for prosthetics, for example. There was lots of laughter, even when they were describing how they got injured – what had been traumatic at the time was now cause for a great and often amusing story. They were excellent examples of being able to get through something really bad; they had all spent a significant amount of time in hospital, but they reminded me that I would get through it, and that it would be worth it in the end.

It was also gratifying to learn that temperature regulation was an issue we had in common. They had also been asking medical staff about it, without ever really getting much of an answer. I wasn't abnormal – it seemed to be an experience shared by other amputees.

The boys enjoyed the visit too. The athletes brought in their gold medals, and put them around the boys' necks. I remember thinking, *Wow. A little piece of London 2012 is here in this room.*

I was also inspired and humbled by others who made contact with me. One was Josh Vander Vies, a Canadian boccia player, discovered by Kate after I had been discussing with her my worries about dressing myself. A day later, she sent Diane a link to YouTube that showed Josh, who has stumps just a little bit longer than mine, dressing himself in a short video he had made to show people how he managed at home. I was starting to understand the generosity that goes with sharing your story – the ideas we were getting about how to do things were only possible because people were brave enough to put themselves out there.

Diane contacted Josh directly through his website, and he sent a really helpful response, with useful links and tips on how to do things. His advice was timely: 'What I have found is that the simplest solution is often the best.'

I was reminded that I might be different now, but I am not alone. There are lots of other people like me – people I possibly never really noticed before – making the best of things that have happened to them.

*

At home, preparations for my return were in full swing. Rachel had put a call out for people to help dig the pit needed for the lift shaft. The response had been amazingly generous – friends came from everywhere to assist with 'the Big Dig', which took an entire day. Our friends John Bain, Anthony Lea and Andrew Kudzius were now working on the next step – building the lift shaft in our garage.

Rather than build the lift tower on the outside of the house, we had opted to lose a car space, as we now only have one car, and space from a study area upstairs. The study became a narrow room just wide enough for my wheelchair and a specially built bench high and narrow enough to allow me to sit and use the computer more easily (kindly manufactured and installed by Richard Prove, one of the dads from school). Andrew and his mate Karl Schottler were also busy working on installing the lift, and we were planning modifications that would allow me to open and close the doors remotely.

Diane and I were learning that the acquisition of a disability brings with it an unexpected burden of paperwork. Life was now all about classification, eligibility and access. Disability care in Queensland is managed by two departments – the Department of Communities, Child Safety and Disability Services, and the Department of Health, better known as Queensland Health. Disability services are generally accessible through the former, while mobility aids are accessible through Queensland Health.

The system was and remains complicated and hard to understand, but we found people working within it who were overwhelmingly helpful and committed to providing great support. Fortunately, there are organisations such as the limb services and carers associations to help people like us. The need for these organisations became very obvious, and without them and, particularly, their support of Diane, I wonder where we would be today.

One of the things we applied for was an assistance dog. Of all the paperwork we've had to do, and all the hurdles we've encountered, this was probably one of our greatest challenges.

Diane's aunt Claire McMahon spent six hours over a couple of days helping me fill in the 33-page application. She would ask me each question on the form, and fill out the answer on my behalf.

We had to create a DVD that included footage of the inside and outside of our home, so the assessors could see the yard, the house and the family. We had to talk about why we wanted a dog. Everyone had a vested interest. The kids got out their soft toy puppies, introduced them and talked about why they thought Daddy needed to have an assistance dog.

It was disappointing to receive a rejection letter not too long after this, with no further consultation or contact. I can understand that demand is high, but a shorter screening process would be a great help – it was frustrating to go through the whole process with no result, especially when filling out any form is difficult for me.

The letter was short, and it didn't go into a lot of detail. I think it was a shock because we hadn't been interviewed, and no one had called to clarify any details. And while the letter didn't tell me that I was too disabled to get a dog, reading between the lines, that's how I took it.

In my head, I'm not disabled. But in the eyes of others, I would be in the 'most physically disabled' category for swimming at the Paralympics (S1), and I'm too disabled to get an assistance dog. It's humbling when I'm reminded of it.

Some things just come as a blow. It's a good thing that we've become pretty adept at rolling with the punches.

At the time, I really wanted the dog. I saw it providing me with a lot more independence – even basic things like picking something up or bringing something to me so I wouldn't need to rely on a carer, Diane or the kids would be a tremendous help. Since being knocked back, however, I think I've found ways to get some aspects of the independence that a dog might have provided me, even if there are still a couple of key ways in which a dog could help, such as if I fall over at home on my own.

We've since learned, after further communication with the organisation that manages assistance dog placements, that I might actually be eligible for a dog. In retrospect, the original assessment was probably correct. I possibly wasn't stable enough – things were changing for us at the time around the house – and maybe it was too soon. I still really want a dog, but whether we will persist with an assistance dog remains to be seen.

*

One of the questions at the back of my mind as I was preparing to go home was, *Can this happen to me again? Am I more susceptible to infection as a result?* This was something that had been worrying me from the time I woke, and which also seemed to interest the medical staff. People would often talk about how strong I was to survive this, but if I was strong, then how did I get so ill?

I had consulted an immunologist to see if there was a problem with my immune system. Diane and I were concerned that I might be susceptible to another infection or have a genetic predisposition that may put the kids at risk.

The immunologist had done a series of comprehensive tests, and when the results came in he contacted us to say that there was nothing Diane and I needed to worry about.

'We're asking the wrong question,' he told us. 'The question shouldn't be "Why was Matthew so badly affected by the bacteria?" Rather, the question should be, "What was it about Matthew's immune system that was so good that it saved him?"'

I had been fit when I became ill. I cycled to and from work occasionally, and we ate well. Aside from probably being a bit stressed with work, I looked after myself. I have never been a heavy drinker or a smoker. If I had been older, or had a different makeup, perhaps I would have fallen more quickly rather than battling on.

We will never know what caused the original infection, but it was good to know that looking to the future, I could be confident that there was nothing wrong with my immune system.

*

There were a few occasions while I was in rehab when I was able to be a part of the family routine during the week. Emily's first day of kindy in early 2013 was one of these.

She was not convinced she needed to go. We were. With all that had happened, she had become very attached to Diane. I wanted to make sure Diane had the opportunity to have some time to herself.

Normally I would go home on a Saturday night, but on this particular occasion I modified the plan so I went home on the Sunday to return on Monday morning. It would be the first time I would participate in the normal 'get ready for school' routine. Up to that point, I had only been at home for extended periods over the school holidays.

Taking Emily to kindy was a big moment. I wanted to be there for Diane and Emily. Diane was always emotional at important milestones such as when the children went to kindy or started school.

We woke up, had breakfast, and the boys got ready for school as they usually did. All was going well until it came time to get Emily ready. She was in floods of tears because Diane had suggested she wear a t-shirt and shorts, which was a departure from the princess dresses she had been wearing consistently for the past year.

The t-shirt Diane was trying to get Emily to put on had a rainbow on the front, but it was not a dress. Emily wanted a dress.

So Emily was crying because she didn't like the outfit Diane wanted her to wear and Diane, in turn, was in tears because her baby was growing up.

We needed to change direction.

'Diane, I think you need to go and get the boys ready for school. I'll talk to Emily,' I said. Diane agreed, and left me with Emily while she went to assist the boys.

It was time to negotiate with my three-year-old.

'Emily, what's the problem?'

'I want to wear a dress.' Soft sobs were still shaking her little body.

'Emily, you need to wear something to play in at kindy. How about you wear a skirt and a t-shirt?'

She looked at me, and considered the possibility.

'This skirt?' She ran off to get a ballerina skirt out of her wardrobe. It was pink, made of tulle, and very frilly.

'Yes, if you wear the t-shirt Mummy wants you to wear.' I was trying to stay firm.

'No. This one.' She pulled out the matching t-shirt to the skirt.

It was a compromise, in a sense. It wasn't a dress, but it was as close to a dress as you could get. It wasn't Diane's preferred t-shirt, but it was a t-shirt. We were making progress. We're talking about a child I hadn't seen, ever, in a pair of shorts once she could dress herself.

We managed to get ourselves to school and then kindy to deliver Emily for her first day, where Diane again burst into tears.

It was wonderful to be there for Emily's first day and to support my two girls.

And it had been great to be part of the normal weekday routine for once. As Diane dropped me back at rehab, I remember thinking, *Wow. That's right. It's really noisy in the mornings.* I missed that noise.

*

As time passed, the limitations of my leg prosthetics emerged – actually, they were painfully obvious, in a literal sense.

I couldn't sit down in my prosthetics because they would cut into me so badly that I would lose my breath. As I walked, the sockets would pull my skin, and on some occasions my testicles would be sucked into the socket and squeezed as I was walking. The pain was excruciating, as you might imagine.

At other times, the sockets would grab one piece of pubic hair, and pull tighter with each step. When the sockets weren't pulling on my testicles or pubic hair, they would be chafing me. The discomfort was relentless. At one end of my body I had phantom pain in my arms, and at the other, I had tenderness and chafing.

I had a conversation with David, my prosthetist, because there was the potential to change socket systems. I could have gone with silicon liners, and all sorts of weird and wonderful things. But trying the first system made me realise that my leg stumps were too short for socket-based prosthetics.

'I can't imagine, mechanically, how any socket system can effectively hold on to my leg.'

David, who is a very gentle soul, agreed.

Jacqui and I talked about whether what I was doing in rehab was as good as it gets.

I came to the conclusion that I had given my legs enough of a go to know that they weren't going to be functional outside hospital.

'I can't see how I am going to be able to balance well enough in these prosthetics to be able to use them functionally,' I said.

Jacqui agreed, too.

I decided I wasn't going to spend my time trying to perfect something that wasn't going to work. I made that call around four to six weeks after returning to hospital, and then started the discharge process.

I needed to question why I wanted legs. It's not actually because I want to walk (although I haven't given up hope yet). My key goals have always been to be able to feed myself and go to the toilet. It's quite simple – without legs, I can't get on a toilet, and therefore I'm not going to be independent in the daytime.

I know I will always need help to get ready in the morning (until they invent an automatic person-washing machine), but my aim is to be independent for the rest of the day. Having legs would help me transfer from one place to another, and there would obviously be lots of other benefits – if I could walk around a bit, my health would be better, and I might be able to get in and out of normal cars and get on a plane without a wheelchair. If I could, for a few hours, be independent of the wheelchair, then that would give me huge scope for doing things more easily.

I was reminded of why I wanted legs on one of my bus rides with

Ben and Luke. The bus was turning corners and my wheelchair was sliding around on the floor, as it is inclined to do. This time, I was feeling a bit shaken and was desperately trying to back the chair into a spot where it wouldn't slide around.

'It's okay. I've got you, Dad.'

It was Ben, at the age of nine, trying to hold my chair so it wouldn't slide into other passengers.

I decided that if, in addition to being able to go to the toilet on my own, I was able to get on to the bus and sit down, with no possibility of sliding and no need for help from others, then legs were still a goal worth pursuing.

And despite the realisation that the length of my stumps was working against me, I knew the door was not yet closed.

It was finally time to go home, and to start exploring other options.

CHAPTER 14

A NEW LIFE

I had left rehab before, and I would be returning the following week as a day patient, so the transition wasn't as hard as it had been from ICU, although we did have another farewell party. I had also been home before, a lot, so I wasn't expecting things to be too difficult, but it wasn't until that first night at home that I realised the enormity of what was ahead.

It was one of those moments of clarity – what had happened really hit me. This time, I wasn't going back to hospital. This was it – our new life, and we had to make the best of it.

The lift had not yet been installed, so we were all still living downstairs and I was unable to go upstairs. Diane and I were in Luke's room, while the boys and Emily camped together in whichever room they wanted.

In the mornings, carers would come, and I would hear everyone upstairs, where the kitchen and living room were, getting ready for the day.

Life was busy because school was in. I had rehab on Monday, Tuesday and Wednesday, and Diane would drop me there after the school run. Thursday was my medical appointment day, and if I didn't have any appointments, I would catch up on emails. On Fridays, Claire McMahon would come over and help me with the paperwork. I also spent time doing research on prosthetics and lobbying for change.

Nights were initially chaotic. The routine was exhausting, and it became clear pretty quickly that adding me to the equation was a big complication. The boys had an activity most days – piano lessons, tennis, swimming, tae kwon do, soccer/rugby training – and we would often be getting home after dark. Diane needed to feed me dinner – in hospital, Mum had done that while Di was at home with the kids, and this was before we got the Neater Eater – and often, she didn't really eat properly herself. We knew we needed to readjust.

We explained to the boys that we would drop a few activities, and that they could pick a couple to focus on. That streamlined things, and gave us a bit more downtime at home. It allowed us to settle into a routine.

Being home was good for me. I quickly came to realise that a lot of the limitations I felt, I placed on myself. The children's expectations of me hadn't changed.

I had been coaching Will's soccer team when I became ill. Upon coming home, it became apparent that I was expected to pick up where I left off.

'So, Dad, when are you going to be the soccer coach again?'

Will often appeared to completely forget that I didn't have arms and legs. It was lovely. I knew I could be the manager, but I didn't think it would be fair to return as coach – to coach six-year-olds, you need to demonstrate.

So I explained that I couldn't coach, but I would help manage the team. Will was happy with that, but then, Will's happy about most things. He's that sort of kid. I did later become the manager for Will and Ben's cricket team with another dad, Stuart Greaves.

And while I didn't think I was capable of playing games as I had previously, the boys had other ideas.

One afternoon, Luke walked to the back door with a football in his hands.

'I'm going to play some rugby, Dad.'

I was working on my emails, and turned to him.

'Okay.' I looked at Luke, and he looked back at me. Neither of us moved or spoke for a moment.

'Aren't you coming, Dad?'

I had one of my brain explosions. All the negative thoughts, all the barriers, all the reasons why I couldn't play rugby with him at that moment came out: *How am I going to catch a ball? How am I going to score? I might run him over with my chair.*

The way he looked at me convinced me that it wasn't going to be a good idea to turn him down.

'Okay, Luke. I'll see you downstairs.'

I went down in the lift and met him on the back lawn.

'So, Luke, how are we going to do this?'

Luke had a plan. I could carry the ball under my shirt, and score a try by dropping the ball over the line; I would kick off by holding the ball between my stump and my cheek and hitting it with my other stump.

We tried but I kept losing. After a short time, Luke stopped.

'Dad, just wait. I'll be back.' I wondered what he was going to do as he ran off, but a few moments later, he reappeared with the manual wheelchair that we keep at home, sat in it and faced me.

'Okay, now we can play.'

We then played for the next half-hour in the backyard, both of us in wheelchairs, having a great time.

I was blown away. Without saying anything, he had altered the rules, and made the playing field even so we could have a game of rugby. I was so proud of him.

At the end of the game, he touched me on the shoulder as we went upstairs.

'Thanks, Dad. That was fun.'

He just wanted to play rugby with his dad. He wasn't thinking about barriers – I was. In fact, Luke was thinking about how to make the game fair, and adapting it for my benefit. He was making things possible.

It was an important moment for me.

There were moments like this every day. Kids are grounding – their life is so immediate, and their ability to have fun and live in the present can be contagious if you let it.

While it was great to have fun with the kids, though, one of the many challenges of coming home was reasserting my role as a dad and someone who can look after people. The kids are really well behaved as a general rule, but we had sometimes acceded to them just to make life easier. Now I was home, we needed to establish a routine that was consistent and sustainable.

Luke, who had done such a great job while I was in hospital, in particular took a while to adjust to the fact that he didn't have to look after everyone any more.

Diane and I wanted him to get back a sense of being a kid. So, for example, we would pull him up if we heard him trying to tell his brothers what to do.

We would say, 'Luke, if you've got an issue, talk to us about it. We'll look after disciplining the other kids.' Luke has always had a really responsible streak, and he resisted a bit at first, mainly, I think, because he still wanted to help.

One afternoon, I took him aside and we had a conversation about it being okay for him to let go of that responsibility.

'Luke, it's okay. You don't have to look after me or the boys. You can be a kid.' He seemed to relax a bit after that.

While Luke and the boys were happy to have me home, there were times I suspect Emily would have happily sent me back to hospital.

Emily was two when I became ill, and Diane admits that it was often easier just to let her have her way than to have the fight that was possibly needed to manage her behaviour. We knew we hadn't been as consistent with her as we had with the boys. In her way, she ruled the house and when I came home, she challenged me on a number of occasions.

On one of these occasions, we were having words. Emily was being disrespectful, and I told her that if she did something again, I would put her in what we called the quiet corner.

'How, Daddy?'

It's amazing how even girls of her age have that head-wobble thing and the tone of a teenager. She had her hands on her little hips and her head tilted.

She knew she had me. I had no arms to pick her up with and place her down, which is what I might have done before my illness.

Hmmm. What do I do here?

Fortunately, I'm pretty stubborn, and I'm happy to wait.

The boys had learned this from a really early age. Time-outs could last a long time – I think our record was 42 minutes at one point.

We wouldn't send the kids to their rooms. They would just have to sit out, which meant they would sit beside the action and watch their siblings having fun.

We practised the same technique with Emily. Fortunately, Diane had the arms I didn't and she has the same approach as me. She doesn't ever yell, so it was just a case of being consistent, and of us both maintaining the line.

'Emily, you had better go to the quiet corner, as Daddy will out-last you,' Diane told her in her usual calm, happy voice.

Emily realised Diane and I were on the same page and decided to concede.

We were soon back to being friends. It didn't take very long.

*

Grade 2 classes at Will's school have regular show-and-tell sessions, where students take something to show their classmates or they talk about a topic that interests them. Will decided that he would like to take me as his show-and-tell subject. He's very proud of his family – in Grade 1 he had taken Emily, his baby sister, in to show the class.

Will had told his teacher that he would bring me in, but just in case it was going to cause problems, Diane emailed to check that it was appropriate for a dad to come in for show-and-tell. It was. We set a time, and Diane took me to the school.

I rolled into the classroom, and as soon as he saw me, Will came over and jumped on the wheelchair. He can be quite dramatic, and he rode into the room on the wheelchair in a somewhat king-like manner, introducing me as though he was an MC.

'This – is – MY – dad.'

There was potential for it all to be a bit silly, but Will's teacher Natalie was great, and quickly calmed the class down. I drove the wheelchair to the back of the class, and turned around to face every-one, feeling underprepared.

'Hey, Di, I think we maybe should have rehearsed something?' I whispered.

'Don't be silly. We'll be fine,' she whispered back.

Will was the director.

'My dad,' he told the room, 'will now walk across the floor and back again.' He looked at me.

Oh crap. I had my normal pants on. While I had a transfer board to get on and off the chair, I hadn't really been expecting to 'walk'. I knew that when I walked in these pants, they tended to fall off me as I moved forward. I hoped it wouldn't be an issue this time.

I lowered the wheelchair, and waddled off it on my bottom, down onto the floor.

From the moment I started to move, I could feel my shorts starting to slide off. *Great*, I thought. *The only thing these kids are going to remember is Will's dad flashing himself in front of the class.* I quickly had to change my gait and flick what was left of my legs really high in the air so the stumps would catch my pants and stop them falling off.

I was desperately trying to signal to Diane, but she had no idea what I was trying to say. We had always relied on signals when I had hands – two squeezes on the leg, for example, was our signal that either of us wanted to leave somewhere. Since my homecoming, we had tried to establish some new signals, like me winking when I needed to go to the toilet, but this was early in the piece, and Diane was still forgetting them. This time, when I was trying to catch her eye, she thought I needed encouragement.

'Go for it, honey. You're going really well!' She was getting into it, just like the kids.

Great.

The kids were so keen that they kept getting closer and closer, and Natalie had to keep rescuing me by reminding the kids to sit back and give me some room as I shuffled forward.

I managed to walk across the classroom without losing my pants, and fortunately Will had forgotten about the 'and back again' part by the time I turned around; he had decided he wanted me to put on my arms. He helped put the prosthetics on my stumps, and I demonstrated how they worked, and how I could pick up things.

I was trying to prompt Will to talk a bit more; because he was getting so excited, he wasn't saying much. So I opened the floor to questions. Almost every hand went up, including Will's – he was in the crowd of students, jumping up and down on the spot, seemingly desperate to ask a question. I almost laughed out loud.

'Not you, Will. You have to help me answer the questions!'

'Oh? Okay.' I asked him to pick out who to answer, and we started.

The questions were hilarious – they ranged from 'How do the arms work?' to 'Can you play basketball?' There were a lot of 'Can you do' questions until Natalie suggested they ask me to tell them what I could do.

I then talked about going to the beach, and lots of other things we had been doing. Will also got involved, telling them, 'My daddy can do this . . . my daddy can do that.'

There are a few things that stand out about that day. First, that Will was so proud of me. He was jumping out of his skin, and just so happy and impressed that I could do what I did. And second, the kids were so interested, and had such incredibly natural inquiring minds. I gave them straight answers – for example, when they asked me how I went to the toilet, I told them. It made me feel very comfortable to know that in a situation like that, it's okay to be as matter-of-fact and normal as possible.

I would never have expected to be the subject of Will's show-and-tell. I also know that if I had gone in to talk about my previous job, it would have been as boring as anything, and the kids wouldn't have cared less about what I said.

As it was, everybody in the class was hanging on every word. They felt comfortable, I felt comfortable, and so did Will.

It made me very proud that Will was proud of me – proud that I was different, and that I had all these cool things, like wheelchairs and different arms.

After show-and-tell, which had taken almost an hour, Diane and I waited around until the school assembly, which we wanted to attend because Luke was performing onstage. After we had positioned ourselves, the Grade 2 classes started coming in and had to file past us.

Every child from Will's class gave me a huge smile and a wave, calling out, 'Hi, Mr Ames' as they walked past. Diane said it was like sitting next to a rock star. It was so cute.

Will, unexpectedly, got an award that afternoon at assembly for bringing me in for show-and-tell.

The best part of the day was that I was there to see it.

*

The next time I encountered Will's class was when Diane and I volunteered to help at the school sports day.

I had never done any volunteering at the school, whereas Diane had been a regular over the years with each of the boys. I hadn't had the time, or rather, found the time. I had used the excuse that I was too busy to take the hour or so needed to attend the parent induction session, which was held at 8.40 a.m. Attending that session would have set me up to be able to help at school activities throughout the year.

To put this into context, before my illness, activities associated with kids and school were generally organised by Diane. We would usually talk about what was coming up at night, but if I was away, as was often the case, Diane would send me an Outlook meeting request so the occasion could be scheduled in my calendar. I always turned up to sports days, barbeques and concerts, but I found it hard to manage any more than basic attendance during the week.

My effort with the children was primarily at night, on weekends and on holidays because my work was so demanding.

So here I was, in my new life, with new opportunities and priorities.

I decided to go to the next parent helper induction session, where I learned about my responsibilities, and had to sign some forms with a pen in my mouth. I was then set up to help with the kids in the classrooms or any kind of school activity that I would be able to participate in.

Later in the term, forms were sent home asking parents to help with the school sports day. This time Diane and I volunteered.

We were assigned tunnel ball.

Oh great. Tunnel ball, no arms. I wondered how this was going to work. But I agreed, and when the day came, we met with Gwen Lea, who was also assigned to the event, set ourselves up and waited for the children.

Each group was supposed to visit us for around 20 minutes. The kids were grouped into four 'houses', and they would be lined up in these groups. I sat back a bit, not having seen how things worked before.

Pretty quickly, it was apparent that Diane and Gwen's softly softly approach wasn't too efficient. They were trying to demonstrate how to play, and the kids were losing interest and starting to muck around.

I don't have arms and legs, but I do have a big voice when I need it. I was also aware by this stage that the kids already knew how to play the games because they had been practising in sports class. I didn't want to seem like I was taking over, so I talked to Diane, who was happy for me to intervene.

'Right,' I started. Diane and Gwen's 'Oh sweetie, could you just move lines for us,' was replaced by my 'There are too many people in that line. One of you will have to move to the other line. You at the back, move over now, please.' And they did.

I was having fun. Clearly, demonstrating was out of the question, so I delegated that task to one of the lines. They knew what they were doing – they just needed some direction, and they did a great job.

At one point, Will's class arrived for their turn. As they had at the assembly, they all called out, 'Hi, Mr Ames,' and waved as they lined up.

I could do this. The job simply required someone who could start a race, call out who won, run another two races in a similar manner, get the next group, line them up and start again. I got a system going, but it was a team effort, with Diane and Gwen assisting physically if the kids needed help – if they ran into one another or the ball got away, for example.

It gave me confidence that even without limbs I could be useful. And have a lot of fun along the way.

*

Having established that I could be of use, I was then okay when Luke came home and asked me if I would volunteer to be a helper for an excursion to the Botanical Gardens with his class.

It was to be his last excursion with his class, as he was due to change schools at the end of the year, so I agreed after talking with Diane about how it might work.

There were initially too many volunteers, so my spot wasn't assured. To solve the problem, names were put into a hat. Those pulled out would go with the class. My name was on the list.

Diane was accompanying me everywhere as my carer, so she needed to come along too, and we drove because I couldn't get on the bus with my wheelchair. Once we were there, I suggested she go and have a coffee so she could enjoy some quiet time. I really wanted Diane to have some time to herself, and I also wanted to see if I could manage on my own. I would be able to call her if I needed to eat or go to the toilet.

She was reluctant – she says she likes hanging out with the other parents – but I think she sensed it was important to me to see if I could do it on my own, even for a short period.

I had five Year 4 boys to look after, including Luke, and they were so well behaved that everything went very smoothly. I got to watch worm digging and clay sculpting, among other things. It was an incredibly hot day, which is always problematic for me because I have problems cooling myself. I tend to opt for dehydration when we are out so I don't need to go to the toilet so much.

At one stage, the group needed to go into the hothouse. It was the only point during the day when I questioned what I was doing.

Oh no, I thought. *I am going to cook.*

I didn't have my cooling vest with me, but managed to get through the hothouse without becoming a liability to myself or anyone else. Thankfully.

At the end of the day, Luke turned to me as he was heading back to the car.

'Thanks, Dad.'

Diane was funny. She had spent the day drinking coffee, effectively hiding in the background and coming to help me when needed – we both knew how important she had been in getting me there. She was behind me, whispering, 'Hellooo – what about me?' But we knew what Luke meant.

I was asleep before dinner that night.

*

I tried hard to do what I could with the kids, but there were things that didn't make life easy. Like filling in forms, which is now one of my least favourite activities.

A few weeks after coming home, I took Ben to a workshop he had to attend for his confirmation. Diane dropped us off – we would only be an hour or so. Diane was nervous because it was the first occasion she had left me on my own out of the house, but I really wanted to do see if I could do it, and I felt safe. Diane would only be five minutes away, and our friend Nicole Webb had offered to make sure I was okay. She was there with her son Ruben, who was also being confirmed. So Diane left us, and Ben and I proceeded into the hall after saying hello to a few people.

As we walked in, I was handed an envelope full of forms that I placed under my stump.

Oh great, I thought. *Forms. What on earth am I going to do?*

Fortunately, Nicole, who was sitting next to me, had a solution. First, she got coffee for both of us.

Then she filled out two lots of forms. Ben and I were very grateful.

*

As the months went by, I pushed myself a little further towards being as independent as I could be. I started by looking after the kids at home on my own. Looking after the boys was fine, but Emily was too little for me at first. The boys are at an age when I can verbally instruct them if something goes wrong, but Emily isn't quite there yet.

I was putting Emily to bed one evening, and I asked her to turn off the light on her bedside table.

She managed to pull the light off the table. It landed on her and split open her forehead, and she was bleeding heavily.

To see that happen, to see Emily upset, and not be able to do anything was really difficult. I couldn't even give her a cuddle or come to her assistance because she was so distressed that she wasn't really listening to me.

On that occasion, Diane was at home, but I didn't know where she was in the house, so I had to scream at the top of my lungs to get her attention. I didn't know how badly hurt Emily was. She was screaming and I was screaming. It felt like chaos.

Diane and I talked about things later, after calm was restored. The safety of the kids is really the only thing I worry about when it comes to me being left alone with them. We both understand that.

We just need to make sure that there is some sort of procedure in place to cover those situations. It's getting easier as the kids get older. If it's just the boys, it's okay because if one is hurt, the others are old enough to follow directions, and to get things that might be needed. I can instruct them on what to do. We do plan to put the kids through a first aid course in time. If they know the correct techniques to use in an emergency, it will be a lot easier for them to help one another and me if necessary.

Just because things are difficult and uncomfortable doesn't mean they shouldn't be done. I wanted to be able to take the kids to school. It would make a difference to Diane, freeing up half an hour for her in the mornings, and the school was only a 10-minute walk or wheel from our house.

The first time I took the kids to school on my own it was pretty scary.

Getting to the school with the boys was fine, but on the way back, I needed to cross a main road and this required me to press a pedestrian crossing button. I wasn't sure if I would be able to press the button to trigger the light.

I could though, and I was very impressed with myself. It's amazing the small things that make big victories in this new life.

Being on my own is scary because I do think about what might go wrong – if I run out of battery, or the wheelchair gets stuck; whatever it is, I'm vulnerable. Funnily enough, I don't worry about my personal safety – that someone might steal something from me, or attack me. Perhaps I'm naïve, but I've found people to be so helpful that I don't think about that kind of stuff – it's more the failure of logistics that concerns me.

I knew if something went wrong on my school drop-off, there wasn't going to be too much I could do about it. At the time, I didn't have a mount for my phone, so it was in my backpack and I couldn't get it out. My phone is now mounted beside the wheelchair control, so this isn't such a concern any more, but that feeling of not being able to call for help was isolating.

Diane and I mapped out my route before I did my first trip with the kids.

'Di, if I'm not back in half an hour, come and look for me.'

Fortunately, she never had to come and rescue me.

It became important to me that Diane was able to go out, albeit for short periods of time, and leave me at home alone. I wanted Diane to reclaim as much of her life as she could while balancing her role as a carer for me. The extent that Diane could go out, unless we arranged for a carer to assist, was primarily governed by food and my bladder, and this is still the case. The first time she went out and left me at home by myself, we were both nervous. We made sure I was lying down so I couldn't fall, and that my phone was within voice range. We had by then learned to activate my phone through voice command, so as long as it was within range, I could call some-one for help.

Eventually, we got to the stage where Diane would take the kids to their various activities. First, she would just drop off the kids and come back to me, but later she felt comfortable enough to stay a bit longer for some activities, which I encouraged. We took turns – I would take the boys to tae kwon do and Diane would take them to swimming, where she could catch up with Gwen and Lisa, whose children were in the same swimming class.

These are all things I would never have given a second thought to before.

Diane says now that her main problem with our life before I got ill was that my dedication to my career meant my time with the fam-ily was limited. The time I did spend with family was focused on the kids. In our new life, Diane and I are almost literally joined at the hip.

I worry about whether I cramp Diane's style (she says not) – she can't go out for a whole day, and I've encroached on her friendship group. I'm a regular at coffee, shopping, school activities, sports afternoons and gatherings at the park. Diane assures me that she's

happy to have my company. That's a good thing because there's limited choice. It would be a worry if we didn't get on!

While I've always had good friends, I have really enjoyed becoming closer to the school group as a result of what's happened to me.
I knew David Webb, Anthony Lea, Scott Gosling, Stuart Harland
and Stuart Greaves before through Diane and her friends, but now
there's a closeness that's become really important to me.

The guys actually took me on my first 'boys' night out' after
I returned home. I wasn't someone who went out a lot with 'the
boys' before I got sick, but the opportunity presented itself when the
fathers involved with the cricket team were heading out one Friday
evening.

I was invited, and while Diane and I were nervous, I wanted to
give it a go.

David and Scott picked me up. I know they were also nervous
about the responsibility of looking after me, and David was under
instruction from his wife Nicole and from Diane to take good care
of me. It was the first time I had been on a social outing without
Diane since my operations.

Diane handed over the credit card, some cash, and the voucher
for the cab fare, and away we went.

The boys drew straws to determine who would take me to the
toilet, and the job went to Martin Wood. I had never met Martin
before, but the other cricket dads told me that he was a neurosurgeon; they figured that as he had a medical background he would be
familiar with such a task. We laughed – a neurosurgeon being given
toilet duties.

Fortunately, we didn't have to test that during the evening.

I am sure some of the guys with me were a bit overwhelmed,
but they didn't show it. We went to the Lord Stanley Hotel in
East Brisbane. The boys took it in turns to feed me my dinner and
make sure that my beer glass was never empty. I was feeling a bit

embarrassed about having to be fed, but everyone was so relaxed that I soon got over it.

Despite being nervous about the night, the relaxed nature of the people I was with and the way that they included me made it very easy to enjoy myself. We had pre-booked a taxi home, and when the time came, it seemed like we had only been there for a few minutes.

That's always a sign that you've had a great time.

CHAPTER 15

A YEAR ON

Once I was back at home, I didn't have many down days, although I did have sad moments. I see these as being different. Depression is a medical problem, and I think I'm very lucky that it doesn't appear to be in my makeup to get clinically depressed, although it has certainly affected people close to me and in my family. I also live with Diane. It's impossible to be sad for too long in her company.

I found sad moments were triggered by something – I might be bed-ridden for a while, recovering from yet another setback; I might be at a park, watching someone pick up or tickle the kids and hearing laughter that would otherwise have been generated by me. It's a sense of loss, and I make a conscious effort to manage the feeling.

The first thing I do is try to recognise that I'm sad. I don't let myself dwell on the feeling. I think there's a difference between acknowledging and dwelling on something, and for me it comes down to a choice about what I allow myself to spend time thinking about. When I feel myself taking a bit of a slide in the direction of being too sad, I do a few things to prevent the feeling setting in: I let myself acknowledge feelings of sadness and I talk to Diane about them; I focus on the positives; I set a goal, no matter how small it might be, in relation to something I want to do; and then I get busy.

I've always taken on too much and been too busy. At one stage in my life, I had a new baby, a renovation and a new job, all at the same time. I would start work on the house at six in the morning, do an hour's worth of renovations, get ready to go to work, go to work, come home, spend time with the kids, put them to bed, do more on the house and crash at around midnight – only to start all over again the next day.

So once I was at home, my challenge was to keep busy doing things that were possible.

I began trying to make myself useful. We set up the computer with a voice recognition program called Dragon Dictate so I could use voice commands to read and send emails more easily. I had blue-tooth with the new wheelchair, and I based myself at the computer, which we had located in the same open-plan area as the kitchen.

This was a new role for me. Our life had been arranged quite ste-reotypically before my illness – I did the lawn, house maintenance, coached the kids' sport, drove the kids around to various activi-ties; Diane organised the kids for school, did the cooking, cleaning, shopping, and generally organised our home life.

All of that changed. I now took care of email communication, booked appointments, paid bills, liaised with the school, managed our calendar, reminded Diane which child needed what for what day, and periodically did the grocery shopping online. It was a bit of a transition. Di is a 'do it now' person, whereas as an execu-tive, I was used to having someone highlight the important stuff for me. I'm not the best person for detail, and when I started doing the household admin, things were falling through the cracks.

My first question when I read an email is, 'Do I need to respond?' If someone hasn't asked me a direct question, then the email is for information. So I figure that I've received the information, which is great. I move on.

Diane, however, would always reply, even if it was just acknowledgement. That's time-consuming for me – I email at the pace of a snail on drugs, so what might have taken Diane an hour took me a whole day. But I found that if I didn't respond to emails, I would get a second email seeking confirmation or perhaps asking the question that was intended in the first place. I was still attending rehab as an outpatient three days a week at this stage, so time seemed to be compressed when I was home. We missed a few deadlines, parties and appointments until I got a system going, and even now it's a work in progress.

When Diane and I first had Luke, our plan was that whoever was earning the most money would keep working. That just happened to be me at the time, and then my career took off. I always had great respect for what Diane did – but now, I really understood.

I had no idea that just organising life could keep you so busy.

Fortunately we had help. In addition to Diane's aunt Claire coming over on Fridays, Diane's uncle Gary and our friend Peter Malyon would help out with odd jobs around the house. Our long-term friend and babysitter Cheryl Davies came every Wednesday for the day to help with housework and to look after Emily, and one of the cricket dads, Colin Grosvenor, had a lawn-mowing business and offered to do our yard regularly. At one stage, when the gardens needed a significant overhaul above what Colin could do in a couple of hours, we even had a team from the US Army who were in Australia with Exercise Talisman Saber do a backyard blitz.

The food roster continued, even after we sent an email thanking everyone and suggesting that people could stop cooking for us now that I was home. It's down to two days a week now, but there are still 60 families involved, and it's been an amazing help. I don't know how we would manage without it, even now.

My personal recovery was a medical effort. Our recovery as a family was a community effort.

I knew the value of community and of people pulling together. I had seen it and used it at work. But having it applied to us made me realise its true value. We wouldn't be where we are today without it, although it took us a while to teach Emily about where food really came from when we started cooking more dinners ourselves.

Food, she thought, came from an esky, not the kitchen.

*

One of the biggest challenges for me when it came to adjusting to life at home was being a bystander in my kids' lives on occasion. I would watch my brothers-in-law Aaron and Jason doing stuff like playing cricket, and jumping in the pool with all the kids at the yearly round of birthday parties, and would feel a tug – *I wish*. On some occasions it pulled harder than others, but it's not something I would dwell on if I could avoid it.

I found that I didn't experience that sense of exclusion if we were visiting somewhere that was well-designed for someone with a disability. Some places were designed so it was easy for me to be included when having a day out with my own family; other places made it almost impossible to participate as a member of a group and reinforced that sense of exclusion that resulted in a sense of sadness.

Australia Zoo, for example, has wide and generally flat bitumen paths around the entire property and fantastic disabled access to the stadium and restaurant areas. We visited on a Saturday while I was still in rehab. It was a test of sorts, to see how we would go on a family excursion. I fed camels carrots with my mouth – it amazed me how gentle they were – and the kids competed for rides on the wheelchair when they started to get weary towards the end of the day. It was the perfect venue for an outing with the extended family.

Suncorp Stadium in Brisbane is the same, having been designed with people with a disability in mind. Taking the kids to a game of soccer or rugby is an easy afternoon or evening for us. I can go and actually feel part of the family.

Other places are not so great.

While in Sydney to attend the 2013 Pride of Australia awards, for which I was a finalist, Diane and I took the kids to Luna Park for the day thanks to the generosity of Channel Seven, who had organised a family pass for us. I was keen to give the children some 'kid' time after they had been so good at sitting still and behaving themselves for a few hours at the awards ceremony. It's a hard thing to do when you're little.

From the moment we got there, however, it was clear that it was going to be a deflating kind of day for me. Every ride was a no-go zone for someone with no limbs; the only ride I could access was the ferris wheel, and my wheelchair was too heavy for it. When we tried to get into the Coney Island funhouse, I had to tap with my head on the window so an attendant would let me in through the exit door, because there was no other disabled access.

Diane and I have always been pretty hands-on parents. We would normally be on the rides, and if the kids were scared, I would get on the ride with them to help them overcome their fears. I could see that Diane was hanging back so that I wouldn't feel so alone.

But the kids were having a great time. Will again forgot that I have some physical limitations, and this probably helped me buck myself out of any melancholy. At one point, he wanted to race me down the Coney Island slide.

'Daddy, will you race me?' he asked.

We stood at the bottom of the slide, and I looked up at what seemed like hundreds of steps. The slides have been restored but still have that nostalgic feel to them – they were originally built in the first half of the twentieth century.

It's always so lovely that Will doesn't see any reason why I can't do something. But this was one of those times that I had to say no. Although I was happy to consider the possibility of my torso sliding down a slide that appeared to be around ten metres high, getting up the stairs would have taken me a day.

Will was disappointed momentarily, and went up without me.

We continued on and eventually, we found the dodgem cars. It was a quiet day, so the queues weren't too long. We lined up for a dodgem ride, and all the kids said they wanted a turn. It created a bit of a dilemma for us.

Luke and Ben were tall enough to get on the dodgems by themselves, but Will and Emily needed an adult. Diane decided to take Emily first, so that by the time Ben and Luke had finished, they could stay with me to help with Emily while she then took Will on the cars.

Diane explained her plan to Will.

'You wait for me, and I'll take Emily this time, and then I'll come back and take you next time.'

Will instantly burst into tears.

'Why can't Daddy come with me?'

I could not even contemplate getting into a dodgem car, let alone being able to control it, which was the whole purpose of having an adult with the child. I was trying to decide what to say when a man we had never met came up to me.

He must have seen Will crying and figured out what was going on.

'Do you want me to go on it with him?' he asked us.

My initial thought was, *No thanks. We'll be right*. But I stopped myself. The offer was genuine. I couldn't go on the dodgem cars. Will was upset. It would be a great help.

'Yes, actually, that would be great,' I said. 'Thank you.'

Will was happy to have a partner, so the two of them jumped into one car, Diane and Emily in another, and Ben and Luke in the third. They had a great time, although Will's partner (we never did find out his name) might have regretted his offer when he was slammed from one end of the ride platform to the other. Will's smile was priceless. When the cars stopped, the man jumped out, said thanks to Will, waved goodbye to us and went on his way. It was an amazing act of kindness. We'll probably never meet him again, but at that moment, he made Will's day.

It was really hard for me to watch at first, but the kids were obviously having such a good time that it was impossible not to get caught up in the moment.

Later, Luke decided he wanted to go on the pirate ship, which was a big ride, and Ben seemed to want to go too. We could tell he was a bit fearful, though.

Previously, I would have led by example, but I now have to focus on talking the kids through their fears. As a positive, I think they are really proud of themselves when they achieve something on their own. So I talked Ben through his worries. He got on the ride with Luke, and thoroughly enjoyed himself.

In logistical terms, the Luna Park outing was probably my idea of a nightmare, but in a life that's often about my needs, it was a day of great fun for the family generally. And the experience helped us add to the 'What questions do we really need to ask before we go somewhere?' list.

'Will I fit?' is a question that pops up a lot. It seems like it should be a simple question, with an answer based on physical reality, but I've learned that perception also plays a part.

When a priest had to move a coffin at a funeral so I could pass, some months after I came home, I was reminded of the difference between optimism and pragmatism. Diane's optimistic. I'm

pragmatic. That's a good combination generally. Sometimes, however, we get into a little bit of trouble.

Diane and I were attending the funeral of our friend Nicole
Webb's father. I hadn't been able to get into the main part of the
church where the service was taking place. By this stage, I was
used to this kind of thing happening, so it didn't worry me overly.
I parked myself in the pews at the side of the church and Diane sat
on an adjacent pew with some of our other friends. I couldn't see
the centre aisle, and neither of us was too sure if I was going to be
able to get down it in my wheelchair. We knew that at some point
we would need to venture forward to take communion. We couldn't
do a recce because people were still finding their seats, so we waited.

When the time came to take communion, I told Diane I wasn't
going to go ahead without assurance I would be able to make it
down the aisle.

'Okay. I'll go for a recon,' Di said and off she went.

She had a look around, and as she was entering the aisle, turned
back and nodded to let me know that it was going to be okay.
I started moving forward, not realising that Diane had reached the
front of the aisle, and was now trying to signal to me that it wasn't
going to work.

I had already ventured forward down the middle aisle, which was
quite narrow, but manageable, and joined the queue for communion.
There were people in front of and behind me and the line was progressing quickly, so I was driving the chair rather than just nudging it
forward. I was thinking, *Okay. Yep. This is going to be fine.*

Then suddenly everyone parted in front of me – some people
headed to the right, others to the left. They could obviously see
something I couldn't.

Then it became clear. Directly ahead of me, within arm's reach
if I had one, was the coffin. On the other side, the priest was giving
communion.

I stopped. I was blocked, as there was limited room on either side of my wheelchair. Diane had gone ahead and I was on my own. *Oh no.*

I couldn't work out how I was going to get around it. I thought, *Well, I'll see if I can squeeze through*, and I inched forward. I was looking down and back at my wheels. One was hitting the pew, and the other was very close to the coffin's wheelbase.

I had another of my brain explosions. *I'm not going to get through here.* I momentarily thought about persevering, but knew that if I did and it went wrong, the coffin would tip over. I couldn't go back.

The priest must have seen my panic because at this point he stopped what he was doing (giving communion), came forward and slid the coffin sideways so I could pass. It was such a relief.

On our way back from taking communion, I faced the same problem and I didn't want anyone to have to move the coffin again. I decided to return up a side aisle between the pews and the church wall. I was going well. I came to a spot where there was a column on one side and a large, somewhat timeworn organ against the church wall on the other. Other people had followed me. *Just my luck. I'm going to have to go back, past the coffin, while everyone's streaming behind me.* I paused and thought for a moment.

I decided to make a run for it between the column and the organ. It was tight, and I suspect I took paint off both. My tyres were screeching – there may have even been splinters flying. I made it through, though, and was finally able to return to the back pews where I had started.

It made for a great story, and we laughed about it later in the day. With legs, I might end up being a bit more boring.

*

I had been home for four months when the milestone of 'a year since I got sick' came around. It was a big moment for a number of reasons.

My sister Kate's article on me was published in *The Courier-Mail* on Saturday 15 June – a year since I had my first amputation. We woke the following morning to media knocking on the door before dawn, and to a huge outpouring of support and kind words from people we had never met. The following day was the school fete that Diane had attended on her own the year before. This time, I was able to attend.

Any concerns we may have had about talking publicly about what had happened to us quickly abated. The article had told the story in a way that meant I didn't have to keep explaining what had happened to everyone at the fete. People would just come up to say hello, ask how I was going and let Diane and me know they were thinking of us. It also became clear that others had similar stories to tell and found comfort in hearing about me.

I was amazed, and still am today, at just how many people actually die of sepsis and toxic shock. Hearing about other people's experiences reminded Diane and me that we're not the first, and unfortunately probably won't be the last, to be in the situation we're in. I might have the shortest limbs, but we heard many stories that were almost blow-by-blow replicas of our own. It made us sad – if it happens to so many people, how does it happen again and again?

But an anniversary is cause for reflection, and it was an opportunity for us to take stock of where we were at, emotionally and physically. I was about to undergo more surgery on my limbs and was still attending rehab three days a week. Life was good, if still a bit chaotic. All the usual milestones, such as kids' birthdays, anniversaries and Christmas, had passed.

One of the bigger milestones was my fortieth birthday. It had been a quiet affair, at my request, down at Kate and Jason's property south of Brisbane. They had relocated from Rockhampton, bringing with them an array of animals including horses, dogs and poultry, which gave our kids a new experience. They had a dam, a cubbyhouse, bush and the animals and bugs that go with it, a pool and loads of room to run around.

It was the first time in almost two decades that Mum and Dad, Kate, Rachel and I had lived in the same place. It was fantastic to have everyone close by.

The kids were happy and seemed to be going well. I could see Diane's optimism and positive approach to life rubbing off on them, and I loved that. They were also benefiting from the kindness of strangers – they got to meet rugby league idols Darren Lockyer, Shane Webcke and Allan Langer. They also met the Paralympians, the Wallabies and the Australian cricket team after the first test. On the latter occasion, Michael Clarke emptied his personal backpack and gave it to the boys to share (which, amazingly, they do). They met community heroes like Matt Golinski and got to be part of a live telecast when we travelled to Sydney for the Pride of Australia finals. They saw me being acknowledged simply for being brave, and listened to me talk to schoolkids about being positive.

Diane and I reminded the kids if it came up that none of this would have been possible in our old life. Well, it may have been possible, but it would have been highly unlikely. I can't imagine that the Australian cricket team would have sent me a personal video message on my phone after they won the Ashes, which they did. I was excited and humbled when I received the message, but I'm always pretty even-keeled in my reactions to things like this. Diane, on the other hand, was so excited that Luke had to ask her to calm down.

We kept an eye on the kids to see how they were going. We were conscious not to overreact, but were prepared to call for help if we thought they needed it. We noticed, for example, that Emily became obsessed with my arms and legs once it really dawned on her that I didn't have any. She wasn't the only one. Joshua, Kate's son, had a disabled donkey that he carted around in a toy golf cart for a month or so, and all the kids wrote about me in their school journals.

But even for kids, it's relative.

Emily and Lincoln, Rachel and Aaron's youngest son, were playing over at Mum and Dad's house one Friday morning. It was a regular date for them, and at the time they were both three. (Lincoln and Emily were born within four months of one another and share a special connection. They both had a sebaceous cyst removed from the same place on their chests when they were babies, and both have a birthmark in the same place above their upper lip.)

On the day in question, Mum overheard them having a game of one-upmanship.

'Lincoln.' Emily tapped Lincoln on the shoulder.

'What, Emily?'

'My daddy used to have arms and legs, but now he has none.'

Lincoln looked at her and shrugged. 'I know.'

There was a moment's silence. Then:

'Hey, Emily.'

'What?'

'My daddy used to have hair, and now he has none.' (Aaron doesn't have a lot of hair – he wears it closely shaved, which is why he did such a good job on me when he gave me a haircut.)

Emily had no comeback. They found something else to play with.

All the kids were making sense of things in their own way. The older kids would ask me questions, but the younger ones would incorporate what had happened to me in their play. Emily would hold pens and brushes in her mouth to draw and paint; one of the kids would bite the arms and legs off a gingerbread man, and declare that it looked like me; they would wheel one another around the backyard in makeshift wheelchairs, or kneel when walking, as though they didn't have knees or feet. All of this was usually accompanied by squeals of laughter that would in turn make whichever adult was around at the time laugh as well.

Our kids had been assessed formally over the course of the year. On those occasions, they would be taken for a play and a talk with a social worker or counsellor, and asked to draw pictures associated with ideas and concepts. It was interesting to see the progress in their drawings.

In ICU the pictures had been of machines, and me lying in bed.

At a later assessment, the kids were asked to draw their family.

Luke might have been trying to be politically correct when he drew all six of us with only our heads showing.

Ben revealed his view of the family when he drew the two of us together, with no one else in the picture. I had no arms and legs – he was the only child to make reference to it in their drawings.

Will drew the whole family, head to toe. I was still anatomically intact – all my arms and legs were present.

At the one-year anniversary point, I wanted to see how they were all going, so I found moments to ask each of them. The question was something like 'So how have you coped? How are you going?' Ben and Luke knew what I was referring to instantly, and their responses were to the effect of 'Good, Dad. Thanks.'

When I asked Will the same question, he looked at me blankly, as if to say, *What do you mean? What's the problem?*

His response was just so typical of Will.

'Good, Dad. But I didn't get all the Pokemon cards I wanted for Christmas.'

*

I now travel with Diane, straws, a ramp, sometimes a cooling vest (depending on the weather), a voice-activated mobile phone and a plan. Leaving the house with just car keys and a wallet is a distant memory.

It would be easy to just stay at home, or opt for being antisocial. As an able-bodied person, it never occurred to me how much effort it took for people with a disability to simply get out of the house. I know now that some of the people I pass in the street have, like me, been getting ready for a few hours just to step outside their front door.

But I like to get outside, and I like being with people. I have already spent too many hours of this life lying on my back staring at a ceiling. Being stuck inside is not my preference.

I have never been very good at initiating contact with people, although I'm very happy to catch up and always love to talk if someone calls. It's something I've been conscious of my entire life. I was humbled and very glad, therefore, that so many people made an effort to socialise with me after I came home. People would drop in to say hi, invite us out to dinner as a family, or meet us somewhere so the kids could play or families could spread out.

I don't know why I was surprised that people would still want to know me, but I was a little. With all of our close friends, it felt as if things just went back to normal once I was out of rehab.

In some cases, though, we made a few adjustments. John and Belinda Bain are longstanding friends of ours. We have been in awe of them for many years, as they have five children, including a set of triplets, and retain a great sense of humour about the chaos of life with small children. The kids are similar ages to our kids, so the nine of them have a great time together. John, Belinda and all of their kids had visited me while I was in rehab, and I greatly valued their friendship and efforts to maintain contact with me and the family.

Prior to my illness, we would go camping at Belinda's family property in Tenterfield every year over Easter. I returned home permanently just before the Easter break but had decided that camping was in the too-hard basket. John and Belinda had other ideas. Tenterfield was a bit ambitious, but they invited us to their place for the weekend so we could all go camping.

The plan was for Diane and me to stay in their room, while everyone else, including our kids, camped in the backyard. It sounded doable, so we gave it a try. The tents came out, the kids ran around like crazy playing games, and the four adults kicked back and relaxed. We could have been anywhere. It was another example of our friends going above and beyond to help us get through the changes that had happened in our lives. It felt normal, and great to be around friends.

I had occasionally turned my attention to work over the course of the year, but it was impossible because of my rehabilitation commitments, so I put those thoughts aside. Everyone I worked with understood the situation. I knew I had been replaced instantly – no one's indispensable, and as a manager I was acutely aware that ultimately, things will go on without you. It's hard, though, to express in words how much my colleagues did for me and how supportive they were from the moment I disappeared from their world so unexpectedly.

My workmates had visited me in rehab, helped dig the lift pit and were active in kicking off the fundraising effort that became important later in my journey. Three of my closest colleagues, Graeme Bartrim, Rob Ully and Rosahlena Robinson, had been regular visitors while I was in rehab, and once I got home, I asked them to meet me in my old haunt, Park Road, in the inner north-west suburb of Milton.

I had frequented the busy cafe strip when I was working, so it felt a little strange to be going back in different circumstances. On this particular day, we met up for lunch, and we didn't really talk about work at all. Our conversations were about people – Graeme's kids, the imminent birth of Rob's baby, Rosahlena's family and impending move to Chile, and how my kids were going. To this day, they contact me regularly and I feel really fortunate that they make the effort.

I don't know yet if I'll go back to what I was doing – a lot of those sorts of questions remain unanswered for the time being. But I do know that the relationships I have formed as a result of my career are valuable and worthwhile, and the support I have received from the industry in general has been incredible. The initial fund-raising by my colleagues at Origin helped me to see beyond what was in front of me in terms of rehabilitation.

It gave me the impetus to look ahead and think about possibility rather than reality.

CHAPTER 16

LOOKING AHEAD

One of my earliest memories is of learning to ride my bike in North Queensland, trying to negotiate the puddles in my training wheels. I have always had a fascination with bikes, and I still do.

I remember being particularly fascinated by bikes that had been placed upside down on their handlebars. On one occasion in the early 1980s, while living in our Victoria Plantation mill house just outside Ingham, my sisters and I decided to turn a bike upside down, and mush up this really pretty-looking plant by pushing it through the mudguard.

We spent quite a while under the house – one person pulling the branches off the plants, one feeding the shrubbery through the mudguard, and one swinging the pedals around. All of us waiting, with excitement, to see what came out the other side of the mudguard.

The plants, we later discovered, were chilli bushes. The prettiness came from the colours of the chillies hanging by the hundreds on the branches.

Perhaps I'm suffering from trauma, because I actually don't remember the after-effects. My sisters can recall seeing me sitting in a bath full of milk while my mother contemplated taking me to hospital. My eyes were swollen almost shut and my skin blistered red. I must have been around seven or eight. I just remember how much fun it was.

I always get the urge to turn bikes upside down, even now.

I used to ride a bike before I became ill, but as a commuter, not a recreational cyclist. My bike, fitted with a child seat, still hangs on the wall in our garage.

It didn't really occur to me that I could ride a bike again after my operation until Diane and I visited a bike shop in Carina. I wanted to buy new handlebar grips for my wheelchair because the kids hang off the back and they needed something to hold on to. I asked the guy in the shop about handlebar grips, and then out of the blue, I said, 'So, I was thinking about buying a bike next year.'

I was looking around the shop, not directly at him as I explained that we had bought bikes for the kids there last year and had been really happy with the service. I kept talking, and eventually looked up. The shop assistant's face was quite contorted, and it dawned on me that he probably had no idea how I could possibly ride a bike.

I wasn't wearing any prosthetics, and was simply sitting in my wheelchair. I could see why he was confused. I stopped and clarified that I was going to get prosthetic arms and legs in the future that would possibly allow me to ride a bike, at which point he went, 'Ahhh.'

I could see the relief on his face. He had obviously wanted to ask, 'How in the world are you going to ride a bike?', but not known how.

As it turned out, he was building a recumbent bike for a client with cerebral palsy. He took Diane and the kids downstairs to have a look at it, and gave us some really good advice about where we could buy bikes online. If we bought a bike, he would then be able to put it together for us.

So it became a serious conversation. I'm pretty certain that at some stage, it will happen. I plan to give it a go. I have an idea of how I could possibly cycle, and I've worked out how I can steer with one arm, but I haven't yet figured out how I can brake. It depends on what my prosthetics can do.

I may not be able to walk, but I should be able to ride.

*

By the time I was an outpatient in rehab, I was managing my own recovery, in a sense. I wasn't present for the specialists' weekly case conference, but generally, I was able to discuss issues with each individual specialist. They would then work with one another to achieve the particular outcome I was seeking.

I already knew a little about osseointegration. My prosthetist, David Sweet, had mentioned it as a possible option when he was casting my legs because we had talked about the difficulties with the arms. At that stage, though, there was still a lot of hope for the legs, so while I did some research, I was happy to persevere with trying socket-based prostheses.

Osseointegration is a technique whereby titanium is grafted to bone. The bone integrates with the metal implant, to which a bolt (or abutment) is attached. The bolt pokes through the skin and acts as an extension of the bone. Prosthetics can then be attached to the bolt. The procedure is typically performed on above-knee or above-elbow amputees. It had never before been done on someone with four limbs missing.

I spoke with Saul and his deputy registrar, Dr Claire Panagoda, seeking their views. They acknowledged that they didn't know much about it, but were fantastic about helping me find more information on the subject. Claire found some papers on the OPRA (Osseointegrated Prostheses for the Rehabilitation of Amputees) system, which was being used by a team at The Alfred Hospital in

Melbourne. I had also found quite a lot on the ILP (Integral Leg Prosthesis) system used by the Osseointegration Group of Australia, based in Sydney. OPRA and ILP are the two main osseointegration systems that are applied in Australia. Both looked promising.

Saul held a training conference at the Princess Alexandra Hospital to discuss my situation. At the conference, Diane and I met Debra Berg, manager of the Queensland Artificial Limb Service, which coordinates the distribution of funding for prosthetics. Debra had been responsible for signing off on my interim prosthetics, and had been liaising with David since late 2012. She had been following my case, and the following week, when she was conducting training at the Mater Hospital, she also gave us a brochure on osseointegration. So we were receiving a lot of information about this option, and a lot of support in investigating it.

I knew I wasn't going to be able to use any form of socket-based prosthetics on my legs because they were just too short. If I couldn't attach prosthetics to my limbs, then I couldn't get prosthetics. That meant I would be wheelchair dependent, and independent toileting would be impossible. Diane and I felt it was important to investigate the options.

We spent the best part of three months in the first half of 2013 investigating the two osseointegration systems available in Australia. We met with Dr Al Muderis and his team in Sydney who work with the ILP system, and Steven Gray and his team in Melbourne who work with the OPRA system. We had the chance to speak to other patients, and to discuss my specific circumstances with surgical and rehabilitation teams. It became clear that both systems offered significant advantages over socket-based prosthetics, but both carried risks. The systems differed slightly, and in my opinion the OPRA system provided a superior soft-tissue solution with reduced infection risk.

I was still confused about the risks regarding alternative bone attachments. We sought advice from Dr Tim McMeniman, one of the orthopaedic surgeons who operated on me during my amputations. Tim referred us on to Dr Scott Sommerville, the orthopaedic surgeon who had trained him.

The biggest concern for me was the potential risk of infection, which might result in further amputation of what stumps I had left. But Scott put things into perspective for me. He reminded me that I didn't have any legs anyway, and that I wasn't going to be able to walk with them as they are. So while there were risks to both procedures, the worst-case scenario was that I would have no legs and wouldn't be able to walk. Which is where I am now. No better, but probably no worse.

The decision was a lot easier when it was put to me as clearly as that. We chose the OPRA system because we felt it was better suited to my circumstances, and advised Saul and Claire, who were in agreement and happy to support me. I was very grateful that everyone had been so forthcoming and helpful – it was a big decision, and in the end one that Diane and I felt comfortable with.

In my mind, the real journey to independence was now only just beginning.

*

It's one thing to have an idea of what you need and want. It's another thing to be able to fund it.

The realisation that I would need close to $3 million (in today's money) to pay for prosthetics over my lifetime was sobering and confronting, especially as it became evident that funding to cover the personal cost of my recovery was going to be limited. This is because my amputations are the result of an infectious disease as opposed to a car or workplace accident, in which case rehabilitation costs would be covered by insurance.

It had also become apparent that very basic prosthetics wouldn't be suitable because of the short length of all four of my stumps.

I needed joints to be able to function independently, for even short periods of time.

The National Disability Insurance Scheme was often mentioned to me as a possible source of assistance, but even now at the time of writing, there is no promise of what's to come for someone like me, and no guarantees for future funding of my case. In Queensland, the NDIS won't be enacted until 2016 to 2019, which is still at least two years away.

Diane and I were very conscious that we were lucky. We had both worked hard for a decade before having children and had private health insurance. My rehabilitation in a private unit had been largely funded by BUPA. I also receive a percentage of my income from my employer's insurance scheme, but this ceases if I die. So we were okay for living expenses.

We know this was because we had worked hard and made good decisions, but we also know that had it been the other way around – if this had happened to Diane – we would have been faced with selling our house, and possibly bankruptcy, just to survive because we had not foreseen the scale of what can go wrong. Even though I did receive a Total and Permanent Disability payout, it was obvious quite early on that we would have difficulty meeting my long-term future needs in terms of prosthetics and associated costs.

The initial cost of setting ourselves up, for example, was enormous.

The wheelchair cost $26000, the new lift $40000, an electric bed $8700, the modification of our existing car over $33000 – the list went on: commodes, modifying the house, shower, ramp, software for the computer. It seemed endless. We were grateful for assistance from various government schemes, but this was fairly minimal, in the order of $15000.

And that's not including prosthetics. I have been advised that a full set of limbs costs around $500000, the arms being the most expensive component at around $150 000 each. The limbs have a lifetime of five to seven years, if I'm lucky, before the cost of servicing them becomes too high and they have to be replaced.

I am currently 41. So by the age of 70, I will need six sets, costing around $3 million in today's money. Assuming I'll be wheelchair bound after that, I will still want arms and these are the most expensive prostheses – at today's prices, a pair of myoelectric arms would set me back $300 000. They are expensive because they use motors to move the elbow, wrist and hand, and include complex electronics to control the limbs. Sensors pick up muscle movement in what remains of my bicep and tricep muscles to control the motors that drive the arms. They hold the key to potential independence for me.

My biggest fear through all of this was using everything we have on my prosthetics and leaving Diane in a position where if anything happens to me, she loses the house and has difficulty supporting the kids. I know this happens to other people, usually through no fault of their own. Funding the prosthetics was something we needed to consider as additional to managing our daily living costs. We couldn't save enough on what we now get to support the expense of the prosthetics.

They say never work with friends or family, and up until the point of my illness, I never had. But I happen to be very fortunate in my two older sisters, one of whom, Rachel, has spent 20 years in accounting and finance, and the other, Kate, who has worked for the same amount of time in communication and media. Rachel's the General Manager, Corporate Services of AgForce, and Kate is a senior lecturer in communication at Central Queensland University.

While I was in a coma, they started to put their skills to use. Rachel helped Diane negotiate the mountain of paperwork associated with sudden onset disability, and Kate set up a blog for family and close friends, to help the family get through and make it easy to inform people about what was happening. The blog was private and people had to request access.

It was clear that people wanted to help. Rachel was working with our friends Dan Alexander, Martyn Robotham and Gayle Schabe to establish a foundation through which funds could be raised for my prosthetics, as we were okay for living costs, and my colleagues at Origin had assisted with funds for setting up the house. Members of communities with which we had become involved were also looking to raise funds on my behalf and we were extremely appreciative of the support. So fundraising efforts were gaining momentum.

As the realisation dawned that prosthetics were a possibility and we started to move down the road towards osseointegration and myoelectric prosthetics, I wondered what the impact would be on my personal relationships – with the kids and Diane. Would the prosthetics be a physical barrier between us? Could the bolts be painful for others? Would I hurt Diane while we slept? Would I still be able to cuddle the kids? My dad is a hugger, and I've always been the same with my kids.

It was going to be another adjustment, and I was thinking ahead.

I had spent a lot of time after coming home trying to work out different ways to connect with the boys, and physical contact had proved to be important for Ben. I needed to figure out how to achieve this, because Diane and I knew that of all the boys, he had taken what had happened to me to heart.

Ben has always been the least outwardly expressive of the boys; he's very like me in that respect. I know that behind a very quiet exterior there's a lot going on. Ben had become quite withdrawn while I was in hospital, and we could see that he was struggling to cope – he spent a lot of time drawing, and while sometimes it didn't appear that he was taking things in, his pictures showed us that he was. While I was in hospital, all his drawings had included the machines to which I was attached, and one of his letters to me had read, 'See you in heaven, Dad, maybe.'

Everyone would tell me how withdrawn Ben was, but he was

never like that around me, and he noticeably perked up when I got home. He was more animated, engaged, and seemed much happier generally. He was showing a passion for tae kwon do, which he had taken up after dropping cricket and soccer while I was ill – before that, I had coached his cricket team.

Ben and I developed a wrestling game that we played on a blue exercise mat on the floor at home. The aim of the game was to see if Ben could push me over while we were wrestling. It was great for developing my core strength, and for Ben it was a different way to play with his dad.

The results were split evenly. He would win half of the time and I would win the other half.

It was great fun. I couldn't help worrying about what would happen if my leg stumps had metal protruding from them, though. If that was the case, I wouldn't be able to play games like this without destroying the room, and hurting someone.

While we didn't know what the future held, it was important that we didn't go backwards.

CHAPTER 17

NEW LIMBS

I have always been intrigued by how things work. It's a trait I've inherited or learned from Dad. I was his assistant growing up, and I've had a lot of practice thinking about how to put things together.

I have memories from when we lived in Sydney of holding tools and pieces of gyprock, and of Kate, Rachel and myself dressed in garbage bags with holes at the seams for our arms, helping Dad paint a new rumpus room he had built onto the back of our house.

By the time I was at high school, I was helping Dad renovate the old Queenslander he and Mum had bought when we moved to Brisbane. We were building a major extension, which involved lifting floors, altering rooflines and building a back deck. Dad and I would hang from the roof, working hard, occasionally looking into the lounge room where we could see the girls sitting around drinking coffee with friends who might have dropped in.

I had been free labour until, one afternoon, I mentioned to Dad that I thought it was unfair that my sisters didn't have to help – although I knew they had been part of Dad's construction crew when they were younger and less sociable. Dad agreed, and from that point I earned pocket money for the hours I helped him with the house. I was only 13 or so at the time, but a few years later, I had saved up some money.

I needed a car. I had been driving Kate's Mazda 1500 while she was overseas for a few years, but she had returned and swiftly repossessed it.

Rachel had a 1960 Hillman Minx that she wanted to sell. It had a column shift, white leather seats and was ember red with white wings. It was part of the family, and we called it Harriet (the Chariot). It had a rumble in the engine that meant you could hear it coming from blocks away, and I was interested. It wasn't worth much to anyone else, and was costing Rachel a fortune, so for $50 she agreed it could be mine.

The engine was having problems, so I decided to buy a manual, strip the engine and rebuild it. People asked me why, but my response was, 'Why not?'

I took it apart under our house, labelled each piece, and laid them all out on the concrete floor in the garage area. I recognise now how patient my parents must have been to give up the entire area where the cars normally parked for the duration of my project.

Piece by piece, I put the engine back together. I thought I had followed the instructions perfectly, but at the very end, I had a few extra nuts and bolts left over. It didn't surprise me then that it *almost* worked when I started it up. I didn't want to have to take the car apart again, so I called the RACQ for help, telling them my car wouldn't start.

The RACQ mechanic turned up. He took one look at the car, and one look at me.

'You've been rebuilding the engine, haven't you?' He looked me in the eye. I thought for a moment about my response, but decided to confess.

'Yep. I couldn't quite work out how to put the distributor back in properly again.'

The mechanic paused, and looked at the car.

'We're not supposed to do this, but I haven't seen one of these for ages.'

He spent around three hours helping me with the final touches of the rebuild and we got the car going. It worked well.

So the theme of renovation and rebuilding stuff has been with me for most of my life. That's where the idea for the name of the blog that Kate maintains with Rachel – Renovating Matthew – came from.

I guess I just never envisaged a day when bolts and nuts would stick out of my arms and legs. Fortunately, there are people as experienced as that RACQ mechanic looking after me.

*

Having made a decision about osseointegration, I began what seemed like an endless series of surgeries. Meanwhile, an army of people were raising funds to assist with purchasing prosthetics.

What began with support from work colleagues grew into something much bigger, supported by Rachel, who by this stage had registered the Renovating Matthew Foundation to manage funds raised for the specific purpose of purchasing prosthetics and associated care. Rachel was busy – people from everywhere who had heard my story were keen to do something on my behalf, and we had some amazing people do amazing things. John McGilvray rode his bike 500 kilometres from Junee to Bathurst, and Emma Franks threw her frisbee across Canada, while others donated money in lieu of Christmas and birthday presents.

Four major Renovating Matthew fundraisers were held in 2013. The first was a film night in February organised by my colleagues from Origin and URS Corporation. The movie was *Lincoln*, and I have a distinct memory of the collective gasp from the crowd in the scene where a young soldier pushes a wheelbarrow full of human arms and legs to a pile before dumping them. I laughed, for no other reason than that it was exactly what I had been telling the kids had happened to my limbs.

It was an emotional night for me – I was overwhelmed that so many people had turned up (the event was sold out). I remember rolling out of the lift into the foyer of the cinema at The Barracks in Brisbane and seeing this sea of people in front of me, and choking up. It was fantastic to catch up with so many of my former work-mates, friends and family in one go.

The next fundraiser was a charity gala held by the Holland Park Hawks soccer club later in the year after I had returned home. Obviously, Diane came with me to these events, and on this occasion we had a great night meeting up with members of our local community. Shortly afterwards, we attended a soccer game, where we were presented with a cheque for the funds that had been raised. Will was so excited – it was his soccer club, and he got to lead the men's team out onto the pitch.

Diane and I were particularly looking forward to the masquerade gala ball in late August, which had been organised by members of the school community. This was, outside my family, probably our most important immediate support network and the one that had shared our journey the most closely. Diane said she was looking forward to this night more than any other besides our wedding night. She and my sister Rachel had been involved with the organising committee, and every week I would get an excited update on how everything was going.

Unfortunately for Diane, a gastroenteritis bug that had been sweeping through the kids caught up with her on the day. Diane's hairdresser Katie Munro came to the house to do Diane's hair as a gift, and after Katie had finished, Diane said she was feeling faint. She shrugged it off and hoped it was just because she was tired.

As soon as we got to the school, it was clear that Diane wasn't going to make it too far into the night. She didn't eat or drink much, and said she was feeling queasy. She managed to hold on through my speech, but as soon as it was finished, she had to run outside and vomit in a garden bed. Diane knew she couldn't make it through the evening but she insisted I stay.

Lots of people volunteered to look after me, so Diane drove home after taking me to the toilet. While I get lots of lovely offers of help with toileting from friends who are nurses or who have a carer's background, it's something I try to resist unless I really have no choice. I suppose it's about dignity and independence for me. I'm okay with Diane or a carer, but haven't yet become comfortable with the idea of anyone else being part of that routine.

The fact that I could be at the ball on my own and feel safe and happy was a reminder of the value of community. I was looked after so well and had a fantastic time. I stopped drinking so I wouldn't fill my bladder, and spent a lot of time talking with people and dancing with a whole heap of feet, including those belonging to Gwen, Nicole and Lisa. At one point I asked Lisa's husband, Stuart Harland, to put me back into the chair. I thought he would get someone to help, but he said, 'Okay,' and instantly grabbed me in a bear hug and hoisted me from the floor into the chair.

A crowd of people walked me home at the end of the night. I was probably the most sober in a rowdy group – Diane says she could hear us coming from the corner of our street. I was setting a cracking pace by the end of the trip, as I was desperate to go to the toilet. We must have been a sight – me leading in a wheelchair travelling at maximum speed followed by a group of people in varying states of inebriation, some jogging in bare feet to keep pace with me, in the early hours of the morning.

Two weeks later, we lined up for the Renovating Matthew Ball, which was organised by friends and colleagues from my industry with the support of my sister Rachel. The 500 tickets available sold so quickly that some of my close friends actually missed out. Diane and I stayed the night at the hotel where the ball was being held. I remember looking at Diane all dressed up, while she was doing my tie, and thinking, *I am blown away that you love me so much and have been by my side through all of this.* My love for her and what she has done at times completely overwhelms me.

We were again surprised that so many people would want to attend, and I was excited to meet up with people who had travelled from around the country to share the night. Some of Kate's friends came from Rockhampton, while family friends from Sydney and Fiji made surprise appearances. There were familiar faces, and faces of people we had never met. Diane and I danced the night away. It felt like we were back to our old selves for a moment when we were among the last to leave.

The work put in by the organising committees of all the events was simply amazing. Thanks to their efforts, Diane and I had the opportunity to meet a lot of people who had been supporting us in the background, and as the guest speaker at some of the events, I had the opportunity to tell my story to people I didn't know. I found that nerve-racking at first – *Why would people want to hear what I have to say?*

But I came to realise that many people thought about what happened to me in the context of their own lives, asking themselves, *What would I have done? Would I have wanted to be saved?*

I knew I was happy to be here. There was no doubt in my mind that everything was great, but it interested me to hear about other people's reactions, even if I didn't spend time worrying about what they thought.

We knew that while lots of people had prayed for me to live, some had not. Some of our friends have told us that, and that's fine. Diane and I have always tried not to judge others for what they think or do. It was actually great that they were so honest with us – it's been refreshing to have honest conversations about faith, life and death. Our friend David Webb said his original prayer was for me not to live, but he pretty soon changed it to 'Mate, if you want to live, I pray that you do get through this.'

People were also open with us about being torn as to whether they would want to be saved if the same thing happened to them. When people first started to discuss this with us, it came as a shock to Diane that anyone would even question the decision to save me. In her mind, there was never any other option. She says it wasn't until a fair way down the track that she realised that some people would not have made the same decision. Apparently the word at the school was that 50 per cent of people would save their partners, which was really interesting to us. But everyone's different, and it was great to know what people were thinking.

People had to deal with the news in their own way, and I realise how out there it must have been, hearing about this man who had his limbs amputated to save his life. For many of my friends, I was fine the last time they saw me and then I literally disappeared and returned in a different form months later.

So while I'm not worried about what other people think, I was aware that sharing my story might help people realise that for Diane and the rest of my family, there was never going to be any other decision. I knew that the weight of the decision had worried Diane until she saw how I accepted it. There was just no way I would have wanted to die. The thought that my family might have given up on me and that I might not have been given the chance to live is just completely inconceivable to me, and speaking at the fundraising events was an opportunity to show people that actually, life is good. They might end up thinking, *Oh, right. Now I get it.*

While the fundraising was going well, I questioned whether it would be sustainable. All these people, often from the same social network or group, were working so hard and there was still such a long way to go. The four fundraising events, combined, raised around $100 000 – an impressive amount but only enough to purchase three quarters of one myoelectric arm.

Shortly after the ball, however, my story aired on Channel Seven's *Sunday Night*, and as a result of a breathtakingly generous response by viewers, enough money was raised to purchase one or two sets of prosthetics within a week. While there were apparently some substantial donations, overall most donations were small amounts and the result demonstrated the power of numbers. It meant we could commit to purchasing my first set of limbs. What had been a dream was now firming up into reality, thanks to an outpouring from people we had never met but to whom we will be forever grateful.

*

For me, the road to bionics, or more specifically myoelectric arms and microprocessor-controlled legs, had started with the realisation that despite hours and hours of fitting, practice and training, basic prosthetics were not going to help me reach my goals.

Reflecting on it now, I recognise that while I was always looking for functionality, I think I was looking at the 'bionics' first, rather than the mechanics. The idea of bionic arms and legs was exciting because it potentially offered me greater independence, and created all sorts of possibilities in my head, and in the minds of those around me. But as time went by, it became clear that if we couldn't get the mechanical part right – the sockets, attachments, length – then the rest of it was a fairly pointless exercise.

Having decided that osseointegration was my only option, the ability to attach any future prosthetics – bionic or not – to my limbs depended on whether my body would take to the titanium implants that would be embedded in my bones. Each implant is roughly about 80 millimetres in length and 15 millimetres in diameter. The implant is screwed into the bone, and over time, integrates with bone cells so they become fused together. It works in a similar way to a graft – eventually, the two independent parts become one.

If the implant worked, the next stage would be to attach the titanium abutment, which we refer to as the bolt. The bolt is the bit you can see sticking out, and to which I would attach different prosthetics. It is around 70 millimetres long from where it is attached to the implant. The total length of metal, including the bolt and implant, is around 140–150 millimetres.

The surgery for the implants and bolts was done in six separate operations. Each operation required me to travel to Melbourne, where the team who perform this particular type of osseointegration surgery is based. They normally work out of The Alfred Hospital, but my operations were at two other hospitals, which was really interesting for me. I got to see how different hospital units worked, and got a few new ideas from different physiotherapists that helped when I returned to Brisbane.

The first operation, in June 2013, was for an implant in my right arm. It was particularly nerve-racking for Diane, who was in Melbourne with me, and for the children and my family back at home. The last time they had said goodbye to me before a really major operation was when I had the surgery to amputate my limbs. And apparently, operating on me is a challenge because it's difficult to monitor the blood pressure of such a short-limbed amputee (my arm is too short to attach the cuff). So undergoing the surgery was a risk, and we also had to consider post-surgery infection.

I wasn't really nervous. For me, it was the beginning of a new journey. I was relieved, though, when I opened my eyes after the operation and saw Diane. *Whew. I made it. Great.* She shed a few tears of relief when I woke up, and when we later rang the boys to say hello, I could tell they were also very relieved.

There wasn't anything to show for the implant operations other than refreshed stitching at the ends of the stumps, because the implants don't protrude through the skin. They were painful, but not excruciating, and recovery was simply a matter of giving them time. I needed to wait to see whether the bone integrated effectively. It did. Everything was proceeding as planned.

The next operation was for implants in both legs (July 2013), and the third was for an implant in my left arm (September 2013). Six months after the implants were placed in my legs, I was able to get the bolts attached to the implants. This was my fourth major operation, and it meant another trip to Melbourne in December 2013. For someone who had never previously been to hospital before my illness, I was becoming pretty fluent in the routine. Flight, taxi, admission, fasting, surgery, pain relief, bed rest, then rehab for a few days, taxi, flight. This operation was almost four hours long and as it involved both legs I had two teams of surgeons, one on each leg, to reduce my time in surgery. It required me to stay in bed for almost nine weeks.

Because I was going to be in Melbourne for two of those weeks, Dad and Kate tag-teamed before Diane brought the kids down for a few days. It was great to have the company. It meant someone could feed me so that I didn't have to rely on the nurses, and help fill in time between the rehab sessions that started about a week after the operation. In addition to that, hanging out with Dad and Kate was fun – they brought me chocolate, watched cricket with me and accompanied me to rehab to see what I do.

It was interesting to be an observer in a rehab facility that mainly deals with amputee management. I was at Epworth Hawthorn, a centre that specialises in looking after people like me. Conversations in which limbs were referred to as artefacts rather than body parts were the norm: 'Hey, can you look after my leg while I go back to my room for a while?', 'Just throw my legs over the back of the chair', 'Has anyone seen my foot lying around?'

I'm the same now. I often ask the boys to take my legs somewhere. Diane might ask, 'Hey, honey. Do you think you'll need your legs today?' It's not a question I would have ever imagined would be normal for us.

After two weeks in Melbourne, the surgeons let me go home. Diane was taught the ins and outs of managing the wounds, and Saul, Jacqui and Jean Clow (my occupational therapist in day therapy) made themselves available to manage my rehabilitation in Brisbane once I was moving again.

Seeing the bolts sticking out of my legs is weird. They look like big strong steel fencing bolts and emerge from my skin like piercings. It is hard for me to get a proper look at the bolts because I can't really contort myself enough to see the back of my legs. This is where having Diane around is so great.

'So how do they look, Di?' I asked.

'Honey, they look fantastic,' she replied. Of course they did. The thing about Diane is that the statement's genuine – she really did think the bolts looked fantastic sticking out of my legs. As a result, I felt great about them from the start, and so did the kids. How could we not?

For the first few weeks they were heavily bandaged, but even at that early stage I was excited. From the beginning, my left leg felt great. I could rotate the stump with quite a bit of range, and for the first time I could see and feel the possibilities, and understand what everyone had been talking about. I could feel how much better the control would be. Most importantly, I could feel feedback through my bone. Straight after the operation, I could actually feel it when the doctors tapped on the end of the bolts. And when the puck that sat at the end of each bolt rattled, I could feel that too.

Once the bandages were removed, I could tell when someone

was touching the end of the bolt. These were all strange sensations, but I had a renewed sense of where my body ended. It felt good, even though I was in pretty significant pain for a while. It was also immediately evident that the presence of the bolt would relieve the pain that came with hitting the end of my stump against something, whereby my bone would be driven into my soft tissue. The presence of the bolt means this doesn't happen any more, and gave me confidence to move. My concerns about hurting people with the metal abated after we put soft plastic cups over the ends of the bolts. They looked like they were wearing little blue hats, and they became known as my 'blue bits'.

My right hip was more problematic, but it's been the problem leg since I woke from the coma. It was sore, and the skin on my right buttock was particularly tight, so any movement would pull at the wound. There was a constant feeling of pressure, and a small trickle of blood. The wound wasn't healing that well and about a week after I got home Diane and I were a bit worried. I called Steven Gray, the manager of the osseointegration program, who was really good about making himself available and responding quickly. Steven was overseas, but we spoke on the phone for a while and then Diane and I sent the surgical team some photos of the leg. After the team reviewed them, Steven called us to discuss what was happening and provide advice. I also spoke with doctors locally and started a course of antibiotics as a preventative measure, but I was still consigned to extra bed rest – a couple of weeks at least. Steven might well have been able to hear my sigh from where he was on the other side of the world.

I can't read books easily, don't watch daytime television, and too much use of the iPad makes my mouth sore because I use a mouth-stick, so my life could have been excruciatingly boring for those couple of weeks – but time passed quickly. The cricket was on, so I had an excuse to lie back and watch endless test matches, day/night and Twenty20 games, often with Luke camped on Diane's side of the bed. Since meeting the Australian team after the first Ashes test in 2013, courtesy of an invitation from Cricket Australia, we felt we had a vested interest in their success.

My family and friends kept me company, pulling up chairs beside my bed, bringing coffee and telling stories about life on the outside. The kids were pretty happy to have 'electronic time' (time on the computer, television, or electronic gadget) and to do lots of book reading, and there were also plenty of sleepovers with cousins and grandparents to get them out and about while I was static.

When I was finally allowed to stand upright, I was able to wear my original leg prosthetics, which had been modified to attach to the bolts without needing a socket. It was fantastic – there was so much more freedom to move. But before I could put weight on my legs, I had to train the bone to accept the pressure, so every day, I would lie on a tilt table with each leg on a set of scales. I had to increase the pressure by 5 kilos a week, session by session, until I could support my full body weight on each leg. The sessions lasted two and a half hours each day, broken up into two blocks of just over one hour, so during this period most of my rehabilitation was done at home. The kids thought this was really interesting, and seemed to love helping – they would put my legs on and set up the scales. I was a unique form of science lesson for them, and we had a lot of fun. Emily liked to lie back with me, and her dolls would often come for the ride.

Doing this, I could actually appreciate how I would be able to feel the ground with my prosthetic foot. I had heard about the sensation from other osseointegration patients, but didn't really understand how it could happen. I didn't get that feeling when using sockets – it always felt unstable, like my leg was floating even when it was on the ground.

Even though we were using my original legs, the way they could be attached to my body meant they felt normal to me, or as normal as having metal stuck in the end of your legs when you are standing up can. I could feel they were totally foreign and yet totally part of me. When the legs were attached by sockets, I always felt very insecure when standing upright. Even though I hadn't yet done as much with them in their new form as I knew I would in the future, they immediately felt like they belonged.

Once I get used to how long my legs are, I think I will be able to close my eyes and know where they are in relation to the rest of me. Before my amputations, I hadn't appreciated the importance of having spatial awareness of your body, or proprioception, which simply means knowing where you are even if you're not feeling any pressure against your limbs. Because I now immediately feel a vibration when I hit the ground, I have that kind of perception. I don't feel the pressure you might feel with your toe or finger; rather, the feeling is like what you might experience if someone tapped on your glasses – you would feel the pressure on your nose or on your ears.

The two final operations, in April 2014, were to connect bolts to the implants in my arms. There was a sense of relief that this would be the end of the 'construction' phase. It was immediately evident that the tiny bit of extra length that I now had from the bolts opened up a world that I hadn't been able to access since my amputations.

A few days after the final operation, Dad came up with a way to attach an extra length of metal to the newly attached bolts. It was amazing – all of a sudden, I could type emails and text messages, make phone calls, press buttons and turn on light switches. I was particularly excited to reclaim the television remote – a reinforcement that 'Dad was back'. From this experience, I knew that when I received my training arms, life would start to become much easier for me. I used to wish that if I could just have one limb back, it would be an arm. I know now, from this experience, that if I ever have to make a choice in prosthetics, I would pour all available resources into my arms. This is based on knowledge that has come from having access to a metal stick that adds a couple of inches to my life, let alone arms that can do more complex tasks.

Ultimately, if I can walk, great. If I can walk without a walking aid or crutches, I'll be elated. But I don't expect that. For me, the most important thing is being able to put food into my body and manage what comes out independently. I know, for example, that I will need to be supported when I walk because most bilateral amputees require a walking aid. Taking that into account along with the fact that my right hip is still not great, I'm just moderating my expectations. I'm trying to hold them at the lower end – such as simply being able to transfer myself from one point to another – and then hoping for more.

I do hope to be able to drive. That would be great. People look at me like I'm a bit crazy when I talk about possibly getting a new car when I can drive, but that doesn't bother me. Sam Bailey, a quadriplegic with whom I have become acquainted, wants to be the first quadriplegic to fly a helicopter. I reckon a cool goal would be to race him – Sam in his helicopter and me in a car.

I have learned that until you know for sure that you can't do something, it's still a possibility.

And while it's still a possibility, it's worth pursuing.

CHAPTER 18

LIFE AS I NOW KNOW IT

Over the past two years, I have often wondered, 'Who am I?'

I have had a lot of time to reflect on this, between staring at hospital ceilings, lying in bed for long periods of rehabilitation, and thinking of what to say to a group of people to whom I might be giving a talk.

I haven't figured out the answer yet because I'm still a work in progress, but we probably all are. What's unique about me and other people who have survived a near-death experience and gone on to prosper is that we've entered a 'second chance' phase of our lives.

I'm in that phase now.

I have always been someone who 'does' stuff. I thought I was a very involved, active dad, a devoted husband and an industry professional who was making a worthwhile contribution. Those things may have been part of who I was, but I have since learned just how fluid the definition of who you are can be.

A year after my amputations, Diane and I met with Ben's teacher,

Helen, for a parent–teacher interview. Ben had brightened up a lot since I had come out of hospital, but we knew he had struggled before that. We were expecting the interview to be about possible issues he was having, and we were ready to do whatever it was going to take, and work with whomever we needed to work, to ensure he continued to make good progress.

That's not how it went, though. Instead, we heard about how well he was doing, and how his school results were improving. We were thrilled.

As we were about to leave, Helen asked if Ben had told us about what he had written in a recent English test, and we told her that he hadn't.

Helen said Ben's task in the test had been to write about his hero – who that was, and why.

'Ben wrote that you, Matthew, were his hero,' Helen told us. 'You might be interested in why.'

She told us that Ben had given three reasons why his daddy was his hero: 'because he reads to me, he listens to me and he helps me with my homework'.

We all found this interesting because there was no mention of me fighting hard to live, or being brave.

I was a hero to Ben simply because I was there and I gave him time and attention.

It hit me at that moment: in my earlier life, I don't know that he would have been able to write something as meaningful. Diane thinks that Ben would always have written something like that about me. The alternative we'll never know.

*

Even though I'm still a work in progress, I am now first and foremost a husband, a father, a son, a brother and a friend.

In the course of daily life prior to my amputations, my priorities slipped at times. I was a father, an employee, a husband, a son and a brother, probably in that order. I worked long hours and focused my attention on Diane and the kids whenever I could; it was a challenge to be around for the more routine activities such as school sports days.

Diane and I rarely disagree, but if there was ever friction prior to me getting ill, it was because I prioritised work a little too much. I enjoyed the adrenaline rush that comes with corporate life – meeting powerful people, travelling a lot and working on interesting projects that gave me a sense of satisfaction. At the same time, I was completely committed to the family. I was, my friends and family would tell me, 'Mr 100 Per Cent' – I would put 100 per cent into everything. However, because I knew Diane's love was unconditional, she sometimes got what was left over at the end of each day.

I know now that the price I paid for that corporate life, which was limited time with the family, was not worth it. You often hear people say this, and I, like many, hadn't really applied it to myself.

The only people to whom I am indispensable are my family and friends. In the professional sphere, I'm replaceable. I think I lost sight of that. I plan to work again, but in a way that fits in with the other priorities in my life. I would like to support Diane's return to work after Emily starts school, if that's at all possible and what Diane wants to do. I don't know, and it's still too far ahead to think about it too much. What I focus on is what's in front of me, right here, and right now.

Usually, that's Diane and the children.

In the past two years, I've had the chance to meet the most amazing and generous people, including many who, like me, have an acquired disability. I've met inspirational people from all walks of life – from those who have emailed me with their experiences of coping with adversity to fellow nominees in the Pride of Australia and Father of the Year awards.

Everyone has a different story, and I have learned first hand the value of sharing those stories. Even tiny pieces of information about how someone else has overcome something have made a huge difference at various stages of my recovery. So in turn, Diane and I made a choice to tell our story publicly, in the hope that it would help others, and help the children – if people stared at me, it might be in recognition rather than wonder.

A few people with acquired disabilities have mentioned that they get to a place where they wouldn't change what happened to them, that more positives have come from their experience than negatives. While I believe in positivity, I am not there yet, and can't imagine that I will ever get there. But I may.

I know the day might come when someone tells me that there is nothing more that can be done to assist me and that I won't be able to have the level of independence I would like. They'll tell me that what I have is what I have, and that's it. That will be a hard day, if it comes. Hopefully, I'll continue to get over those kinds of setbacks quickly.

Because actually, what I have now is enough.

I'm here.

I have a wife who is the sunshine in our lives, and who amazes me every day, and I have four beautiful children whom I will be able to watch grow older. I hope to walk (or at least roll) my daughter down the aisle one day when she gets married, and watch the garage get hijacked when one of the boys brings his own car home for restoration.

But in the meantime, I'm happy to lie on the couch and read to them, listen to their stories, and just be around.

I get to spend time with my beautiful sisters in a way that I haven't since we were little. We were a great team then because we moved a lot and didn't have cousins or any extended family; we relied on one another for company and fun. As it turns out, we make a great team now, too, with our partners and children as well.

I always loved my parents deeply, but it's been nice to see other people also recognise how incredible they are. I've had conversations with Mum and Dad about life that we may never have had otherwise, and the support they have given Diane and me has been immeasurably valuable, especially in the absence of Diane's parents.

I know I am lucky. There are so many others who haven't had the support I've had, or who have lost members of their family through tragedy or illness, and I don't know how they do it. I would not have been able to travel this road without Diane and the children. I am where I am today because of them, and I'm in complete awe of those who have found the strength to continue wholly within themselves.

There has always been a community around me, but now I am more aware of it every day. From the bus driver who takes the time to be really careful going around corners because she knows I'm there to the stranger who helps me or my kids when we're out. It's everywhere, every day.

I am grateful for all of these lessons.

*

When our children were being baptised, Diane and I wrote each of them a letter, telling them what we hoped for their future.

Will's read:

You are very special to us. We pray that you will always smile your gorgeous smile; laugh out loud; love with all of your heart; embrace those around you; jump with joy; follow your dreams; always play like a child; have the compassion of an angel; walk with those less fortunate; be at one with nature; look for the beauty in all; be warmed by the love of your family; be true to yourself; and above all else we pray that you will live life to the fullest with peace and happiness.

We will always be there for you; to share; to guide; to
hope, and most importantly, to love. We are the caretakers
of a beautiful soul. The destination is unknown and will
only be determined by you. We pray that the journey is rich
and diverse and that our guidance helps you on your way.
We will love you for all the days of our life.

Love, Mum and Dad

Perhaps I lost sight of some of my own message after writing that
letter, but through this journey, I have relearned how to play like
a child, and the value of compassion. I've added complexity to the
'rich and diverse life' we intended for the children but, importantly,
I am still here to provide guidance.

Diane and I understand that the children's lives are now harder
than they would have been and that there will be things I may not
be able to do with them in the future, such as kick a ball on a beach,
or go walking in the rain. But that's where family and friends have
stepped in, and in doing so, added an extra layer of richness to our
lives.

Diane and I work every day to lighten any possible burden on
the children, but we know that in a way they will be better people
because of what's happened to me. They'll have empathy with others worse off than them, and they'll know how hard it can be for
some people to simply get out of bed every day, because they watch
me do it each morning.

They'll know the value of community, and the importance of
being active and giving back, because they've seen how our lives have
been enhanced by being part of, and contributing to, a community.
They'll know the importance of asking for help when it's needed, but
also that it's a good idea to try things out for themselves at the start.

They'll know that while declarations of love and commitment

are great, words alone are not enough, and action is everything.

They will have seen the value of fighting for the wellbeing of others, because they saw how hard medical specialists worked to find the answers they didn't know in order to help me succeed.

They'll know that no matter how hard or confronting it is being with someone who has a disability, it's important to try to communicate and be honest about your fears. They'll also know not to feel sorry for someone with a disability – yes, life may be harder, but that doesn't mean it's worse.

They'll know to smile whenever someone makes eye contact because they have seen how much it means to me, and they'll be the first to offer a helping hand to someone else because they have been at the receiving end when things were difficult.

They'll know that what you can achieve as an individual is nothing compared to what can be achieved as a team. And they'll know that having a professional identity can be fulfilling, but shouldn't come at the expense of those you love.

They'll know to pursue possibilities and accept what life offers, but also that our only power over life is to choose what to do with it. They will be able to see all that is good in the world, rather than focus on that which is not. It's impossible for me to think that with Diane as their mother, they'll be able to look at life any other way.

Most importantly, they'll know that Diane, the doctors and the rest of the family made the right decision.

It gave me a chance to be a better husband, a better father, a better son, a better brother and a better friend. The decision to save me was a chance for life – a different life, a harder life in some ways, a better life in others.

But whichever way I look at it, I know it was a gift. And for every day, I am grateful.

AFTERWORD

It's the beginning of a new year, and while we're still trying to get into a routine, there's a sense of calm in the house. Matthew is reading to Emily. The two of them are lying on his tilt table while Matthew does his exercises. Emily is tilted back with him, holding up the book so he can read, and Ben and Will are monitoring the weight on Matthew's prosthetic legs. They put the legs on for him earlier, and are taking their role seriously.

Luke is sitting at the table doing his homework. He's at a new school, which is a big change for him, and he is adjusting well and trying to manage the tiredness. Earlier this evening, Matthew spent a bit of time talking with Luke about some of the issues that go with growing up, and Luke, as always, took the advice on board.

I am in the kitchen, which opens onto our lounge and dining room. It's been a normal day, which has resulted in the normal chaos, so I'm taking my time to clean up and prepare for tomorrow.

Once the tilt table session is over, Matthew will read to the boys and help me put everyone to bed. Then Matthew and I will get into bed ourselves, and we'll have a chance to talk about the day. We'll also possibly talk about how we're travelling as a family. It is a conversation we have regularly and the type of discussion we've always had in the evenings, even before Matthew's illness.

Life is different, and it is hard, but it's the new normal.

There's lots of love in the house, and we're surrounded by wonderful support from our family, friends and community.

I don't have big moments where I think I'm glad we made the right choice. The thought is with me every second of every day, and has been since we were given the option to save Matthew.

While it is my wish that Matthew had never become sick and still had his limbs, this is the life we have now.

We are all glad every day that he is here with us.

He had the will to live. He has the will to be strong and positive for us.

His being here makes a difference.

A NOTE FROM THE WRITER

My first memory of Matthew was watching him through a window. He was a newborn baby, and I had been hoisted onto someone's shoulders. Our family had come to Sydney from Fiji, where we were living, so Matthew could be born at Manly Hospital. For my sister Rachel and me, Matthew was not only our baby brother; we have both also described him as our first love.

We had what some might describe as an idyllic childhood. Our early years were spent in cane fields in Fiji and North Queensland, as our father worked in the sugar mills. Afternoons were spent in sugar piles and 'testing' fresh molasses, riding in the back of Dad's ute with our dogs, helping Mum beat away wildlife escaping cane fires, and catching tadpoles in stormwater drains – it was an outdoors life.

We moved to Sydney to be closer to our grandparents, with whom we played backyard cricket and learned to ice-skate at Narrabeen ice-skating rink. Our summers were marked by trips to

Dee Why Beach and long afternoons at the Sydney Cricket Ground watching cricket greats Dennis Lillee and Greg Chappell take on the West Indies and England.

In late 1985, Dad's work took us to Hawthorne, in Brisbane's inner east – years before it became the gentrified suburb it is today. Our parents bought an old Queenslander, which Dad renovated, taking Matthew along for the ride.

In a household full of fiery females, Matthew was always a picture of calm. He and Dad would retreat to work on their projects under the house, do a bit more renovating and ask really good questions about why 'the girls' weren't being rational about something or other.

Rachel and I thought Matthew was pretty malleable, but it was more that he was happy to go along with whatever games we had planned if he didn't have anything else he would rather do. He has always been laidback in his demeanour, but we learned early on that in Matthew's case there was a big difference between being easygoing and being compliant. From the moment he could talk, he knew what he wanted, and if something was important to him, he would pursue it until he was satisfied with the outcome.

I left home at 20, the day after my final university exam, and set off for London with a great family friend. Matthew had just finished his first year of university, Rachel was doing her second year of accounting at UQ and Diane was just arriving on the scene. I travelled for two years, hearing stories of Matthew and Diane's romance from afar. Our grandmother Ninna, who lived at home with the family, was a particular fan of Diane's, but my parents had also fallen in love with this beautiful brown-eyed girl from the northern suburbs.

We nicknamed Diane 'Pollyanna'. She was always so happy and positive. Coming from a family of extreme pragmatists, Rachel and I sometimes questioned, very early on, whether anyone could possibly be that happy and positive all the time.

We grew to learn that yes, they could. We also grew to learn that it's contagious.

While Diane had been touched by tragedy with the untimely deaths of her parents in 2009, our side of the immediate family had been touched by luck. Relatively long lives, no accidents, great health – it seemed we were quite blessed, a lucky group of people born into good times in good circumstances.

Our luck changed on 16 June 2012, when what seemed to be the perfect life was shattered after a sudden and seemingly innocuous illness. Faced with the possibility that Matthew might die, pragmatism merged with positivity – we had to do what we had to do to save him, hoping it would work out.

Matthew emerged from an induced coma three weeks later with no limbs, but surrounded by love, strength and the will of those around him to pull together and do whatever it took to make things work.

We started recording this journey and sharing it with people soon after Matthew became ill, but to bring it together in the form of this book has been an amazingly positive experience. It was something we thought might be too hard – reliving moments of agony again, and reflecting on what might have been. We did cry, a lot, but we also laughed on many occasions, and revisiting what happened reminded us of the overwhelming love and support we all received along the way.

Spending time with Matthew and Diane is always rewarding, but getting the chance to talk deeply and frankly with them about their memories – from growing up to how they felt at particular moments over the past two years – is something for which I feel very grateful. We had a lot of fun and consumed a huge amount of coffee.

Just as this is Matthew's journey, it has also been the journey of our family, a community and a very large group of wonderful friends. In the final stages of writing this book, our aunt Ruth passed away. Our family is a small one, and Ruth was the only surviving extended relative. She would have loved to see Matthew get up and walk, but we're sure she is looking down from heaven and cheering him on in spirit.

While we shouldn't need events like this to help put things into perspective, Matthew's story is a reminder to all of us about what's important. This story isn't finished yet, and we still don't know how it will end.

But we do know that good things can come from bad, that every extra day we have is a blessing and that actions based on pure good-will and generosity of spirit make a really big difference.

*

Here's an update on Matthew's progress.

In April 2014, he completed all of his osseointegration surgery, and will spend the next twelve months building strength in his bones prior to fitting of his first full set of final prosthetics. He is being assessed for his ability to drive myoelectric arms, as this depends on how strong the signals are in his remaining arm muscles. Signs are mixed, but he remains hopeful. He is also investigating new technology that can maximise the control of any future prosthetic such as Targeted Muscle Reinnervation (TMR) and direct nerve connection.

He needs to build significant strength in his leg bones before he can be assessed for micro-processor controlled legs, and he's working on it. He continues with his rehab as an outpatient at the Mater Private Hospital in Brisbane, and spends many hours on the tilt-table doing weight-bearing exercises.

As well as working on his physical rehabilitation, Matthew is staying active in the community. He has become a Rotarian and in his spare time gives talks to schoolkids and disability groups about coping with challenges. He also spends time lobbying government for better services for people with disabilities. And he's still a regular at the park on Friday afternoons.

Matthew and Diane's family, friends and community continue to rally around them as Matthew pursues his goal of independence.

He's hoping to be walking by June 2015 – three years after his amputations.

After that, he says, who knows?

*

The Renovating Matthew blog continues to receive messages and requests for help from people sitting beside hospital beds around the world as a loved one battles toxic shock or sepsis. To follow Matthew's journey, visit:

Blog – renovatingmatthew.com

Twitter – @renovatingmatt

ACKNOWLEDGEMENTS

From Matthew and Diane

We have been on an amazing journey over the past couple of years. This would not have been possible without our team of incredible people.

To Luke, Ben, Will and Emily – we are blessed to have such awesome children. You give us the inspiration to strive to be our best. We love you with all of our hearts.

To Roy and Christine Ames – thanks for putting your lives on hold to get us up and running again, for being an incredible set of grandparents for our children, and for picking up the load where we were not able to. Thanks to Christine for never giving up and to Roy for your unending optimism.

To Kate Ames and Jason Feeney and Rachel and Aaron Fraser and their families – we are so fortunate to have you as our support team leaders. We are in awe of your capacity to give unconditionally to help us – Rachel, for your time and effort in 'making things happen' for us, and Kate, for documenting our journey so that our children, in time, will be able to understand what happened, and for your belief in the worth of telling our story so that it may help others.

To Jenny and Bill Graham, Claire McMahon, Gary McMahon, Jan Leighton, Judy Steenbeeke and their extended families – your continued support made a wonderful difference as we learned to manage our new lives. To Peter and Robyn Leighton. Thank you for your part in our journey.

To Bill and Mary Leighton – thank you for teaching us how to live our lives with strength and love. To Ruth Ames. Thanks for always being there for us. We will miss you all forever.

To Gwen and Anthony Lea, Nicole and David Webb, and Lisa Moroney and Stuart Harland – your unwavering support and constant thoughtfulness helped us establish the new normal for our family and allowed our children to enjoy their childhood.

To our fantastic friends – you have helped us in everything, from visiting us in hospital and helping with our children to delivering delicious home-cooked meals for the past two years. Sharing your time with us gave us strength and helped us understand how widely we were supported. We would especially like to thank: Cheryl Davies, Kim Ibbott, Nicky Rolls, Dan and Annette Alexander, Martyn and Steph Robotham, Gayle and David Schabe, Peter and Claire Malyon, Angelique and David McKillop, and Mandi and Scott Gosling.

To Matthew's amazing workmates at Origin, URS and Santos – In your very busy lives you always found time to assist us. We would especially like to thank: Graeme Bartrim, Rosahlena Robinson, Rob Ully, Sandra Schulte and Fiona Allen. Special thanks to the people at Origin, especially Paul Zealand – your support of me demonstrates exceptional care for people. We would also like to thank Rachel and Kate's colleagues at AgForce and Central Queensland University for their understanding, particularly Brent Finlay, Scott Bowman and Helen Huntly.

To our local communities, that gave of their time and support so willingly – thank you. We would especially like to thank our boy's primary school community, the Environment Institute of Australia and New Zealand, and Holland Park Hawks, who were the first to bring the community together to give us hope. Through you all, we were reminded that an organisation's heart is its people. We would especially like to thank: Lauren and Peter Audet and their Gala team, Danielle Bolton and her Renovating Matthew Ball team, Len Catalano and David Reid and their Hawks team.

To the Mater Public Intensive Care team – thank you for believing in the importance of saving Matthew, and for your exceptional care. We would like to especially thank: Dr Tim McMeniman; Dr Brett Collins; Dr Shane Townsend; Dr John Morgan; Dr Amod Karnik; Dr Jeff Presneill; Dr Mike Ranger; Christie Barrett; Sally McCray; and the nursing and support team, particularly Chris, Anne, Eamonn, May, Murray and Chloe.

To the Mater Private Rehabilitation Unit – your faith in Matthew has helped him achieve his best, and allowed our family to share his experience. A special thanks to: Dr Saul Geffen, Deirdre Cooke, Jacqui O'Sullivan, Jean Clow, Nick Flynn, Dr Claire Panagoda, Janice Kruesmann and David Sweet.

To the Melbourne OPRA Osseointegration team, led by Steven Gray – thank you for willingly taking on a case as complex as Matthew's and always treating us with respect.

To the team of people that have supported us to stay in our own home. – thank you, especially: Andrew Kudzius and Karl Schottler, Colin Grosvenor, Liz Ainsworth and the team at St Michael's Home Modifications.

To the teams at *Sunday Night* and Penguin – thanks for supporting us in sharing our story and being so wonderful to work with, especially Lisa Ryan, Andrea McNamara, Louise Ryan and Anyez Lindop.

Along the way, we have been privileged to meet people who have gone out of their way to show us kindness, share their stories, and remind us that we are not alone. Meeting every one of you has made an impact.

To those who contributed to the Renovating Matthew Foundation, and who have made contact with us along the way – without your support, we would not be facing as bright a future as we are now. We have been amazed by the heartfelt messages and generosity of people we know and those we have never met. You have reminded us of the amazing humanity that still exists in the world.

Finally, to anyone who has ever shared a smile or a kind word with us when out and about – thank you. On each and every occasion, it has made our day.

From Kate

I extend my sincere thanks to everyone around me while I was pulling this book together. To Matthew and Diane, for trusting me with your story, and to Luke, Ben, Will and Emily, for sharing your parents with me on so many occasions.

To my husband, Jason, for being there to pick up the pieces and keep our lives moving forward on regular occasions, and children, Maeve and Joshua, for sharing me so extensively with others for a little while. To Joe and Cherrie Feeney, your selfless support of us all through this journey has been amazing.

To Mum, Dad, Rachel, Aaron, Lincoln and Ethan – I love you, and thanks for such great feedback. In a sense, this was a collective effort.

To Matthew and Diane's close friends and the medical staff involved in Matthew's treatment and recovery, thank you for making time to share your stories and provide feedback along the way.

To my wonderful friends in lots of different places, thanks for being there with us from the start, and to Ally and Sara, you know how important you are. I don't know what I would have done without your support.

To my colleagues at Central Queensland University – your kind words, generosity of time and spirit, and willingness to help has reminded me why I've worked with you all for almost half of my life and plan to continue to do so.

To the team at Penguin led by Andrea McNamara, thank you for your faith in me, and for your enthusiasm and support along the way. To Lynda Hawryluk, Celeste Lawson and Lisa Ryan – just thank you. Your belief in the worth of this story from the outset has been important.